About the Authors

Jane Kelly trained as a Chartered Management Accountant while working in industry. Her roles ranged from Company Accountant in a small advertising business to Financial Controller of a national housebuilding company. Jane has subsequently specialised in both using and teaching others how to use Sage software and also teaching people the bookkeeping basics.

Jane is the author of *Sage 50 Accounts For Dummies* and *Bookkeeping Workbook For Dummies* (Wiley).

John A. Tracy is Professor of Accounting, Emeritus, at the University of Colorado in Boulder. Before his 35-year tenure at Boulder, he was on the business faculty for 4 years at the University of California in Berkeley. He has served as staff accountant at Ernst & Young and is the author of several books on accounting and finance, including *Accounting For Dummies* (Wiley). Dr. Tracy earned his MBA and PhD degrees from the University of Wisconsin.

Dedication

From Jane: I would like to dedicate this book to my daughter, Megan. I hope that she will be proud of her mum and maybe even write a book of her own one day – even if it is about Disney princesses and fairies!

From John: In memory of Gordon B. Laing – a gentleman and editor of the first rank.

Authors' Acknowledgements

From Jane: I hope that this book will help many small businesses understand the basic concepts of accounting. I can't emphasis enough the importance of setting up proper systems. With the right accounting systems in place, you'll have a better chance of surviving the current economic climate. If you have any comments or suggestions about this book or maybe have a question, please contact jane@sycamoreonline.com.

I would like to thank all those at Wiley who have made this publication possible: here's to the next project.

Finally, I would like to thank my husband, Malcolm, and my daughter, Megan, who have put up with my extended periods of absence while I've been pounding the keyboard!

From John: I'm deeply grateful to everyone at Wiley who helped produce this book. Their professionalism, courtesy and good humour were much appreciated. This book would not have been possible but for the success of *Accounting For Dummies* (Wiley). I owe Wiley and the several editors an enormous debt of gratitude, which I am most willing to acknowledge.

Thanks to all of you! I hope I have done you proud with *Accounting Workbook For Dummies*.

Publisher's Acknowledgments

We're proud of this book; please send us your comments through our Dummies online registration form located at www.dummies.com/register/.

Some of the people who helped bring this book to market include the following:

Acquisitions, Editorial, and Media Development

Project Editor: Rachael Chilvers

Development Editor: Kelly Ewing

Copyeditor: Andy Finch

Content Editor: Jo Theedom

Commissioning Editor: Samantha Spickernell

Assistant Editor: Jennifer Prytherch

Production Manager: Daniel Mersey

Cover Photos: © INSADCO Photography/Alamy

Cartoons: Ed McLachlan

Composition Services

Project Coordinator: Lynsey Stanford

Layout and Graphics: Carl Byers, Nikki Gately, Joyce Haughey, Christine Williams, Erin Zeltner

Proofreader: Laura Albert

Indexer: Claudia Bourbeau

Contents at a Glance

Table of Contents

Introduction

First of all, we have to admit that accounting has an image problem. Be honest: What's the first thing that pops into your mind when you see the word 'accountant'? You probably think of a nerd wearing a bad suit. Well, we've never worn a bad suit, and can assure you that we're not nerds. We own iPods, have a good sense of humour and to be honest we're pretty normal!

This book offers a different take on accounting – one that offers new insights and perspectives. We don't go out of our way to be contrary or confrontational, but accounting isn't an exact science. Accounting is full of controversy and differences of opinion. In this book, we state our opinions forcefully and (we hope) clearly.

About This Book

Whether it's a small family business or a large corporate, every business keeps track of its financial activities and its financial condition. You can't run a business without an accounting system that tells you whether you're making a profit or suffering a loss, whether you have enough cash to continue or your bank account balance is approaching zero, and whether you're in good financial shape or are on the edge of bankruptcy.

Accounting Workbook For Dummies is largely about business accounting. It explains how business transactions are recorded in the accounts of a business and the financial statements that are prepared for a business to report its profit and loss, financial condition and cash flows. It also explains how business managers use accounting information for decision making. (The book doesn't delve into business income taxation, which is the province of professional accountants.)

Most business managers have limited accounting backgrounds, and most have their enthusiasm for learning more about accounting well under control. But, deep down, they're likely to think that they should know more about accounting. Business managers will find this book quite helpful even if they just dip their toes in.

If you're a business bookkeeper or accountant, you can use this book to review the topics you need to know well. It can help you upgrade your accounting skills and lay the foundation for further advancement. One great thing about *Accounting Workbook For Dummies* is that it offers alternative explanations of accounting topics that are different from the explanations in standard accounting textbooks. The many questions and problems (with clearly explained answers) offer an excellent way to test your knowledge, and nobody knows your exam results but you.

If you're a student presently enrolled in a beginning accounting course, you can use this book as a supplementary study guide to your textbook, one that offers many supplementary questions and exercises. Perhaps you took an accounting course a few years ago and need to brush up on the subject. This book can help you refresh your understanding of accounting and help you recall things forgotten.

Foolish Assumptions

Mastering accounting is like mastering many subjects: First, you must understand the lingo and the fundamentals. In accounting, you have to work problems to really get a grasp of the topic and technique. Passive reading just isn't enough. In writing this book, we've assumed that you aren't a complete accounting neophyte. We designed the book as a second step that builds on your basic accounting knowledge and experience. If you have no previous exposure to accounting, you may want to consider first reading *Accounting For Dummies* (Wiley).

You don't have to be a maths wizard to understand accounting; basic school algebra is more than enough. However, you do have to pay attention to details, just as you have to pay close attention to the words when you study Shakespeare. Accounting involves calculations, and using a business/financial calculator is very helpful. In our experience, many people don't take the time to learn how to use their calculators. But that's time well spent. In many of the questions and problems posed throughout the book, we explain how to use a scientific calculator for the solution.

How This Book Is Organised

Accounting Workbook For Dummies consists of four parts that cover topics including recordkeeping basics, financial statements, accounting for business managers, and investment accounting. We wrap it all up with some advice about financial statements and tips for management accounting.

Part I: Business Accounting Basics

The general theme of the chapters in this part is how an accountant records the transactions of a business (its financial activities) in an accrual-basis accounting system and how the effects of transactions are reported in the three primary financial statements of a business – the profit and loss statement, the balance sheet and the cash flow statement. This part also includes a review of the bookkeeping cycle, from recording original entries through the adjusting and closing entries at year-end.

Part II: Preparing Financial Statements

This part examines the accounting issues and procedures involved in preparing the three primary financial statements of a business. Compared with the standard textbook approach to these topics, we put much more emphasis on the interconnections between the three financial statements. The statements fit together like a tongue-and-groove joint, and the chapters focus on these connections. This part closes with the decisions every business must make in choosing which accounting methods to use for recording profit.

Part III: Managerial, Manufacturing and Capital Accounting

This part of the book examines how managers use accounting information when making business decisions. In addition to financial statements, managers need profit models for their decision-making analysis, and accountants should take the lead in designing useful profit models for managers. This part also explains how the product cost of manufactures is determined and the difficult accounting issues involved in measuring product cost. The last chapter of this part discusses the accounting measurement of interest and return on investment. Most people have a basic understanding of interest and return on investment, but when it gets right down to a specific situation, they're fuzzy on the details.

Part IV: The Part of Tens

Like all *For Dummies* books, *Accounting Workbook For Dummies* ends with a couple of chapters that provide tips to help you recall and apply important points sprinkled throughout the book. We provide two such chapters in this book – one being ten things you should know about business financial statements, and one being a ten-point checklist for management accountants.

Icons Used in This Book

Throughout this book, you can find useful 'pointers' that save you the trouble of buying a yellow highlighter pen and using sticky notes. These icons draw your attention to certain parts of the text. Think of them as road signs on your journey through accounting.

This icon marks the spot of an example question that explains and illustrates an important point. The answer follows the question. It's a good idea to make sure that you understand the answer before attempting the additional questions on the topic. To get the most out of the example questions, don't read the answer right away. First, try to answer the question, and then compare our answer with yours and how you got it.

This icon points out helpful information that might save time to make you a better accountant.

We use this icon to indicate that you need to bear these points in mind as you work your way through the book.

Simply put, this icon is a red flag that means 'Watch out'. This warning sign means that the topic explained is a serious and troublesome issue in accounting, so pay close attention and handle it with care.

Where to Go from Here

Accounting Workbook For Dummies is designed to maximise modularity. Each chapter stands on its own feet to the fullest extent possible. Of course, it makes sense to read the chapters in order, but you can jump around as the spirit moves you.

You may be a business investor who's interested in interpreting return on investment (ROI) (Chapter 12), or you may want to review manufacturing cost accounting (Chapter 11). You may be a business manager who needs to know about analysing profit behavior (Chapter 10), or you may be confused about cash flow (Chapters 7 and 8). If you're a student studying for your first accounting exam, we suggest that you start with Part I and read the chapters in order.

In our view, a scientific calculator has become as essential as a TV remote control, and we highly recommend that you invest in one (a calculator, that is, not a remote control). Hewlett-Packard (HP) and Texas Instruments (TI) make very good ones. If you can avoid it, don't buy the cheapest model; the next one up usually has better financial functions and a good display.

Part I
Business Accounting Basics

'So for all you eager investors, our latest
financial report will be read to you by our
new accountant, Mr Mesmero.'

In this part . . .

Accountants are the scorekeepers of business. Without accounting, a business couldn't function; it wouldn't know whether it's making a profit; and it wouldn't know its financial condition. Bookkeeping – the recording-keeping part of accounting – must be done well to make sure that all the financial information needed to run the business is complete, accurate and reliable. This part of the book walks you through the basic bookkeeping cycle – from making original entries through adjusting entries, to financial statements. Before jumping into the mechanics of bookkeeping, however, we explain the financial effects and the manifold effects of sales and expenses on assets and liabilities.

Chapter 1

Elements of Business Accounting

The starting point in accounting is to identify the entity that you're accounting for. A business entity can be legally organised as a partnership, limited company (Ltd) or a public limited company (PLC). Alternatively, a business entity simply may consist of the business activities of an individual, in which case it's called a sole proprietorship. Regardless of how the business entity is legally established, it's treated as a separate entity or distinct person for accounting purposes.

Keeping the Accounting Equation in Balance

The accounting equation (Assets = Liabilities + Owners' capital) says a lot in very few words. This equation is like the visible part of an iceberg – loads of important points are hidden under the water.

Notice the two sides to the equation: assets on one side of the equals sign and claims against the assets on the other side. These claims arise from credit extended to the business (*liabilities*) and capital invested by owners in the business (*owners' capital*). (The claims of liabilities are significantly different to the claims of owners; liabilities have seniority and priority for payment over the claims of owners.)

Suppose that a business has £10 million total assets. These assets didn't fall down like manna from heaven (as one of the authors' old accounting professor was fond of saying). The money for the assets came from somewhere. The business's *creditors* (to whom the firm owes its liabilities) may have supplied, say, £4 million of its total assets. Therefore, the owners' capital sources provided the other £6 million.

Business accounting is based on the two-sided nature of the accounting equation. Both assets and sources of assets are accounted for, which leads, quite naturally, to *double entry accounting*. Double entry, in essence, means two-sided, and is based on the general economic exchange model, as follows: in economic transactions, something is given and something is received in exchange. For example, we recently bought an iPod from Apple Computer. Apple gave us the iPod and received our money. Another example involves a business that borrows money from its bank. The business signs a loan agreement promising to return the money at a future date and to pay interest over the time the money is borrowed. In exchange for the loan agreement, the business receives the money. (Check out Chapter 3 for how to implement double entry accounting.)

Q. Is each of the following equations correct? What key point does each equation raise?

   a. $250,000 Assets = $100,000 Liabilities + $100,000 Owners' capital

   b. $2,345,000 Assets = $46,900 Liabilities + $2,298,100 Owners' capital

   c. $26,450 Assets = $675,000 Liabilities – $648,550 Owners' capital

   d. $4,650,000 Assets = $4,250,000 Liabilities + $400,000 Owners' capital

A. Each accounting equation offers an important lesson.

a. Whoops! This accounting equation doesn't balance, and so clearly something's wrong. The Liabilities, owner's capital or some combination of both is $50,000 too low; or the two items on the right-hand side may be correct, in which case total assets are overstated $50,000. With an unbalanced equation such as this one, the accountant definitely needs to find the error or errors and make appropriate correcting entries.

b. This accounting equation balances, but, wow! Look at the very small size of liabilities relative to assets. This kind of contrast isn't typical. The liabilities of a typical business usually account for a much larger percentage of its total assets.

c. This accounting equation balances, but the business has a large negative owners' capital. Such a large negative amount of owners' capital means the business has suffered major losses that have wiped out almost all its assets. You wouldn't want to be one of this business's creditors (or one of its owners).

d. This accounting equation balances and is correct, but you should notice that the business is *highly leveraged*, which means that the ratio of debt to capital (liabilities divided by owners' capital) is very high, more than 10 to 1. This ratio is quite unusual.

1. Which of the following is the normal way to present the accounting equation?

    a. Liabilities = Assets – Owners' capital

    b. Assets – Liabilities = Owners' capital

    c. Assets = Liabilities + Owners' capital

    d. Assets – Liabilities – Owners' capital = 0

Solve It

2. A business has £485,000 total liabilities and £1,200,000 total owners' capital. What is the amount of its total assets?

Solve It

£485,000 + £1,200,000 =

= £1,685,000

3. A business has £250,000 total liabilities. At start-up, the owners invested £500,000 in the business. Unfortunately, the business has suffered a cumulative loss of £200,000 up to the present time. What is the amount of its total assets at the present time?

Solve It

Assets = 550,000

Liab = 250,000

owner £500,000
        200,000
        300,000

4. A business has £175,000 total liabilities. At start-up, the owners invested £250,000 capital. The business has earned £190,000 cumulative profit since its creation, all of which has been retained in the business. What is the total amount of its assets?

Solve It

Liab = 175,000

owners = 250,000 440,000
        190,000

Ass = £615,000.

Distinguishing Between Cash- and Accrual-Based Accounting

Cash-based accounting refers to keeping a record of cash inflows and cash outflows. Individuals use cash-based accounting when keeping their chequebooks, because people need to know their day-to-day cash balance and need a journal of their cash receipts and cash expenditures during the year for filing their annual income tax returns.

Individuals have assets other than cash (such as cars, computers and homes), and they have liabilities (such as credit card balances and home mortgages). Hardly anyone we know keeps accounting records of their noncash assets and their liabilities (aside from putting bills to pay and receipts for major purchases in folders). Most people keep a chequebook, and that's all as regards their personal accounting.

Although it's perfect for individuals, cash-based accounting just doesn't make the grade for the large majority of businesses. Cash-based accounting doesn't provide the information that managers need to run a firm or the information necessary to prepare business tax returns and financial reports. Some small businesses are able to use cash-based accounting for the filing of their VAT returns. There's a turnover limit applied to VAT cash accounting; it can only be used if your estimated taxable turnover during the next tax year is not more than £1.35 million (correct at the time of writing).

Most businesses apply *accrual-based accounting* methods. This method ensures that the business records revenue at the time the sale is made (rather than when the cash has been received for the goods), and records expenses to match with the sales revenue or at least in the period benefitted.

Most firms keep track of their cash inflows and outflows, of course, but accrual-based accounting allows them to record all the assets and liabilities of the business. Also, accrual-based accounting keeps track of the money the owners invested in the business and the accumulated profit retained in the business. In short, accrual-based accounting has a much broader scope than cash-based accounting.

A big difference between cash- and accrual-based accounting concerns how they measure annual profit of a business. With cash-based accounting, profit simply equals the total of cash inflows from sales minus the total of cash outflows for expenses of making sales and running the business, or in other words, the net increase in cash from sales and expenses. With the accrual-based accounting method, profit is measured differently because the two components of profit – sales revenue and expenses – are recorded differently.

When using accrual-based accounting, a business records sales revenue when a sale is made and the products and/or services are delivered to the customer, whether the customer pays cash on the spot or receives credit and doesn't pay the business until sometime later. Sales revenue is recorded before cash is actually received. The business doesn't record the cost of the goods (products) sold as an expense until sales revenue is recorded, even though the business paid out cash for the products weeks or months earlier. Furthermore, with accrual-based accounting, a business records operating expenses as soon as they're incurred (as soon as the business has a liability for the expense), even though the expenses aren't paid until sometime later.

Cash-based accounting doesn't reflect economic reality for businesses that sell and buy on credit, carry stocks, invest in long-lived operating assets and make long-term commitments for such things as employee pensions and retirement benefits. When you look beyond small cash-based business, you quickly realise that businesses need the comprehensive recordkeeping of accrual-based accounting. We like to call it 'economic reality accounting'.

The following example question focuses on certain fundamental differences between cash-based and accrual-based accounting regarding the recording of sales revenue and expenses for the purpose of measuring profit.

Q. You started a new business one year ago. You've been busy dealing with so many problems that you haven't had time to sit down and look at whether you made a profit or not. You haven't run out of cash (which for a start-up venture is quite an accomplishment), but you understand that the sustainability of the business depends on making a profit. The following two summaries present cash flow information for the year and information about two assets and a liability at year-end:

Revenue and Expense Cash Flows For First Year

£558,000 cash receipts from sales

£375,000 cash payments for purchases of products

£340,000 cash payments for other expenses

Assets and Liabilities at Year-End

£52,000 debtors from customers for sales made to them during the year

£85,000 cost of products in stock that haven't yet been sold

£25,000 liability for unpaid expenses

Compare the profit or loss of your business for its first year according to the cash- and accrual-based accounting methods.

A. Profit according to cash-based accounting equals the cash inflow from sales minus the total of cash outflows for expenses (and the total of cash outflows for expenses equals the purchases of products plus other expenses). Thus, under cash-based accounting, your business has a loss for the year:

Sales revenue: £558,000

Less expenses: £715,000

Loss: £157,000

Under accrual-based accounting, you record different amounts for sales revenue and the two expenses, which are calculated as follows:

Sales revenue: £610,000 (£558,000 cash receipts from sales + £52,000 year-end debtors)

Cost of Goods Sold: £290,000 (£375,000 cash payments for purchases – £85,000 year-end stock)

Other expenses: £365,000 (£340,000 cash payments for other expenses + £25,000 year-end liability for unpaid expenses)

Loss: £45,000

To answer Questions 5 to 8, please refer to the summary of revenue and expense cash flows and the summary of two assets and a liability at year-end presented in the preceding example question.

5. What would be the amount of accrual-based <u>sales revenue</u> for the year if the business's year-end debtors had been £92,000?

Solve It

loss ⚡ 5000

£ 558.000 + £ 92000 =

£ 650.000

6. What would be the amount of accrual-based <u>Cost of Goods Sold</u> expense for the year if the business's cost of products held in stock at year-end had been £95,000?

Solve It

loss ⚡ 375000

£ 280.000

7. What would be the amount of accrual-based other expenses for the year if the business's liability for unpaid expenses at year-end had been £30,000?

Solve It

loss - £ 50.000.

£ 340000 + £ 30000 =

= £ 370000

8. Based on the changes for the example given in Questions 5, 6 and 7, determine the profit or loss of the business for its first year.

Solve It

Not profit, Not loss.

£ 0.00.

£ 650.000 ,

370.000 } £ 650.000
280.000 }

0.00

Summarising Profit Activities in the Profit and Loss Statement

As crass as it sounds, business managers get paid to make profit happen. Management literature usually stresses the visionary, leadership and innovative characteristics of business managers, but these traits aren't worth much if the business suffers losses year after year or fails to establish sustainable profit performance. After all, businesses are profit-motivated, aren't they?

Therefore, the Profit and Loss Statement takes centre stage in business financial reports. The Profit and Loss Statement summarises a business's revenue and other income, expenses, losses and bottom-line profit or loss for a period. The Profit and Loss Statement gets top billing over the other two primary financial statements (the balance sheet and the cash flow statement), which we discuss in the later sections 'Assembling a Balance Sheet' and 'Partitioning the Statement of Cash Flows'. The Profit and Loss Statement is referred to informally as the Profit & Loss or P&L statement, although these titles are seldom used in external financial reports.

Financial reporting standards demand that a Profit and Loss Statement is presented annually to owners. But financial reporting rules are fairly permissive regarding exactly what information should be reported and how it's presented (see Chapter 5 for the full scoop on Profit and Loss Statement disclosure).

Q. Take a look at this extremely abbreviated and condensed Profit and Loss Statement for a business's most recent year. (***Note:*** a formal Profit and Loss Statement in a financial report must disclose more information than you see here.)

Profit and Loss Statement for Year

Sales revenue	£26,000,000
Expenses	£24,310,000
Net income	£1,690,000

This business sells products, which are also called *goods* or *merchandise*. The cost of products sold to customers during the year was £14,300,000. Expand the condensed Profit and Loss Statement to reflect this additional information.

A. Profit and Loss Statement reporting requires a business to show the Cost of Goods (products) Sold as a separate expense and deduct it immediately below sales revenue. The difference must be reported as *gross margin* (or *Gross Profit*). Therefore, the condensed Profit and Loss Statement should be expanded as follows:

Profit and Loss Statement for Year

Sales revenue	£26,000,000
Cost of Goods Sold	£14,300,000
Gross margin	£11,700,000
Other expenses	£10,010,000
Net income	£1,690,000

9. One rule of the Profit and Loss Statement reporting is that interest expense and income tax expense is reported separately. The £10,010,000 'Other expenses' in the Profit and Loss Statement for the answer to the example question includes £350,000 interest expense and £910,000 income tax. Rebuild the Profit and Loss Statement given the information for these additional two expenses. **Hint:** profit before interest expense is usually labelled 'operating earnings', and profit after interest and before income tax expense is usually labelled 'earnings before income tax'.

Solve It

10. Please refer to the Profit and Loss Statement for the answer to the example question. Suppose the business distributed £650,000 cash to its shareowners from its profit (net income) for the year. Is this cash disbursement treated as an expense?

Solve It

Assembling a Balance Sheet

The *balance sheet* (also called the statement of financial position) is one of the three primary financial statements that businesses report (the other two being the Profit and Loss Statement and the cash flow statement). The balance sheet summarises the assets, liabilities and owners' capital accounts of a business at an instant in time. Prepared at the close of business on the last day of the profit period, the balance sheet presents a 'freeze frame' look at the business's financial condition.

Preparing and reporting a balance sheet takes time, so by the time you read a balance sheet, it's already somewhat out-of-date. The business's stream of activities and operations doesn't stop, which means that from the date at which the balance sheet was prepared to when you read it, the business will have engaged in many transactions. These subsequent transactions may have significantly changed its financial condition. For more on the balance sheet, turn to Chapter 6.

In accounting, the term *balance* refers to the sterling amount of an account, after recording all increases and decreases in the account caused by business activities. The balance sheet reports the balances of asset, liability and owners' capital accounts, but it also refers to the equality, or balance, of the accounting equation (see the section 'Keeping the Accounting Equation in Balance' earlier in this chapter).

Q. The following list summarises the assets and liabilities of a business at the close of business on the last day of its most recent profit period:

Amounts owed by customers to the business: £485,000

Cost of unsold products (that is to be sold next period): £678,000

Cash balance on deposit in current account with bank: £396,000

Amounts owed by business for unpaid purchases and expenses: £438,000

Loans owed to bank (on which interest is paid): £500,000

Original cost of long-term operating assets that are being depreciated over their useful lives to the business: £950,000

Accumulated depreciation of long-term operating assets: £305,000

Using this information, prepare the business's balance sheet.

A.

Cash	£396,000	Creditors	£438,000
Debtors	£485,000	Loans owed	£500,000
Stock	£678,000	Owners' Capital*	£1,266,000
Fixed Assets (Net of Accumulated Depreciation)	£645,000		
Total Assets	£2,204,000	Total Liabilities and Owners' Capital	£2,204,000

*Owners' capital is determined by deducting the sum of liabilities from total assets.

Note: This balance sheet isn't classified into current assets and current liabilities. Also, owners' capital isn't classified. (Chapter 6 explains the balance sheet in greater detail.)

Now use the balance sheet shown in the preceding example to answer Questions 13 to 16.

11. Suppose £950,000 of owners' capital consists of profit earned and not distributed by the business. What is this amount usually called in the balance sheet? And, what is the other amount of owners' capital called in the balance sheet?

Solve It

12. The business appears unable to pay its liabilities. The two liabilities total £938,000, but the business has a cash balance of only £396,000. Do you agree?

Solve It

13. Can you tell the amount of profit the business earned in the period just ended?

Solve It

14. In a balance sheet, assets usually are listed in the order of their liquidity (how quickly they convert to cash). Cash is listed first, followed by the asset closest to being converted into cash and so on. Is the sequence of assets correct according to the normal rules for presenting assets in balance sheets?

Solve It

Partitioning the Cash Flow Statement

You can argue that the cash flow statement is the most important of the three primary financial statements. Why? Because in the long run, everything comes down to cash flows. Profit recorded on the accrual basis of accounting has to be turned into cash – and the sooner the better. Otherwise, profit doesn't provide money for growing the business and paying distributions to owners.

By themselves, the Profit and Loss Statement and balance sheet don't provide information about the cash flow generated by the business's profit-making, or operating, activities. But people who use financial reports (business managers, lenders and investors) want to see cash flow information. In short, financial reporting standards require a cash flow statement.

Accountants normally categorise the cash flow into three different types:

- ✔ Cash flows from operating activities, which include inflows from sales and cash outflows from expenses.

- ✔ Investing activities, which include the purchase and construction of long-term operating assets such as land, buildings, equipment, machinery, vehicles and tools. If a business realises cash from the disposal of such assets, the proceeds are included in this category of cash flows.

- ✔ Financing activities, which include borrowing money from debt sources and paying loans at maturity as well as raising capital from shareowners and returning capital to them. Cash distributions from profit are included in this category of cash flows.

Q. The cash flow statement for a business's most recent year is presented as follows. Based on the information provided, can the amount of cash flow be determined from operating activities?

Cash flow from operating activities:	?????
Cash flow from investing activities:	
Capital expenditures	(£2,345,000)
Proceeds from disposal of property	£225,000 (£2,120,000)
Cash flow from financing activities:	
Increase in debt	£1,625,000
Issue of capital stock shares	£550,000
Cash dividends to shareholders	(£400,000) £1,775,000
Net cash increase during year	£355,000

A. You can determine the amount of cash flow from operating activities by the following calculations:

£2,120,000 net cash needed for capital expenditures + £355,000 cash balance increase = £2,475,000 total cash needed

£2,475,000 total cash needed – £1,775,000 net cash provided from financing activities = £700,000 cash flow from operating activities

Cash flow from operating activities is explained in more detail in Chapter 8.

You can condense a cash flow statement, such as the one for the example, into its four basic components as follows (negative numbers appear in parentheses):

Cash flow from operating activities	£700,000
Cash flow from investing activities	(£2,120,000)
Cash flow from financing activities	£1,775,000
Net increase in cash during the year	£355,000

If you know three of the four components in a condensed cash flow statement, you can determine the fourth factor. Suppose that you know the increase or decrease in cash during the year (which is easy enough to determine by comparing the ending cash balance with the beginning cash balance). And suppose that you can quickly determine the cash flow from investing activities and the cash flow from financing activities (because not many transactions of these two types exist during the year).

Knowing these three factors, you can quickly determine the cash flow from operating activities. The remainder of the increase or decrease in cash during the year is attributable to operating activities.

Questions 15 to 18 give you three of the four components in a condensed cash flow statement and ask you to solve for the unknown factor.

15. Three of the four components of cash flow for the year of a business are as follows:

Cash flow from operating activities	£450,000
Cash flow from investing activities	(£725,000)
Cash flow from financing activities	£50,000
Net increase (decrease) in cash during the year	????

Determine the increase or decrease in cash during the year.

Solve It

16. Three of the four components of cash flow for the year of a business are as follows:

Cash flow from operating activities	£2,680,000
Cash flow from investing activities	????
Cash flow from financing activities	£1,250,000
Net increase (decrease) in cash during the year	£400,000

Determine cash flow from investing activities for the year.

Solve It

17. Three of the four components of cash flow for the year of a business are as follows:

Cash flow from operating activities	$650,000
Cash flow from investing activities	($925,000)
Cash flow from financing activities	????
Net increase (decrease) in cash during the year	($65,000)

Determine cash flow from financing activities for the year.

Solve It

18. Three of the four components of cash flow for the year of a business are as follows:

Cash flow from operating activities	????
Cash flow from investing activities	($480,000)
Cash flow from financing activities	($150,000)
Net increase (decrease) in cash during the year	$150,000

Determine cash flow from operating activities for the year.

Solve It

Tracing How Dishonest Accounting Distorts Financial Statements

Obviously, a business needs to keep its accounting system as honest as the day is long. In preparing its financial statements, a business should be forthright and not misleading. Unfortunately some businesses cheat in their accounting and financial reporting. Now, there's cheating and then there's real cheating. So what's the difference?

Many businesses perform cosmetic surgery on their accounts, touching up their financial condition and profit performance. This practice is popularly called *massaging the numbers*. Professional investors (as in mutual fund managers) and lenders (as in banks) know that many businesses employ a certain amount of accounting manipulation, and as a practical matter not much can be done about it.

On another level, some businesses resort to accounting fraud to put a better sheen on profit performance and conceal financial problems. Accounting fraud is popularly called *cooking the books*. Think of massaging the numbers as fibbing or putting a spin on the truth and cooking the books as out-and-out lying with the intent to deceive and mislead.

In recent years the incidence of accounting fraud has risen alarmingly. (Does Enron ring any bells?) Accounting fraud is illegal and perpetrators are subject to prosecution under criminal law. Plus, victims can sue the persons responsible for the fraud.

EXAMPLE

Q. Suppose that a business has engaged in some accounting fraud to boost its profit for the year just ended. Assume that the business didn't commit any accounting fraud before this year (which may not be true, of course). As the result of fraudulent entries in its accounts, the £2,340,000 bottom-line profit reported in its Profit and Loss Statement was overstated £385,000. How does this dishonest accounting distort the business's balance sheet?

A. Owners' capital is overstated £385,000 because profit increases owners' capital. And the overstatement of profit may have involved the overstatement of assets, the understatement of liabilities or a combination of both. To correct this error, owners' capital should be decreased £385,000. In addition, assets should be decreased £385,000 or liabilities should be increased £385,000 (or some combination of both).

19. Suppose a business commits accounting fraud by deliberately not writing down its stock of £268,000, which is the cost of certain products that it can no longer sell and are going to be thrown in the junk heap. How should its balance sheet be adjusted to correct for this accounting fraud, ignoring income tax effects? (Use the answer template provided.)

Cash	Creditors
Debtors	Loans Payable
Stock	Owners' Capital
Fixed Assets (Net of Accumulated Depreciation) _____	
Total Assets	Total Liabilities and Owners' Capital _____

Solve It

20. Suppose a business commits accounting fraud by deliberately not recording £465,000 liabilities for unpaid expenses at the end of the year. How should its balance sheet be adjusted to correct for this accounting fraud, ignoring income tax effects? (Use the answer template provided.)

Cash	Creditors
Debtors	Loans Payable
Stock	Owners' Capital
Fixed Assets (Net of Accumulated Depreciation) _____	
Total Assets	Total Liabilities and Owners' Capital _____

Solve It

Answers to Problems on Elements of Business Accounting

Here are the answers to the practice questions presented earlier in this chapter.

1 Which of the following is the normal way to present the accounting equation?

c. Assets = Liabilities + Owners' capital

The other three accounting equations are correct from the algebraic equation point of view. However, the accounting equation is usually shown with assets on one side and the two broad classes of claims against the assets on the other side. *Note:* you see answer (b) (Assets – Liabilities = Owners' capital) when the purpose is to emphasise the *net worth* of a business, or its assets less its liabilities.

2 A business has £485,000 total liabilities and £1,200,000 total owners' capital. What is the amount of its total assets?

Total assets = £1,685,000, which is the total of £485,000 liabilities plus £1,200,000 owners' capital.

3 A business has £250,000 total liabilities. When it was started the owners invested £500,000 in the business. Unfortunately, the business has suffered a cumulative loss of £200,000 up to the present time. What is the amount of its total assets at the present time?

Total assets = £550,000, which is the total of £250,000 liabilities plus £300,000 owners' capital.

Notice that the original £500,000 that the owners invested in the business is reduced by the £200,000 cumulative loss of the business, and the owners' capital is now only £300,000.

4 A business has £175,000 total liabilities. Originally, at the time of starting the business, the owners invested £250,000 capital. The business has earned £190,000 cumulative profit since it started (all of which has been retained in the business). What is the total amount of its assets?

Total assets = £615,000, which is the total of £175,000 liabilities and £440,000 owners' capital.

Notice that in addition to the original £250,000 capital invested by owners, the business has earned £190,000 profit, so its total owners' capital is £440,000.

5 What would be the amount of accrual-based sales revenue for the year if the business's year-end receivables had been £92,000? (For the original numbers, see the earlier section 'Distinguishing Between Cash- and Accrual-Based Accounting'.)

Sales revenue (£558,000 cash receipts + £92,000 year-end debtors) = £650,000

6 What would be the amount of accrual-based cost of products sold expense for the year if the business's cost of products held in stock at year-end had been £95,000? (For the original numbers, see the earlier section 'Distinguishing Between Cash- and Accrual-Based Accounting'.)

Cost of products sold (£375,000 cash payments – £95,000 year-end stock) = £280,000

7 What would be the amount of accrual-based other expenses for the year if the business's liability for unpaid expenses at year-end had been £30,000? (For the original numbers, see the earlier section 'Distinguishing Between Cash- and Accrual-Based Accounting'.)

Other expenses (£340,000 cash payments + £30,000 year-end liability) = £370,000

8 Based on the changes to the example given in Questions 5, 6 and 7, determine the profit or loss of the business for its first year.

In this case, the total of the two expenses (cost of products sold and other expenses) happens to be £650,000, which is exactly equal to sales revenue. So the business breaks even for the year. This outcome is unusual, of course; the total of expenses for the year is almost always different to the total sales revenue for the year.

9 One rule of Profit and Loss Statement reporting is that interest expense and income tax expense is reported separately. The £10,010,000 'Other expenses' in the Profit and Loss Statement for the answer to the example question includes £350,000 interest expense and £910,000 income tax. Rebuild the Profit and Loss Statement given the information for these additional two expenses. **Hint:** profit before interest expense is usually labelled 'operating earnings' and profit after interest and before income tax expense is usually labelled 'earnings before income tax'.

Profit and Loss Statement for Year

Sales revenue	£26,000,000
Cost of Goods Sold	14,300,000
Gross margin	£11,700,000
Other expenses	8,750,000
Operating earnings	£2,950,000
Interest expense	350,000
Earnings before income tax	£2,600,000
Income tax expense	910,000
Net income	£1,690,000

Burying interest expense or income tax expense in a broader expense category such as 'other expenses' or 'general expenses' is unacceptable. Interest and income tax expenses are reported towards the bottom of the Profit and Loss Statement. They're viewed as *nonoperating expenses*, which means that they depend on how the business is financed and its income tax situation.

10 Please refer to the Profit and Loss Statement for the answer to the example question. Suppose the business distributed £650,000 cash to its shareowners from its profit (net income) for the year. Is this cash disbursement treated as an expense?

No, cash distributions from profit to the shareowners of a business aren't an expense. In other words, net income is before any distributions to shareowners.

Profit and Loss Statements generally don't disclose information regarding distributions from profit (net income) during the year. To be more accurate, a Profit and Loss Statement doesn't *have to* disclose this information. However, some businesses don't end their Profit and Loss Statements at bottom-line net income: they add net income to the retained earnings balance at the start of the year and deduct distributions from net income during the year to arrive at the year-end balance of retained earnings. But such disclosure isn't common practice. Distributions from net income usually are reported in a separate financial statement called the Statement of Changes in Owners' Capital, which we discuss in Chapter 8.

11 Suppose £950,000 of owners' capital consists of profit earned and not distributed by the business. What is this amount usually called in the balance sheet? And, what is the other amount of owners' capital called in the balance sheet?

The £950,000 of owners' capital over and above the amount of capital invested by the owners typically is called *retained earnings*. To be more precise, business corporations and limited liability companies use this term. (If a business is organised legally as a partnership, it follows different practices for reporting the partners' capital.) The remaining balance is called capital invested.

12 The business appears unable to pay its liabilities. The two liabilities total £938,000, but the business has a cash balance of only £396,000. Do you agree?

A business isn't expected to hold cash equal to the total of its liabilities. In our opinion, this business wouldn't be judged insolvent, although this judgement depends on how conservative or strict you are in evaluating solvency. The business's cash flow prospects are the key factor. The debtors accounts will be collected in the short-run, and this incoming cash will be available for paying the business's liabilities. Also, the stock held by the business will be sold during the short-run and generate cash flow.

13 Can you tell the amount of profit the business earned in the period just ended?

No, a balance sheet doesn't report profit (net income) for the most recent period. You look to its Profit and Loss Statement for this key figure.

14 In a balance sheet, assets usually are listed in the order of their liquidity (how quickly they convert to cash). Cash is listed first, followed by the asset closest to being converted into cash and so on. Is the sequence of assets correct according to the normal rules for presenting assets in balance sheets?

Yes, the sequence is correct according to conventional rules for reporting assets in a balance sheet. Cash is listed first, followed by assets according to their liquidity. In the example, cash is first, debtors are listed second, after cash, because debtors will be collected in the short-term. Stock is listed after debtors because this asset consists of products that have to be sold before they can be converted into cash.

15 Based on the three of four components of cash flow for the year of a business that follow, determine the increase or decrease in cash during the year.

Cash flow from operating activities	£450,000
Cash flow from investing activities	(£725,000)
Cash flow from financing activities	£50,000
Net increase (decrease) in cash during the year	????

Cash decreased £225,000 during the year.

16 Based on the three of four components of cash flow for the year of a business that follow, determine cash flow from investing activities for the year.

Cash flow from operating activities	£2,680,000
Cash flow from investing activities	????
Cash flow from financing activities	£1,250,000
Net increase (decrease) in cash during the year	£400,000

Cash flow from investing activities for the year is a *negative* £3,530,000. In other words, the net cash *decrease* from investing activities was £3,530,000 during the year.

17 Based on the three of four components of cash flow for the year of a business that follow, determine cash flow from financing activities for the year.

Cash flow from operating activities	$650,000
Cash flow from investing activities	($925,000)
Cash flow from financing activities	????
Net increase (decrease) in cash during the year	($65,000)

Cash flow from financing activities for the year is $210,000. In other words, the net cash increase from financing activities was $210,000 during the year.

18 Based on the three of four components of cash flow for the year of a business that follow, determine cash flow from operating activities for the year.

Cash flow from operating activities	????
Cash flow from investing activities	($480,000)
Cash flow from financing activities	($150,000)
Net increase (decrease) in cash during the year	$150,000

Cash flow from operating activities for the year is $780,000. In other words, the net cash increase from sales and expense (operating) activities was $780,000 during the year.

19 Suppose a business commits accounting fraud by deliberately not writing down its stock of $268,000, which is the cost of certain products that it can no longer sell and are going to be thrown in the junk heap. How should its balance sheet be adjusted to correct for this accounting fraud, ignoring income tax effects?

The changes in the balance sheet to correct the fraudulent error are:

Cash		Creditors	
Debtors		Loans Payable	
Stock	($268,000)	Owners' Capital	($268,000)
Fixed Assets (Net of Accumulated Depreciation)	_____		_____
Total Assets	($268,000)	Total Liabilities and Owners' Capital	($268,000)

20 Suppose a business commits accounting fraud by deliberately not recording $465,000 liabilities for unpaid expenses at the end of the year. How should its balance sheet be adjusted to correct for this accounting fraud, ignoring income tax effects?

The changes in the balance sheet to correct the fraudulent error are:

Cash		Creditors	$465,000
Debtors		Loans Payable	
Stock		Owners' Capital	($465,000)
Fixed Assets (Net of Accumulated Depreciation)	_____		_____

Total Assets Total Liabilities and Owners' Capital

Chapter 2

Financial Effects of Transactions

. . . .

. . . .

*T*he primary job of accounting is to record faithfully all the transactions of the business so that you can prepare financial statements from the transaction records. Transactions are the heartbeat of every business, which is why accountants, above all else, must know how to record them, and this chapter shows you how to do so.

Note: in this chapter, we don't use debits and credits (which we discuss in Chapter 3). Instead, we keep the focus on the balance sheet, which is the summary of the financial condition of a business.

Relying on Accurate Transaction Records

The following three financial statements are the financial anchors and reference points of every business:

> ✔ **Balance sheet:** Summarises the business's assets, liabilities and owners' capital at the end of a period.
>
> ✔ **Cash flow statement:** Summarises the business's cash transactions for the same period of time.
>
> ✔ **Profit and Loss Statement:** Summarises the profit-making transactions of the business for a period of time.

These three important statements are based on the transaction records you've made. If you're more the visual type, try this illustration on for size:

Transactions → Accounting process → Financial statements

Transactions can best be described as 'economic exchanges' between the business and the groups of people or entities that surround it. Here are the six basic groups with which a business may conduct transactions:

- ✔ **Customers:** Who buy the goods and services that the business sells.

- ✔ **Employees:** Who provide their skills and services to the business in exchange for a salary and benefits.

- ✔ **HM Revenue & Customs (HMRC):** Who expect the business to collect taxes on their behalf and pay them across.

- ✔ **Investors:** Who invest their own money into the business so that they may receive a return on their investment.

- ✔ **Lenders:** Who provide finance to the business usually in the form of a loan and expect interest to be paid on that loan.

- ✔ **Suppliers:** Who sell a wide variety of products to the business so that it may operate its business.

---

1. Name the three main financial statements and describe which individuals may be interested in using them and why.

Solve It

Classifying Business Transactions

Businesses are profit-motivated, and so one basic type of transactions is obvious: profit-making transactions. In a nutshell, *profit-making transactions* consist of making sales and incurring expenses.

Well, if you want to be picky, a business may have other income in addition to sales revenue, and it may record losses in addition to expenses. But the bread and butter profit-making activities of a business are making sales and keeping expenses under control. The profit-making transactions of a business over a period of time are reported in its Profit and Loss Statement (see Chapter 1 for more on the Profit and Loss Statement).

Consider, for instance, the purchase of products for stock. As far as profit is concerned, nothing happens until the business makes a sale of that stock and records the Cost of Goods Sold expense against the revenue from the sale. Because the business needs to have the products available for sale, the purchase of stock is likely to be one of the first few transactions a business undertakes.

In understanding accounting, you first need to be very clear about which type of transaction you're looking at.

A transaction may not necessarily be a profit-making transaction; the business may be undertaking the following activities:

- ✔ **Financing activities:** The business may be borrowing money or repaying amounts borrowed, and these transactions need to be recorded. The firm also has to record transactions in which the owners invest capital in the business, and also when distributions are made to them.

- ✔ **Investing activities:** The business may be purchasing long-term assets such as buildings, land, plant and machinery, to aid the operating activities of the business.

Both investing and financing activities tend to affect the balance sheet rather than the Profit and Loss account, because they involve the increase/decrease of assets and liabilities to the business. The Profit and Loss Statement reflects the revenues and expenses of the business rather than the assets, liabilities and capital.

Investing and financing activities for a particular period are reported in that particular period's cash flow statement (Chapter 1 contains all about the cash flow statement).

2. Describe and give as many examples as you can of **profit-making transactions**.

Solve It

3. Describe and give examples of **investing activities**.

Solve It

4. Describe and give examples of **financing activities** that a business may undertake.

Solve It

Seeing Both Sides of Business Transactions

The accountant's job is to capture all the transactions of the business, determine the financial effects of every transaction, record every transaction in the business's accounts and prepare the financial statements from those accounts.

To carry out their mission, accountants must understand how transactions (and certain other events) affect the financial condition of the business. To illustrate the impact of transactions, consider the case of a business that has been in operation for many years. Its condensed balance sheet at the start of the year appears as follows:

Condensed Balance Sheet

Cash	£250,000	Operating Liabilities	£350,000
Noncash (debtors)	£300,000	Debt	£500,000
Noncash (stock)	£400,000	Owner invested capital	£250,000
Noncash (other assets including plant and machinery, land and buildings, fixtures and fittings)	£550,000	Retained earnings	£400,000
Total assets	£1,500,000	Total liabilities and capital	£1,500,000

Assets have been classified as cash and noncash assets. The cash includes cash at the bank (money contained in all the bank accounts) and cash in hand (petty cash). The noncash assets include the following:

- Computer equipment
- Debtors
- Fixtures and fittings
- Land and buildings
- Plant and machinery
- Stock

The noncash assets are shown in the balance sheet at their net value. The term *net* means that the amount of accumulated depreciation that has been recorded up to this time is deducted from the cost of the assets.

Liabilities are divided into two types based on their sources:

- Those that arise out of operating activities
- Those that result from borrowing money on interest-bearing debt

Operating liabilities are short-term and don't bear interest: they include trade creditors, accrued expenses and amounts owed to HMRC. Owners' capital is shown in two different accounts in the preceding table. The first is for capital invested in the business by its owners. This source of owners' capital is segregated from the other owners' account, which expresses profit that has been earned and retained by the business.

In the preceding table, you can see that the total assets and the total liabilities plus owners' capital appear below the line. This information is the accounting equation of the business. The accounting equation is in balance, as of course it should be.

The following examples use the figures shown in the condensed balance sheet (see the preceding table) and show you how the business's balance sheet would appear under differing conditions.

Q. The business borrows £500,000 and signs a loan agreement from the lender, promising to pay interest over the life of the loan and to return £500,000 at a future date. The condensed balance sheet appears as follows:

Condensed Balance Sheet

Cash	+£500,000	Operating liabilities		
Noncash		Debt	+£500,000	
		Owners' invested capital		
		Owners' retained earnings		
Total assets	+£500,000 =	Liabilities and owners' capital	+£500,000	

A. No interest expense is recorded when the money is borrowed because interest is a time charge for using borrowed money. Interest expenses will be recorded in each future period the money is borrowed, starting at the time the money is borrowed.

Q. The business invests £250,000 in a new machine that it will use for several years and pays for the purchase with a cheque. The condensed balance sheet appears as follows:

Condensed Balance Sheet

Cash	−£250,000	Operating liabilities	
		Debt	
		Owners' invested capital	
Noncash	+£250,000	Owners' retained earnings	
Assets	Nil =	Liabilities and owners' capital	Nil

A. No change in total assets takes place, but rather an exchange among assets: cash decreases £250,000 with the cost of the new machine. Keep in mind that the cost of the machine will be charged as a depreciation expense over future periods in which the machine is used.

Q. The business owners invest an additional £750,000 in the business to aid in its growth and expansion. The entries appear as follows:

Condensed Balance Sheet

Cash	+£750,000	Operating liabilities	
		Debt	
		Owners' invested capital	+£750,000
Noncash		Owners' retained earnings	
Assets	+£750,000 =	Liabilities and owners' capital	+£750,000

A. The business owners have invested £750,000 in the business, which will be paid into the bank account and hence shown as cash on the left side of the balance sheet. The corresponding entry is shown on the right hand side of the balance sheet as owners invested capital.

Q. The business distributes £100,000 of the profit it earned during the year to its shareholders. The entries appear as follows:

Condensed Balance Sheet

Cash	–£100,000		Operating liabilities	
			Debt	
			Owners' invested capital	
Noncash			Owners' retained earnings	–£100,000
Assets	–£100,000	=	Liabilities and owners' capital	–£100,000

A. Profit is recorded in owners' retained earnings. Profit increases this account, and distributions from profit decrease the account.

---

5. Suppose that all revenue transactions during the year increase cash and that all expense transactions during the year decrease cash. In other words, suppose that no other assets and no operating liabilities are affected by the profit-making activities of the business during the year (this scenario isn't realistic and is assumed only for this problem). The net income (bottom-line profit) of a typical business for the year is £950,000. Using the following template, show how profit affects the balance sheet.

Condensed Balance Sheet

Cash		Operating liabilities
		Debt
		Owners' invested capital
Noncash		Owners' retained earnings
Assets	=	Liabilities and owners' capital

Solve It

---

6. During the year, a business borrows £850,000 and uses £750,000 of these funds to invest in new long-term operating assets. Using the following template, show how these transactions affect the balance sheet.

Condensed Balance Sheet

Cash		Operating liabilities
		Debt
		Owners' invested capital
Noncash		Owners' retained earnings
Assets	=	Liabilities and Owners' Capital

Solve It

7. A freak flood causes extensive damage to stock. Unfortunately these losses weren't insured, and the business has to write off $175,000 of its stock. Ignoring the income tax effects of this write-off, use the following template to show how these transactions affect the balance sheet.

Condensed Balance Sheet

Cash	Operating liabilities
	Debt
	Owners' invested capital
Noncash	Owners' retained earnings
Assets =	Liabilities and owners' capital

Solve It

8. A loan is due for repayment during the year, and the business decides not to renew it. Accordingly, the business pays $500,000 to the lender, and the loan account is closed. (All interest expenses on this debt were recorded correctly during the year.) Using the following template, show how paying off the loan account affects the balance sheet.

Condensed Balance Sheet

Cash	Operating liabilities
Noncash – debtors debt	
Noncash – stock	Owners' invested capital
Noncash – other assets	Owners' retained earnings
Assets =	Liabilities and owners' capital

Solve It

Concentrating on Sales

One of the most quoted sayings in business is, 'Nothing happens until you sell it'. (Another is, 'There's no such thing as a free lunch', but we digress.) Well, certainly a business has to make sales that generate enough sales revenue to overcome its expenses and leave a residual of profit. As you no doubt know, this task is a tall order.

The effect that making a sale has on a business's financial condition depends on when cash is collected from the sale. Regarding cash collection, sales come in three types:

- **Advance payment sales:** The customer pays the business before the sale is consummated; that is, before the business delivers the product and/or service to the customer.

- **Cash sales:** Cash is collected when the business makes the sale and delivers the product and/or service to the customer.

- **Credit sales:** Cash isn't collected until sometime after the sale is made; the customer is given a period of time before having to pay the business.

No doubt you're familiar with cash and credit sales. However, you may be a little rusty, from an accounting point of view, on advance payment sales. For this type of sale, at the time of receiving an advance payment, the business doesn't record a sale; instead, it records a liability that stays on the books until the product or service is actually delivered to the customer. This specific liability is one of the business's operating liabilities.

For example, we recently sent a £50 cheque to a magazine publisher as advance payment for delivery of our favourite magazine every month for the coming 12 months. Similarly, if we were avid football supporters, we would buy season tickets for our team, which require us to pay before the season starts. Do you give gift certificates to others as birthday or holiday presents? A gift certificate is another example of an advance payment sale. The liability of the advance payment sale is extinguished as magazines are delivered, games are played and gift certificates are redeemed.

Suppose a business recorded £3,200,000 sales revenue for the year just ended. Can you tell how its balance sheet changes as the result of that sales revenue? No, you can't – unless the business makes only cash sales. If the business makes credit sales or collects advance payments from customers for future sales, the changes in its balance sheet caused by sales are a little more involved. Sorry, but this is a business fact of life.

0. A business makes all three kinds of sales: cash, credit and advance payment. For the latest year, it records £3,200,000 total sales revenue. Its sales causes its debtors balance to increase £75,000 during the year and its operating liabilities balance to increase £50,000 during the year. The balance sheet is affected in the following way:

Its sales cause the following changes in the balance sheet for the business:

Condensed Balance Sheet

Cash	+£3,175,000	Operating liabilities	+£50,000
Noncash – debtors	+£75,000	Interest-bearing liabilities	
		Owners' invested capital	
		Owners' retained earnings	+£3,200,000
Assets	+£3,250,000 =	Liabilities and owners' capital	+£3,250,000

A. Some important points to note in this scenario are:

✔ Credit sales cause debtors to increase £75,000 during the year, and so the year-end balance of debtors (shown as a noncash asset) is £75,000 higher than the start-of-year balance. Generally speaking, debtors increase when sales increase year-to-year.

✔ Advance payment sales cause operating liabilities to increase £50,000 during the year, so the year-end balance of the liability for advance payments from customers is £50,000 higher than the start-of-year balance. Generally speaking, this liability increases when sales increase year-to-year.

The £3,200,000 sales revenue for the year increases owners' retained earnings. But don't forget that the business has expenses for the year. Expenses must be deducted from sales revenue to get to the net effect on owners' retained earnings, which is profit for the year. (Expenses are examined in the section 'Concentrating on Expenses' later in this chapter.)

---

9. A business sells only to other businesses and makes all sales on credit; it doesn't have any cash sales or advance payment sales. During the year, the business makes £35,000,000 sales. From these sales, the business collects £31,500,000 during the year, and also collects the £3,250,000 debtors balance at the start of the year. Using the following template, show the effects of these transactions on the business's balance sheet.

Condensed Balance Sheet

Cash	Operating liabilities
	Debt
	Owners' invested capital
Noncash – debtors	Owners' retained earnings
Assets =	Liabilities and owners' capital

Solve It

10. A business requires advance payments on all sales. In other words, it collects cash from customers before products are delivered to them later. During the year, the business receives £12,500,000 in advance payments from customers. By the end of the year, the business has delivered 85 per cent of products to customers for advance payments received during the year. Also, the business delivers products to customers during the year that fully discharges the £1,500,000 balance in liability for advance payments at the start of the year. Using the following template, show the effects of these transactions on the business's balance sheet.

Condensed Balance Sheet

Cash	Operating liabilities
	Debt
	Owners' invested capital
Noncash	Owners' retained earnings
Assets =	Liabilities and owners' capital

Solve It

11. During the year, a business makes £3,650,000 cash sales. The business has a very liberal product return policy and therefore accepts product returns from customers and refunds £450,000 cash. Using the following template, show the effects of these transactions on the business's balance sheet.

Condensed Balance Sheet

Cash	Operating liabilities
	Debt
	Owners' invested capital
Noncash	Owners' retained earnings
Assets =	Liabilities and owners' capital

Solve It

12. During its first year of business, a firm makes £6,250,000 credit sales. The business collects £5,600,000 cash from customers during the year from these sales. Unfortunately, a few customers don't pay despite repeated requests and threats of legal action. The business cuts off credit to these 'deadbeat' customers and refuses to make any more credit sales to them. The business has to write off £150,000 uncollectible debtors. Using the following template, show the effects of these transactions on the business's balance sheet.

Condensed Balance Sheet

Cash	Operating liabilities
Noncash – debtors	Debt
	Owners' invested capital
	Owners' retained earnings
Assets =	Liabilities and owners' capital

Solve It

Concentrating on Expenses

Just as cash is collected before, after or at the time of sale, cash is paid before, after or at the time that an expense is recorded. The following are some examples of cash payment for expenses:

- **Paying cash before an expense is recorded:** The expense of Cost of Goods (products) Sold isn't recorded until the sale is made. (Products are bought and paid for before they're sold to customers.) Another example is that businesses pay for insurance policies today that provide coverage for six months or more, but the insurance expense isn't recorded until time passes.

- **Paying cash after an expense is recorded:** A business records advertising expenses because the ads have already appeared on TV or in newspapers, but it may not pay the bills for these ads until next year.

- **Paying cash when an expense is recorded:** Wages and salaries expenses are generally recorded at the time employees are paid.

Most businesses invest in long-term operating assets, the cost of which is charged to the depreciation expense over many years. Essentially, a business pays for the asset today, but the cost of the asset is recorded as an expense over several future years.

Suppose we tell you that a business records £3,000,000 total expenses for the year just ended. Does this simply mean that cash decreased this amount? Hardly! Recording expenses involves other assets than just cash – it involves operating liabilities as well.

Q. We are now going to look at how expenses impact the balance sheet. (The impact of sales is discussed in the 'Concentrating on Sales' section). Expenses are now dealt with to close the profit circle. During the year just ended, the business records all three types of expenses – expenses recorded before, after and at the time of paying the expense. For the year, the business records £3,000,000 total expenses. These expenses cause stock to increase £50,000 during the year, other noncash assets to decrease £75,000 (because depreciation on the assets was recorded) and operating liabilities to increase £45,000.

This example shows how the condensed balance sheet is affected by the preceding expense transactions:

Condensed Balance Sheet

Cash	–£2,930,000	Operating liabilities	+£45,000
		Debt	
Noncash – stock	+£50,000	Owners' invested capital	
Noncash – other assets	–£75,000	Owners' retained earnings	–£3,000,000
Assets	–£2,955,000 =	Liabilities and owners' capital	–£2,955,000

A. Some important points to note in this scenario are:

✔ The business records $75,000 depreciation expenses for the year, and so its long-term operating assets (noncash assets) decrease this amount.

✔ The $50,000 *increase* in stock may strike you as an odd effect of expenses. Keep in mind, however, that a business can purchase or manufacture more stock than it sells during the year, in which case its stock balance increases; that's exactly what happened in this example.

✔ The business has $45,000 more operating liabilities at year-end than it did at the start of the year. In other words, its unpaid expenses at the end of the year are $45,000 more than at the beginning of the year.

✔ The retained earnings are reduced by the $3,000,000 spent on expenses.

Note: both sides of the balance sheet must balance, and so you can see from the preceding example that the balance sheet has a negative impact of $2,955,000. The cash balance is a balancing figure when you've entered the impact of all the transactions noted above.

---

13. A business records $4,500,000 total expenses for the year. The expenses cause a $100,000 increase in its operating liabilities, and a $200,000 depreciation expense is recorded in the year. No change in stock takes place during the year (which is unusual). Using the following template, show how the expenses affect the balance sheet. (Again, treat cash as the balancing figure, when you've plugged all the other numbers into the balance sheet).

Condensed Balance Sheet

Cash	Operating liabilities
	Debt
	Owners' invested capital
Noncash	Owners' retained earnings
Assets =	Liabilities and owners' capital

Solve It

---

14. A business leases all its long-term operating assets (buildings, machines, vehicles and so on). Thus, it has no depreciation expense. For the year just ended, the business records $2,450,000 total expenses. Expenses cause a $75,000 increase in operating liabilities. Stock increases $45,000 during the year. Using the following template, show how the expenses affect the balance sheet. (Again, treat cash as the balancing figure, when you've plugged all the other numbers into the balance sheet).

Condensed Balance Sheet

Cash	Operating liabilities
	Debt
	Owners' invested capital
Noncash	Owners' retained earnings
Assets =	Liabilities and owners' capital

Solve It

15. A business is just about ready to prepare its financial statements for the year when a sharp-eyed bookkeeper notices that the business has failed to accrue (record) certain liabilities for unpaid expenses at the end of the year. So, a correcting entry has to be made. The amount of these liabilities for unpaid expenses at year-end is $38,000. Using the following template, show how the accruals affect the balance sheet.

Condensed Balance Sheet

Cash	Operating liabilities
	Debt
	Owners' invested capital
Noncash	Owners' retained earnings
Assets =	Liabilities and owners' capital

Solve It

---

16. A business decides to engage in accounting fraud to improve its profit performance for the year. Of course, doing so is unethical and illegal, but the chief executive of the business is desperate, and the chief accountant agrees to conspire with the chief executive to carry out this accounting fraud. They decide that they can't manipulate sales revenue for the year, and so the accounting fraud has to be done on the expense side of the ledger. The changes in financial condition caused by the actual expenses of the business for the year are given below. How may management go about misstating the expenses in order to boost profit $125,000? (Note: you have to think like a crook to work this problem.)

Condensed Balance Sheet

Cash	−$4,800,000	Operating liabilities	+$275,000
		Debtors	
Stock	+$50,000	Owners' invested capital	
Noncash assets	−$400,000	Owners' retained earnings	−$5,425,000
Assets	−$5,150,000 =	Liabilities and owners' capital	−$5,150,000

Solve It

Determining the Composite Effect of Profit

To determine the profit or loss of a business for the year, you need to blend sales revenue and expenses together. The equation for profit is as follows:

Profit = Sales revenue – Expenses

For example:

Sales revenue	£3,200,000
Less: Expenses	–£3,000,000
Equals: Profit	£200,000

Determining the effects of profit on the year-end financial condition of a business is a little more involved than the profit computation. You merge the two examples of changes in the balance sheet presented earlier in this chapter – one from revenue (see the section 'Concentrating on Sales') and the second from expenses (see the section 'Concentrating on Expenses') – to determine the cumulative effect on assets, liabilities and owners' retained earnings.

Two kinds of balance sheet accounts aren't affected by sales and expense transactions: interest-bearing liabilities and owners' invested capital.

To show the combined effect of both revenue and expense transactions, we combine the two examples shown in the earlier sections 'Concentrating on Sales' and 'Concentrating on Expenses'.

Combining the changes caused from sales with the changes caused from expenses gives the following:

Condensed Balance Sheet – Composite Net Changes From Sales and Expenses

Cash	+£245,000	Operating liabilities		+£95,000
Debtors	+£75,000	Debt		
Stock	+£50,000	Owners' invested capital		
Other noncash	–£75,000	Owners' retained earnings		+£200,000
Assets	+£295,000	= Liabilities and owners' capital		+£295,000

To determine each amount of change, combine the change caused by sales and the change caused by expenses. For instance, sales increase cash £3,175,000 and expenses decrease cash £2,930,000, and so the net change is £245,000 increase.

17. Suppose that expenses for the year cause the following changes in the business's financial condition:

Condensed Balance Sheet

Cash	–£2,880,000	Operating liabilities		+£150,000
Debtors		Debt		
Stock	+£25,000	Owners' invested capital		
Other noncash	–£95,000	Owners' retained earnings		–£3,100,000
Assets	–£2,950,000 =	Liabilities and owners' capital		–£2,950,000

Using the following template, show the combined effect on the balance sheet, using the sales information taken from the example shown in the earlier section 'Concentrating on Sales' and the change in expenses as shown in this question.

Condensed Balance Sheet

Cash	Operating liabilities
Noncash – Debtors	Debt
Noncash – Stock	Owners' invested capital
Noncash – Other assets	Owners' retained earnings
Assets =	Liabilities and owners' capital

Solve It

---

18. Suppose that sales for the year cause the following changes in the business's financial condition:

Condensed Balance Sheet

Cash	+£3,000,000	Operating liabilities		–£50,000
Debtors	+£250,000	Debt		
Stock		Owners' invested capital		
Other noncash		Owners' retained earnings		+£3,300,000
Assets	+£3,250,000 =	Liabilities and owners' capital		+£3,250,000

Using the following template, show the combined effect on the balance sheet, using the purchases information shown in the example from the earlier section 'Concentrating on Expenses' and the changes in the company's financial condition as a result of sales given in the question.

Condensed Balance Sheet

Cash	Operating liabilities
Noncash – Debtors	Debt
Noncash – Stock	Owners' invested capital
Noncash – Other assets	Owners' retained earnings
Assets =	Liabilities and owners' capital

Solve It

19. Starting with the balance sheet at the beginning of the year (see 'Seeing Both Sides of Business Transactions' earlier in this chapter) and the changes caused by its profit-making activities during the year (as we describe at the start of this section), what is the business's financial condition at the end of the year, ignoring other transactions that occur during the year?

To help you work out this problem, the business's balance sheet at the start of the year is repeated here (from the table earlier in this chapter):

Condensed Balance Sheet

Cash	£250,000	Operating liabilities	£350,000
Noncash – Debtors	£300,000	Debt	£500,000
Noncash – Stock	£400,000	Owners' invested capital	£250,000
Noncash – Other assets	£550,000	Owners' retained earnings	£400,000
Assets	£1,500,000 =	Liabilities and owners' capital	£1,500,000

Condensed Balance Sheet

Cash		Operating liabilities	
Noncash – Debtors		Debt	
Noncash – Stock		Owners' invested capital	
Noncash – Other assets		Owners' retained earnings	
Assets	=	Liabilities and owners' capital	

Solve It

---

20. Building on your answer to Question 19, assume that the business has other non-profit transactions during the year, as follows:

✔ Increases its interest-bearing debts by £100,000.

✔ Pays £80,000 distribution from profit to its shareowners.

Taking into account these additional transactions, what is the effect on the balance sheet of the business at the end of the year? (Use your answer to Question 19 to adjust with the transactions shown previously (the increase in interest-bearing debt and the £80,000 distribution of profit).

Condensed Balance Sheet

Cash		Operating liabilities	
Noncash – Debtors		Debt	
Noncash – Stock		Owners' invested capital	
Noncash – Other assets		Owners' retained earnings	
Assets	=	Liabilities and owners' capital	

Solve It

Answers to Problems on Financial Effects of Transactions

Here are the answers to the exercises presented earlier in this chapter.

1 Name the three main financial statements and describe which individuals may be interested in using them and why.

The three main financial statements of a business are:

- **Profit and Loss Statement:** This statement confirms whether the business is making a profit or loss for the period. Managers and owners of the business are interested in this information, because the Gross Profit of a business can be used as a performance indicator when comparing it to competitors in the same industry. The overall profit at the year-end determines the distributable profit available to shareholders and investors, and so they're certainly interested in that figure. Additionally, anyone lending money to the business such as a bank would probably also request that the Profit and Loss Statement is made available to them.

- **Balance Sheet:** This statement summarises the assets and liabilities and capital of the business. It is a snapshot of the business at a particular point in time. Potential investors are interested in viewing the balance sheet, because it offers a financial health check of the business. For example, investors can check the ratio of assets and liabilities, to make sure that the business can service it debts.

- **Cash flow statement:** The managers would use this statement as a useful day-to-day management tool, because it shows the availability of cash on a monthly or even a daily basis. It helps business decisions such as ensuring that enough money is available to meet the payroll obligations at the end of the month. Banks may also want to see a cash flow statement as part of a business plan required to gain additional funding.

2 Describe and give as many examples as you can of **profit-making transactions**.

Profit-making transactions consist of making sales and incurring expenses. In order to maximise the profit potential of a business you should seek to maximise revenue and minimise expenses.

Examples of profit-making transactions:

Sales

- Maximising product sales
- Maximising consultancy fees
- Investigating increasing other income opportunities

Controlling costs

Examples of costs to control are:

- Wages and salaries
- Advertising
- Minimising heat, light and electricity costs where possible

Overall you should be reviewing all other overheads and controlling expenditure where possible.

3   Describe and give examples of **investing activities**.

Investing activities can be described as those activities that involve the purchase of assets to be used for the long-term operating activities of the business. Examples are as follows:

- ✔ Purchase of plant and machinery for the purpose of improving operating activities.

- ✔ Purchase of a factory building to install the plant and machinery and run the business.

- ✔ Purchase of motor vehicles such as lorries and vans to transport the goods to the customers.

4   Describe and give examples of **financing activities** that a business may undertake.

Financing activities are those transactions recorded when a business borrows or repays money loaned to it. Financial activities also include transactions whereby the owner invests in the business or where the business repays monies to the owners and shareholders of a business. Examples are as follows:

- ✔ Loan taken out by the business to fund the purchase of a fixed asset.

- ✔ Repayments made on a bank loan.

- ✔ Capital introduced by the owner.

- ✔ Drawings taken out by the owner.

- ✔ Dividends paid to the shareholders (distributions of profit).

5   Suppose that all revenue transactions during the year increase cash and that all expense transactions during the year decrease cash. In other words, suppose that no other assets and no operating liabilities are affected by the profit-making activities of the business during the year (this scenario isn't realistic and is assumed only for this problem). The net income (bottom-line profit) of a typical business for the year is £950,000. Using the following template, show how profit affects the balance sheet.

Condensed Balance Sheet

Cash	+£950,000	Operating liabilities	
		Debt	
		Owners' invested capital	
Noncash		Owners' retained earnings	+£950,000
Assets	+£950,000 =	Liabilities and owners' capital	+£950,000

6   During the year, a business borrows £850,000 and uses £750,000 of these funds to invest in new long-term operating assets. Using the following template, show how these transactions affect the balance sheet.

Condensed Balance Sheet

Cash	+£100,000	Operating liabilities	
		Debt	+£850,000
		Owners' invested capital	
Noncash	+£750,000	Owners' retained earnings	
Assets	+£850,000 =	Liabilities and owners' capital	+£850,000

Cash initially increases by £850,000 when the loan is originally taken out, but then reduces by £750,000 when the asset is purchased (£850,000 − £750,000 = £100,00).

7 A freak flood causes extensive damage to stock. Unfortunately these losses weren't insured, and the business has to write off £175,000 of its stock. Ignoring the income tax effects of this write-off, use the following template to show how these transactions affect the balance sheet.

Condensed Balance Sheet

Cash		Operating liabilities	
		Debt	
Noncash	–£175,000	Owners' invested capital	
		Owners' retained earnings	–£175,000
Assets	–£175,000 =	Liabilities and owners' capital	–£175,000

The noncash asset refers to stock.

8 A loan is due for repayment during the year, and the business decides not to renew it. Accordingly, the business pays £500,000 to the lender, and the loan account is closed. (All interest expenses on this debt were recorded correctly during the year.) Using the following template, show how paying off the loan account affects the balance sheet.

Condensed Balance Sheet

Cash	–£500,000	Operating liabilities	
		Debt	–£500,000
		Owners' invested capital	
Noncash		Owners' retained earnings	
Assets	–£500,000 =	Liabilities and owners' capital	–£500,000

9 A business sells only to other businesses and makes all sales on credit; it doesn't have any cash sales or advance payment sales. During the year, the business makes £35,000,000 sales. From these sales, the business collects £31,500,000 during the year, and also collects the £3,250,000 debtors balance at the start of the year. Using the following template, show the effects of these transactions on the business's balance sheet.

Condensed Balance Sheet

Cash	+£34,750,000	Operating liabilities	
Noncash (debtors)	+£250,000	Debt	
		Owners' invested capital	
		Owners' retained earnings	+£35,000,000
Assets	+£35,000,000 =	Liabilities and Owners' Capital	+£35,000,000

The business adds £35,000,000 to debtors from its credit sales during the year. It collects £34,750,000 on debtors during the year (£31,500,000 + £3,250,000). Therefore, debtors increases £250,000, as you see in the balance sheet above. Debtors are included as noncash assets.

10 A business requires advance payments on all sales. In other words, it collects cash from customers before products are delivered to them later. During the year, the business receives £12,500,000 in advance payments from customers. By the end of the year, the business has delivered 85 per cent of products to customers for advance payments received during the year. Also, the business delivers products to customers during the year that fully discharges the £1,500,000 balance in liability for advance payments at the start of the year. Using the following template, show the effects of these transactions on the business's balance sheet.

Condensed Balance Sheet

Cash	+$12,500,000	Operating liabilities	+$375,000
		Debt	
		Owners' invested capital	
Noncash		Owners' retained earnings	+$12,125,000
Assets	+$12,500,000 =	Liabilities and owners' capital	+$12,500,000

The business fulfils 85 per cent of its advanced payment for sales during the year, which means it records $10,625,000 sales revenue. Also, the business earns $1,500,000 by delivering products to 'pay off' the balance in the Liability Account for advance payments at the start of the year. Sales revenue is the sum of the two, or $12,125,000. The business has not delivered on 15 per cent of its $12,500,000 advance payment sales during the year, which gives a $1,875,000 year-end balance in this liability. The year-end balance is $375,000 higher than the beginning balance in this liability. By the way, if you got this answer right the first time around, congratulations! This is a tough problem.

11 During the year, a business makes $3,650,000 cash sales. The business has a very liberal product return policy and therefore accepts product returns from customers and refunds $450,000 cash. Using the following template, show the effects of these transactions on the business's balance sheet.

Condensed Balance Sheet

Cash	+$3,200,000	Operating liabilities	
		Interest-bearing liabilities	
		Owners' invested capital	
Noncash		Owners' retained earnings	+$3,200,000
Assets	+$3,200,000 =	Liabilities and owners' capital	+$3,200,000

12 During its first year of business, a firm makes $6,250,000 credit sales. The business collects $5,600,000 cash from customers during the year from these sales. Unfortunately, a few customers don't pay despite repeated requests and threats of legal action. The business cuts off credit to these 'deadbeat' customers and refuses to make any more credit sales to them. The business has to write off $150,000 uncollectible debtors. Using the following template, show the effects of these transactions on the business's balance sheet.

Condensed Balance Sheet

Cash	+$5,600,000	Operating liabilities	
Noncash – debtors	+$500,000	Debt	
		Owners' invested capital	
		Owners' retained earnings	+$6,100,000
Assets	+$6,100,000 =	Liabilities and owners' capital	+$6,100,000

In its Profit and Loss Statement for the year, the business reports $6,250,000 sales revenue and $150,000 bad debts expense for the debtors written-off during the year. So, the net effect on owners' retained earnings is an increase of $6,100,000.

13 A business records $4,500,000 total expenses for the year. The expenses cause a $100,000 increase in its operating liabilities, and a $200,000 depreciation expense is recorded in the year. No change in stock takes place during the year (which is unusual). Using the following template, show how the expenses affect the balance sheet. (Again, treat cash as the balancing figure, when you've plugged all the other numbers into the balance sheet.)

Condensed Balance Sheet

Cash	−$4,200,000	Operating liabilities	+$100,000
		Debt	
		Owners' invested capital	
Noncash	−$200,000	Owners' retained earnings	−$4,500,000
Assets	−$4,400,000 =	Liabilities and owners' capital	−$4,400,000

The noncash asset is the movement in net book value of the assets due to the increase in accumulated depreciation, which is deducted from the cost of the assets in the balance sheet.

14 A business leases all its long-term operating assets (buildings, machines, vehicles and so on). Thus, it has no depreciation expense. For the year just ended, the business records $2,450,000 total expenses. Expenses cause a $75,000 increase in operating liabilities. Stock increases $45,000 during the year. Using the following template, show how the expenses affect the balance sheet. (Again, treat cash as the balancing figure, when you've plugged all the other numbers into the balance sheet.)

Condensed Balance Sheet

Cash	−$2,420,000	Operating liabilities	+$75,000
		Debt	
Noncash – Stock	+$45,000	Owners' invested capital	
		Owners' retained earnings	−$2,450,000
Assets	−$2,375,000 =	Liabilities and owners' capital	−$2,375,000

15 A business is just about ready to prepare its financial statements for the year when a sharp-eyed bookkeeper notices that the business has failed to accrue (record) certain liabilities for unpaid expenses at the end of the year. So, a correcting entry has to be made. The amount of these liabilities for unpaid expenses at year-end is $38,000. Using the following template, show how the accruals affect the balance sheet.

Condensed Balance Sheet

Cash		Operating liabilities	+$38,000
		Debt	
		Owners' invested capital	
Noncash		Owners' retained earnings	−$38,000
Assets	=	Liabilities and owners' capital	

The income tax effect of recording the additional $38,000 expenses isn't reflected in this answer. The additional $38,000 is deductible to figure taxable income, and so the income tax expense for the year decreases.

16 A business decides to engage in accounting fraud to improve its profit performance for the year. Of course, doing so unethical and illegal, but the chief executive of the business is desperate, and the chief accountant agrees to conspire with the chief executive to carry out this accounting fraud. They decide that they can't manipulate sales revenue for the year, and so the accounting fraud has to be done on the expense side of the ledger. The changes in financial condition caused by the actual expenses of the business for the year are given below. How may management go about misstating the expenses in order to boost profit $125,000? (Note: you have to think like a crook to work this problem.)

Condensed Balance Sheet

Cash	Operating liabilities	−$125,000
	Debt	
	Owners' invested capital	
Noncash	Owners' retained earnings	+$125,000
Assets =	Liabilities and owners' capital	

Thinking like a crook, we probably would manipulate liabilities for unpaid expenses; we would deliberately not record $125,000 of these liabilities. The effects of this manipulation are shown in the condensed balance sheet above. As you see, operating liabilities are understated $125,000. Therefore, total expenses for the year are $125,000 lower, and net income is $125,000 higher (before income tax is taken into account). Doing accounting fraud this way may deceive auditors because no record exists of these unrecorded liabilities in the accounts. However, a sharp auditor may notice something missing if she looks carefully for unrecorded liabilities.

17 Suppose that expenses for the year cause the following changes in the business's financial condition:

Condensed Balance Sheet

Cash	−$2,880,000	Operating liabilities	+$150,000
Debtors		Debt	
Stock	+$25,000	Owners' invested capital	
Other noncash	−$95,000	Owners' retained earnings	−$3,100,000
Assets	−$2,950,000 =	Liabilities and owners' capital	−$2,950,000

Using the template, show the combined effect on the balance sheet, using the sales information shown in the example in the earlier section 'Concentrating on Sales' and the change in expenses shown in the question.

Condensed Balance Sheet

Cash	+$295,000	Operating liabilities	+$200,000
Noncash – debtors	+$75,000	Debt	
Noncash – Stock	+$25,000	Owners' invested capital	
Other noncash	−$95,000	Owners' retained earnings	+$100,000
Assets	+$300,000 =	Liabilities and owners' capital	+$300,000

18 Suppose that sales for the year cause the following changes in the business's financial condition:

Condensed Balance Sheet

Cash	+$3,000,000	Operating liabilities	−$50,000
Debtors	+$250,000	Debt	
Stock		Owners' invested capital	
Other noncash		Owners' retained earnings	+$3,300,000
Assets	+$3,250,000 =	Liabilities and owners' capital	+$3,250,000

Using the following template, show the combined effect on the balance sheet, using the purchases information shown in the example from the earlier section 'Concentrating on Expenses' and the changes in the company's financial condition as a result of sales given in the above question.

Condensed Balance Sheet

Cash	+$70,000	Operating liabilities	−$5,000
Noncash – Debtors	+$250,000	Debt	
Noncash – Stock	+$50,000	Owners' invested capital	
Other noncash	−$75,000	Owners' retained earnings	+$300,000
Assets	+$295,000 =	Liabilities and owners' capital	+$295,000

19 Starting with the balance sheet at the beginning of the year (see 'Seeing Both Sides of Business Transactions' earlier in this chapter) and the changes caused by its profit-making activities during the year (as we describe at the start of the section 'Determining the Composite Effect of Profit'), what is the business's financial condition at the end of the year, ignoring other transactions that occur during the year?

Condensed Balance Sheet

Cash	$495,000	Operating liabilities	$445,000
Noncash – Debtors	$375,000	Debt	$500,000
Noncash – Stock	$450,000	Owners' invested capital	$250,000
Other noncash	$475,000	Owners' retained earnings	$600,000
Assets	$1,795,000 =	Liabilities and owners' capital	$1,795,000

20 Building on your answer to Question 19, assume that the business has other non-profit transactions during the year, as follows:

- Increases its interest-bearing debts by $100,000.
- Pays $80,000 distribution from profit to its shareowners.

Taking into account these additional transactions, what is the effect on the balance sheet of the business at the end of the year? (Use your answer to Question 19 to adjust with the transactions shown above.)

Condensed Balance Sheet

Cash	$515,000	Operating liabilities	$445,000
Noncash (Debtors)	$375,000	Debt	$600,000
Noncash (Stock)	$450,000	Owners' invested capital	$250,000
Other noncash	$475,000	Owners' retained earnings	$520,000
Assets	$1,815,000 =	Liabilities and owners' capital	$1,815,000

Chapter 3

Getting Started in the Bookkeeping Cycle

In This Chapter

▶ Establishing a chart of accounts

▶ Recognising the difference between balance sheet and profit and loss nominal accounts

▶ Appreciating the centuries-old debits and credits method

▶ Making journal entries for business transactions

*T*he bookkeeping and recordkeeping system of a business requires an accountant to do the following jobs:

✔ Establish the *chart of accounts* in which the transactions of the business are recorded.

✔ Record *original entries* for transactions of the business as they occur day by day.

✔ Use the *debits and credits* system for recording transactions in order to keep the books (accounts) of the business in balance.

✔ Record additional *adjusting entries* at the end of the period to adjust revenue and Expense accounts in order to make profit correct.

✔ Record certain 'housekeeping' entries, called *closing entries*, to bring the profit accounting process for the year to a close.

This chapter explains the first three elements: the chart of accounts, original entries and debits and credits. Chapter 4 completes the bookkeeping cycle by explaining the last two elements: adjusting entries and closing entries.

Whether the bookkeeping process is handled by a person recording entries by hand (popularly envisioned wearing a green eyeshade and arm garters and making entries with a quill pen) or a 21st-century bookkeeper working at a computer keyboard, the process is fundamentally the same: adopt a chart of accounts, make original entries using debits and credits to keep the books in balance, make adjusting entries to get profit for the period right and close the books at the end of the year. Multinational companies do the same process as your local corner shop: 'the more things change, the more things stay the same'.

Constructing the Chart of Accounts

Accounts are the basic building blocks of an accounting system. An *account* is a category of information, like a file in which a certain type of information is stored. The reason for establishing an account is that the business needs specific information pulled together in order to prepare a financial statement or some other accounting report.

The first step in setting up an accounting system is to identify the particular accounts that are needed. The financial effects of transactions are recorded as increases or decreases in accounts, and you can't make an accounting entry for a transaction without having accounts to increase or decrease. In short, no accounts mean no accounting!

Suppose that you're the chief accountant of a brand new business and you're on your first day on the job. After you find the coffee machine and the toilets, where do you begin? (Don't say lunch!)

Your initial task should be to establish the chart of accounts to be used to record the transactions of the business. The chart of accounts becomes the official set of accounts that you use to record the effects of transactions. Unless you authorise the creation of a new account, the accounts in the chart are the only ones you use.

The need for one account in the chart of accounts, the cash account, is pretty obvious. A business needs to know how much money it has in its bank account, and so it must establish a cash-at-bank account and record cash receipts and payments in the account.

Which other accounts are needed? That's the million dollar question. To answer it, the chief accountant looks to the information the business needs to report in its financial statements and tax returns (the two major information demands on the accounting system of a business). Each business is very different, and the accountant needs to review business operations very carefully to work out what accounts are going to be needed for reporting purposes.

Have a look at your business and find out whether a chart of accounts already exists. If so, obtain a copy and study the accounts that are currently there. If you feel that any are missing, make a note of them below. If you're new to business and don't currently have a chart of accounts set up, don't worry; we reveal all in this chapter and the next!

Limited companies and certain other organisations including clubs and societies need to complete a Company Tax Return form (CT600). They pay corporation tax on the taxable profits for that company.

The following information is required for the tax return in order to calculate the correct amount of tax:

- Turnover – total profit plus expenses.
- Other income – such as bank/building society interest, income from UK land and buildings, overseas income and so on.

Expenses also need to be analysed for your own benefit but ultimately the taxable profit is used to calculate the corporation tax payable.

If you're a sole trader or partnership, you have to complete an income tax return with details about your income and expenditure. In addition to highlighting the different forms of income, the income tax return requires you to split your expenditure between different expense headings such as:

   ✔ Accountancy, legal and professional fees

   ✔ Bad debts

   ✔ Bank charges and interest

   ✔ Client entertaining (be aware that this expense isn't an allowable cost for tax purposes)

   ✔ Cost of Goods Sold

   ✔ Depreciation

   ✔ Equipment hire and rental

   ✔ General expenses

   ✔ Insurance

   ✔ Maintenance, repair and renewals

   ✔ Motor expenses

   ✔ Rent and rates

   ✔ Staff entertaining

   ✔ Telephone, printing and stationery

   ✔ Travelling expenses

   ✔ Wages and salaries

In order to provide the relevant information for HMRC you need to ensure that your accounts system can collate the required information. Therefore, you must check that your chart of accounts has the appropriate accounts set up, so that correct analysis can be carried out at the year-end and your tax returns completed satisfactorily.

If you're using a computerised accounting system such as Sage, a standard chart of accounts is available that can be used and then customised to suit your business. Therefore, you don't have to start from scratch with a completely new chart of accounts (although this option is available if you want it, why make life more difficult for yourself?).

---

1.   Imagine that you've just taken on the role of accountant for a chain of shoe shops. What kind of accounts may you expect to see in the chart of accounts?

Solve It

Discussing Nominal Accounts

You may have heard of the term nominal (general) ledger. This phrase refers to the complete set of accounts that a business creates and maintains. The nominal ledger consists of a number of nominal accounts. For example, you'll have a nominal account for sales, purchases, rent, rates and so on. The chart of accounts (see the preceding section) is a formal index of these accounts.

The chart of accounts is split into balance sheet nominal accounts and profit and loss nominal accounts. Basically the balance sheet nominal accounts are used to construct the balance sheet and the profit and loss nominal accounts are used to construct the Profit and Loss Statement.

Balance sheet nominal accounts contain the balances of accounts such as assets, liabilities and owners' capital. The balance sheet is a financial snapshot at a particular moment in time. The balances for each relevant account are used at that same moment in time to construct the balance sheet.

Profit and loss nominal accounts are those reported in the Profit and Loss Statement, which is the summary of the revenue and expenses of a business for a period of time.

Balances in these accounts are cumulative over a period of time. Take the balance in the sales revenue account at the end of the year, for example. This balance is the total amount of sales over the entire year. Likewise, the balance in advertising expenses is the total amount of the expense over the entire year. At the end of the period, the accountant uses the balances in the profit and loss nominal accounts to determine a business's net profit or loss for the period.

The closing balance for each profit and loss nominal account is transferred to the retained profit account for the year. Therefore, the individual account is effectively zeroed down and the account starts with a zero balance at the start of the new accounting period.

Balance sheet nominal accounts are different; they don't zero down at the end of the year. Instead, you note your ending balance for each account, so that you can prepare a balance sheet, and then you carry forward the balances to the new accounting period. For example, if you had a loan showing as a liability in the balance sheet, you wouldn't write this amount off at the end of the first year, because money is still owed. The balance owing simply moves across to the next accounting period and the balance reduces as the loan is paid off.

Q. Imagine your local supermarket. Can you picture yourself standing in the car park and looking at the shop? Imagine yourself walking around the aisles and doing your shopping. What do you see? What kind of items appear before you that you would also find in the company's accounts?

A. Following are the kinds of profit and loss accounts and balance sheet accounts that you're likely to encounter. Obviously plenty more exist, but these few give you a flavour.

Balance Sheet accounts

Fixed assets

Shop premises (including land and other buildings)

Shop fitting equipment

Motor vehicles (including delivery vans)

Current assets

Stock

Cash

Note: This kind of business is unlikely to have debtors because most people pay by cash or debit/credit card

Current liabilities

Money owed to suppliers

Accruals

VAT owed

PAYE owed

Long-term liabilities

Bank loans

Mortgages

Owners' capital

Shareholders' funds

Retained profit

Dividends payable

Profit and Loss accounts

Income

Sales from shops (both cash and credit)

Expenses

Cost of Goods Sold

Staff costs and wages

Heat, light and electricity for all the shops

All the other overhead costs associated with running a business

2. Using the supermarket example, imagine that you're at the start of a new financial year. List three accounts that have a zero balance at the start of the year and explain why. Then, list three accounts at the start of the year that have an opening balance and explain why.

Solve It

3. Consider two different accounts for a business that makes credit sales. The first is a balance sheet account, debtors. The second is a profit and loss nominal account, sales revenue. Would you record increases and decreases in both accounts during the year, or are only increases recorded during the year?

Think about the type of transactions that are posted through these accounts to answer the question.

Solve It

4. A good friend is reading the most recent financial report of your business. In the balance sheet, your friend comes across an account called 'Owners' capital – Retained earnings'. You're asked, 'Is this an Asset account? If it is, is it money in the bank?' How do you answer this question?

Solve It

Knowing Your Debits from Your Credits

Business transactions are economic exchanges because something of value is given and something of value is received. By its very nature, an economic exchange is a two-sided transaction. For example, a business sells a product for £400. It receives the money (immediately or later) and gives the product to the customer. In another example, a business buys a piece of machinery. The bookkeeper needs to record the fixed asset purchase and also record the method used to pay for the machinery (asset). For example, a cheque is recorded showing the bank payment for this transaction.

Accountants and bookkeepers use an ingenious scheme to record transactions while keeping the accounting equation constantly in balance – it's called *double-entry accounting*. This system dates back to 1494 where a book was published describing the method.

 Double-entry accounting records both sides of a transaction, and the accounting equation remains in balance as transactions are recorded. For example, if a transaction decreases cash £25,000, the other side of the transaction is a £25,000 increase in some other asset, or a £25,000 decrease in a liability, or a £25,000 increase in an expense (to cite three possibilities).

To keep the accounting equation in balance as they record transactions, accountants use the system of debits and credits. The famous German writer Goethe is reputed to have called double-entry accounting 'one of the finest inventions of the human mind'. Well, we're not sure that this bookkeeping technique deserves such high praise, but undeniably this debits and credits method has been in use over six centuries.

Table 3-1 summarises the basic rules for debits and credits. By long-standing convention, debits are shown on the left and credits on the right. An increase in a liability, owners' capital, revenue and income account is recorded as a credit, and so the increase side is on the right. The recording of all transactions follows these rules for debits and credits.

You must follow certain rules when applying double-entry bookkeeping. If you adhere to the rules listed in the following table, you won't go far wrong.

- ✓ If you want to increase an asset, you must debit that account.
- ✓ To decrease an asset, you must credit that account.
- ✓ To increase a liability, you credit that account.
- ✓ To decrease a liability, you debit that account.
- ✓ If you want to record an expense, you debit the expense account.
- ✓ If you need to reduce an expense, you would credit that expense account.
- ✓ If you want to record income, you credit the income account.
- ✓ If you want to reduce income, you debit the income account.

You can remember these rules using the table below. You can copy this table and keep a copy somewhere handy for you to refer to.

Table 3-1	Bookkeeping Rules	
Account Type	*Debits*	*Credits*
Assets	Increase	Decrease
Liabilities	Decrease	Increase
Income	Decrease	Increase
Expenses	Increase	Decrease

Practically everyone has trouble with the rules of debits and credit (we certainly did!). Frankly, the rules aren't very intuitive. Discovering the rules for debits and credits is just something you have to bite the bullet with and get on with! The only way to really understand the rules is to make accounting entries – over and over again. After a while, using the rules becomes like tying your shoes – you do it without even thinking about it.

In the following example question, the number of accounts is limited to simplify the problem; even a small business typically needs more than 100 accounts.

0. Suppose a small business has the following ten accounts. Notice the horizontal and vertical lines under the accounts in the following example. These lines form the letter 'T'. Although the actual accounts maintained by a business don't necessarily look like T accounts, accounts usually have one column for increases and another column for decreases. In other words, an account has a debit column and a credit column. Also an account may have a running balance column to keep track continuously of the account's balance.

The business conducts the following transactions during the year:

a. Makes sales during the year for £2,400 (all are cash sales).

b. Cost of Goods Sold during the year is £1,600.

c. Incurs a £425 telephone bill, which will be paid sometime later.

d. Obtains a £10,000 bank loan (ignore the interest expense on this note).

e. Issues a cheque for £275 to pay for rent of the business premises; these particular expenses are recorded as paid and haven't been recorded previously in a Liability account.

f. Makes sales on credit of £1200.

How should the above transactions be recorded in the business's accounts?

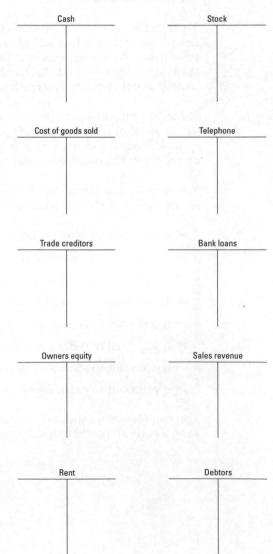

A. The following figure shows how the transactions are recorded in the business's accounts. (The letters in the entries correspond to the transactions listed in the question.) In each transaction, the debit amount equals the credit amount.

In every account, debits are on the left, and credits are on the right. And don't forget that increases in assets and expenses are recorded as debits, and increases in liabilities and sales revenue are recorded as credits. These few transactions are a very small sample of the large number of transactions the business makes over the course of one year.

Questions 5 to 9 use the same ten accounts given in the preceding example question.

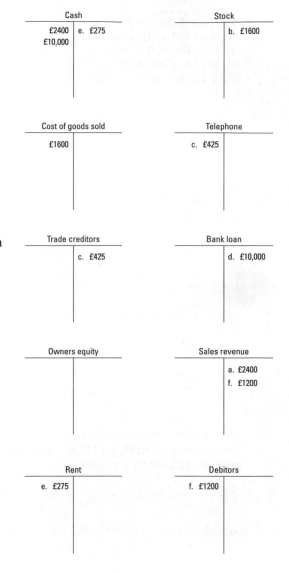

5. A business purchases products for stock and pays £3,500 cash for the purchase. How should this transaction be recorded in the accounts?

Solve It

6. A business pays a telephone bill for £425, which is currently being shown as a trade creditor because it wasn't paid straight away. How should this transaction be recorded in the accounts?

Solve It

7. The business pays £1200 off the bank loan (ignore interest expense). How should this transaction be recorded in the accounts?

Solve It

8. The owners invest an additional £25,000 in the business. How should this transaction be recorded in the accounts?

Solve It

9. The business receives a cheque for £300 from a customer who is paying for goods received but not previously paid for. How would this transaction be recorded in the accounts?

Solve It

Making Original Journal Entries

To explain and illustrate double-entry bookkeeping in the preceding section, we enter the effects of transactions directly into accounts. By keeping the number of accounts to a minimum, you can see the 'big picture' because all assets, liabilities, owners' capital, revenue and expenses fit on one page. Looking at accounts this way is a useful first step in understanding the rules of debits and credits.

However, with a large number of accounts, recording the effects of transactions directly in the accounts of a business isn't practical. The debits are in one account and the credit are in another account, and the accounts may be far removed from one another. A much more useful method is to record every transaction such that both sides of the transaction are in one place; keep the debit(s) and credit(s) in the entry for the transaction next to each other.

Therefore, the standard practice is to record transactions first in journal entries so that both sides of a transaction (both the debits and credits of the transaction) are recorded in one place. A journal is like a diary in that it's a chronological listing of transactions. After journal entries have been recorded, the debits and credits of the transactions are recorded in the accounts of the business. The debits and credits are delivered to their proper addresses, which in accounting parlance is called posting to the accounts.

The journey from transactions to financial statements is as follows:

Transactions → Journal entries → Posting to accounts → Financial statements

One reason for keeping journals instead of recording the effects of transactions directly in accounts is that a business needs a chronological listing of all its transactions in one place. With journals, each transaction is stored in one place and is available for inspection and review. At a later date, a question or challenge may arise regarding how a transaction was recorded, and the journals allow direct access to original recording of the transaction, which is especially important for audit purposes.

Businesses use several specialised journals, usually one for each basic type of transaction. A typical business has a sales journal, purchases journal, cash receipts journal, cash payments journal, payroll journal and perhaps other journals as well. In addition, a business needs one general journal in which it records low frequency and non-routine accounting entries. Adjusting and closing entries made at the end of the year (as we discuss in Chapter 4) are recorded in the general journal.

Today, businesses use computer-based bookkeeping/accounting systems in place of manual journals and accounts. Using computerised systems, accountants continue to do what they always did in traditional bookkeeping systems, including constructing a chart of accounts, recording journal entries for transactions, posting the debits and credits of journal entries in the accounts, making end-of-period adjusting entries and using the accounts to prepare financial statements.

Q. A business makes £2,350 cash sales for the day. What is the journal entry for these sales?

A.

	Debit	Credit
Cash	£2,350	
Sales Revenue		£2,350

This journal entry follows the conventional format for journal entries in that debits appear first and on the left and credits come second and are shown on the right. In this journal entry, the cash account is debited, because it shows an increase in assets of £2,350; the sales revenue account is credited with £2,350, because income accounts are credited if increased. The journal entry is the same whether recorded manually or via a computerised accounting system.

---

10. By looking at the following journal entry, describe the transaction that has taken place.

	Debit	Credit
Stock	£48,325	
Creditors		£48,325

Solve It

11. By looking at the following journal entry, describe the transaction that has taken place.

	Debit	Credit
Cash	£250,000	
Bank Loan		£250,000

Solve It

---

12. By looking at the following journal entry, describe the transaction that has taken place.

	Debit	Credit
Rent Expense	£48,325	
Cash		£48,325

Solve It

13. By looking at the following journal entry, describe the transaction that has taken place.

	Debit	Credit
Trade Creditors	£19,250	
Cash		£19,250

Solve It

Recording Revenue and Income

When making sales, a business receives cash at the time of making the sale, after the time of sale or before the time of sale (as we discuss in Chapter 2). What about credit card sales? As you know, individuals use credit cards for a large percentage of their purchases from businesses. As far as businesses are concerned, credit card sales are virtually the same as cash sales. The business immediately transmits its credit card sales to its bank for deposit into its bank account.

A business doesn't get 100 per cent of the value for its credit card sales. Banks discount the credit card amounts. For example, assume a bank discounts 1.5 per cent from the credit card amount. Therefore, for a £100.00 credit card sale, the bank puts only £98.50 in the business's bank account. The credit card discount rate can be higher or lower depending on several factors.

In addition to sales revenue, a business may have other sources of income. A prime example is investment income. Many businesses invest their spare cash in bank deposit accounts that pay interest. Some businesses make loans to officers and employees and charge interest on the loans, which generates interest income, of course.

Q. For a particular business, the day's sales are summarised as follows:

Cash sales	£3,500
Credit card sales	£14,800
Credit sales	£23,400

Its bank discounts 1.75 per cent from credit card sales. In journal entry form, record the sales activity of the business for the day.

The separate journal entries for the three types of sales for the day are:

Cash sales for the day

	Debit	Credit
Cash	£3,500	
Sales Revenue		£3,500

Credit card sales for the day discounted by the bank

	Debit	Credit
Cash	£14,541	
Credit Card Discount Expense	£259	
Sales Revenue		£14,800

Credit card sales for the day

	Debit	Credit
Debtors	£23,400	
Sales Revenue		£23,400

A. Here are a few things to note in these entries:

- These account titles are typical but not universal. Different businesses use slightly different account titles.

- Credit card discount expense is recorded for the credit card sales; in this case, the calculation is £14,800 face value of credit card charges × 1.75 per cent discount fee charged by bank = £259. Sales revenue is recorded gross, or before the bank's discount is deducted.

14. For the day, a business makes £38,900 credit sales to other businesses. How should these credit sales be recorded? (Use the journal entry format shown in the preceding example answer.)

Solve It

15. For the day, a business makes £48,000 credit card sales to individuals. It immediately sends the credit card information to its bank, which deducts 1.5 per cent on credit card charges and puts the remainder in the business's bank account. How should these credit card sales be recorded? (Use the journal entry format shown in the preceding example answer.)

Solve It

16. Over the course of a business day, a few customers return products to the business. For the day, the total of customer returns is £2,300, and the business refunds cash to these customers. How should the product returns be recorded? (Use the journal entry format shown in the preceding example answer.)

Solve It

17. A business invests in a deposit account to earn income on excess cash that it doesn't need for its day-to-day operations. It just received £450 interest for interest earned over the last six months. None of this income has been recorded yet. How should this income be recorded? (Use the journal entry format shown in the preceding example answer.)

Solve It

Recording Expenses and Losses

How many Expense accounts should a business maintain? We can't give you an easy answer to this question. The glib answer is 'as many as it needs'. To make a profit, business managers have to control expenses, and this task requires a good deal of specific information about expenses.

To get an idea of the broad range of expenses a business may have and therefore needs to account for, imagine a business with £10 million annual sales revenue. With that much revenue, you know right off that this enterprise isn't a small operation. The business probably has more than 50 employees and hundreds or thousands of customers. The business may manufacture the products its sells, or it may be a retailer that buys products in condition for resale. Most likely, it buys insurance coverage to protect against various risks and advertises the products its sells. For a £10 million business like this one, we would expect to find several hundred different Expense accounts – even 1,000 or more wouldn't be surprising.

Most businesses with £10 million annual sales revenue have total annual expenses over £9 million, or more than 90 per cent of their sales revenue. Few businesses earn 10 per cent or higher bottom-line profit on their sales revenue. As you may have already figured out, it takes a lot of accounts to keep track of over £9 million expenses.

Using the double-entry bookkeeping system, accountants record expenses, and by doing so, they decrease assets or increase liabilities. Sounds straightforward enough, doesn't it? Well, it isn't! Many different assets and liabilities are credited in making expense entries. To help you understand which Assets and Liability accounts may be affected, see the expense account below.

The following account presents a broad overview of expenses. This summary matches expenses with the balance sheet accounts that are credited in recording the expenses. For instance, in recording the Cost of Goods Sold expense, the stock Asset account is credited. Many different expenses are recorded when cash payments for the expenses are made. You can see that a specific Expense account is recorded when a cash payment is made. The expense can be one of many in the business's chart of accounts.

Expense account debited	*Balance Sheet account credited*
	Assets
Expense accounts paid cash	Cash
Bad debt expense	Debtors(Accounts receivable)
Cost of goods sold expense	Stock
Expense accounts where pay up front	Prepaid expenses
Depreciation expense	Fixed Assets
	Liabilities
Expenses paid later	Trade creditors (accounts payable)
Expenses where bill not yet received	Accrued expenses
Employee expenses payable	PAYE/NI
Credit card expenses	Credit cards payable
	Owners Equity
Dividends paid to shareholders	Retained earnings
Capital repaid to owner	Invested capital

Q. A business has three expenses that it must record:

- ✔ The business issued a £45,000 cheque to its advertising agency for spot commercials that appeared on local television during last month; this cost hasn't been recorded yet.

- ✔ The accountant calculates that depreciation for the period is £306,500.

- ✔ The accountant calculates that the cost of holiday and sick pay accumulated by employees during the period just ended is £15,400; employees have taken none of this time yet.

What journal entries should be recorded for these expenses?

A. The following journal entries are recorded for the three expenses:

	Debit	Credit
Advertising	£45,000	
Cash		£45,000

Because no expense has been recorded before the time of making cash payment, the advertising Expense account is debited (increased) at the time of making payment.

	Debit	Credit
Depreciation	£306,500	
Accumulated Depreciation		£306,500

The cost of a *long-term operating asset*, also called a *fixed asset*, is allocated over the estimated useful life of the asset, and so a fraction of the cost is charged to the depreciation Expense account each period. The fixed asset is credited (decreased) – not by a direct credit in the Asset account but by a credit in the contra account, accumulated depreciation. The balance in this contra account is deducted from the original cost of the fixed asset.

	Debit	Credit
Employees' Benefits Expense	£15,400	
Accrued Expense Liability		£15,400

Some expenses accrue, or build up over time, even though the business doesn't receive a bill for the expense. A good example is holiday and sick pay accumulated by employees. Rather than waiting until individual employees actually take time off to record the expense, the creeping liability for this expense is recorded each period. When the employees are paid for holiday and sick time, the liability is debited (decreased).

18. The business's Cost of Goods Sold for its sales during the period is £938,450. The sales revenue for these sales has been recorded. What journal entry should be made for this expense?

Solve It

19. The business just received an invoice for £15,000 from the outside security firm that guards its warehouse and offices. No entry has been made for this expense yet, and the business normally waits several weeks to pay this bill. What journal entry should be made for this expense?

Solve It

20. Its actuarial firm informs the business that the cost of its employees' retirement pension benefit for the period is £565,000. According to the contract with its employees, the business decides to transfer £300,000 to the trustee of the pension plan and to defer payment of the remainder until a later time (which it has the option to do). No entry has been made for this expense yet. What journal entry should be made for this expense?

Solve It

21. Unfortunately, one of the major customers of the business declares bankruptcy. This customer owes the business £35,000. The business has already recorded the credit sale to the customer and the Cost of Goods Sold for the sale. After careful analysis, the business comes to the conclusion that it won't be able to collect any money from this customer. The business doesn't record an expense caused by uncollectible debts until it actually writes off the debt. What journal entry should be made for this expense?

Solve It

Recording Investing and Financing Transactions

Suppose a business records 10,000 transactions during the year. The large majority are sales and expense transactions, and perhaps fewer than 100 are investing and financing transactions. Though few in number, investing and financing transactions are very important and usually involve big chunks of money. In fact, these two types of transactions are reported in the cash flow statement – and that ought to tell you something.

Investing activities include the purchase and construction of fixed assets, such as land, buildings, machines, equipment, vehicles and so on. In general, these investments are called *capital expenditures*. (The term capital refers to the large amounts of money invested in the assets as well as the long-term nature of these investments.)

These assets aren't held for sale in the normal course of business; instead, they're held for use in the operations of the business. When grouped together in a balance sheet, fixed assets are typically labelled property, plant and equipment. Eventually, the business disposes of these assets by trading them in for new assets, selling them off for residual value or just having the junk collector come and haul them away.

Investing transactions include acquisitions of other long-term assets, such as intangible resources (patents, for example) and research projects in the development stage.

Financing activities basically fall into three basic categories:

- ✔ A business borrows money on the basis of interest-bearing debt and pays these loans at their maturity dates or renews them.

- ✔ A business raises capital (usually money) from shareowners and may return some of the invested capital to them.

- ✔ A business distributes cash to its shareowners based on its profit performance.

Large public companies may well engage in much more complex and sophisticated financing deals and instruments than these basic types, but those activities are beyond the scope of this book.

0. The investing and financing activities for the year of a new, start-up business are summarised as follows:

✔ Receives £10,000,000 from a venture capital (VC) firm; in exchange, the business signs a £5 million loan agreement (interest-bearing, of course) to the VC firm and issues shares of stock to the VC firm equal to 10 per cent of the total number of shares of stock issued by the business.

✔ Purchases various fixed assets for total cash payments of £6,000,000.

Make the journal entries for these investing and financing activities.

A. The journal entries for these investing and financing activities are as follows:

	Debit	Credit
Cash	£10,000,000	
Loan		£5,000,000
Owners' Capital – Invested Capital		£5,000,000

	Debit	Credit
Fixed assets	£6,000,000	
Cash		£6,000,000

One-half of the money invested in the start-up business by the VC firm is secured by a loan agreement on which the business has to pay interest. This transaction is recorded in the loans payable Liability account to indicate that the business has the legal obligation to pay interest and to pay the loan at its maturity date.

The other half of the money that the VC firm put in the business is attributed to the account for capital stock shares issued by the business. The account title property, plant and equipment is a generic title for fixed assets. The business would maintain more-specific accounts for each major asset purchased, such as buildings, machinery, vehicles and so on.

22. A business needs more capital to expand and grow, and so it issues additional stock shares for a total of £25,000,000. What journal entry should be made for this financing transaction?

Solve It

23. A business has a very good year; its £58,000,000 net income for the year is an all-time high. Being in a generous mood, its board of directors declares a whopping cash distribution of £30,000,000 based on the business's record-setting performance. What journal entry should be made for this financing transaction?

Solve It

Answers to Problems on the Bookkeeping Cycle

Here are the answers to the questions presented earlier in this chapter.

1 Imagine that you've just taken on the role of accountant for a chain of shoe shops. What kind of accounts may you expect to see in the chart of accounts?

The following represents the typical accounts that you may find in a shoe shop.

Income

- Sales from shoes, split into cash sales and credit card sales, which can be further split into:

  • Accessories (including polishes, and so on)

  • Children's shoes

  • Handbag sales (often found in shoe shops)

  • Men's shoes

  • Women's shoes

Expenses

- Admin expenses
- Finance charges (including bank interest)
- Heat, light and power
- Premises costs – such as maintenance
- Rent and rates for the shops
- Staff salaries

Can you think of any more?

Balance sheet

- Accruals
- Bank loans
- Capital invested
- Cash (from the tills)
- Dividends
- Land and buildings (if the shops are owned)
- Motor vehicle costs (possibly delivery vans)
- PAYE owed to HMRC (from the payroll)
- Retained profits
- Stock

2 Using the previous supermarket example, imagine that you're at the start of a new financial year. List three accounts that have a zero balance at the start of the year and explain why. Then, list three accounts at the start of the year that have an opening balance and explain why.

The following accounts are likely to have a zero balance at the start of the year. They are the profit and loss accounts such as:

- Sales
- Cost of Goods Sold
- Rent and rates
- Heat light and power for the supermarket
- Wages and salaries
- Office admin expenses
- Any other overheads associated with the business

All profit and loss accounts are zeroed down at the end of the year and the balance is transferred to the retained profits account.

The following balance sheet accounts have balances at the start of the year because you never zero these ones down:

- Cash
- Loans outstanding
- Owners' capital – invested capital
- Stock
- Fixed assets, such as cost of shops, capital expended for shop fitting expenditure
- PAYE due to HMRC
- VAT due to HMRC

3 Consider two different accounts for a business that makes credit sales. The first is a balance sheet account, debtors. The second is a profit and loss nominal account, sales revenue. Would you record increases and decreases in both accounts during the year, or are only increases recorded during the year?

Think about the type of transactions that are posted through these accounts to answer the question.

This question focuses on just two accounts taken from the chart of accounts of a business that makes credit sales. (Even a small business keeps hundreds of accounts.) The first is a balance sheet account, debtors. The second is a profit and loss account, *sales revenue*.

Both increases and decreases are recorded in the debtors account, because increases are recorded for sales made on credit, and decreases are recorded when debtors pay their invoices. A continuous flow in and out of this account takes place. In contrast, the sales revenue account records mostly increases during the year, which is the sales invoices issued to the customers. However, some decreases may be recorded in this revenue account, if credit notes need to be issued, but they're the exception rather than the rule. For example, after recording sales revenue, an error may be discovered that requires a decrease in the account to correct the error (this would be done by way of a credit note).

4   A good friend is reading the most recent financial report of your business. In the balance sheet, your friend comes across an account called 'Owners' capital – Retained earnings'. You're asked, 'Is this an Asset account? If it is, is it money in the bank?' How do you answer this question?

No, no, no, no! Many people assume that retained earnings is an Asset account and, in particular, that it's money stashed away someplace. (The title of the account may suggest this misleading interpretation.) You should stress that assets are listed under assets in the balance sheet and that assets aren't tucked under owners' capital on the other side of the balance sheet. Retained earnings are created from the business earning profits over the years. This is the profit remaining after any distributions are made to its shareowners.

5   The business purchases products for stock and pays £3,500 cash for the purchase. How should this transaction be recorded in the accounts?

5.

Stock	
Cash £3500	

Cash	
	Stock £3500

6   A business pays a telephone bill for £425, which is currently being shown as a trade creditor, because it wasn't paid straight away. How should this transaction be recorded in the accounts?

6.

Trade creditors	
Cash £425	

Cash	
	Trade creditors £425

7   The business pays £1200 off the bank loan (ignore interest expense). How should this transaction be recorded in the accounts?

7.

Bank loan	
Cash £1200	

Cash	
	Bank loan £1200

8   The owners invest an additional £25,000 in the business. How should this transaction be recorded in the accounts?

8.

Cash	
Owners equity £25,000	

Owners Equity	
	Cash £25,000

9 The business receives a cheque for £300 from a customer who is paying for goods received but not previously paid for. How would this transaction be recorded in the accounts?

9.

Debtors		Cash	
	Cash £300	Debtors £300	

10 By looking at the following journal entry, describe the transaction that has taken place.

	Debit	Credit
Stock	£48,325	
Creditors		£48,325

This entry records that the business purchased stock on credit and the goods will be paid for at a later date.

11 By looking at the following journal entry, describe the transaction that has taken place.

	Debit	Credit
Cash	£250,000	
Bank loan		£250,000

This entry shows that the firm has received £250,000 *by way of a business loan.*

12 By looking at the following journal entry, describe the transaction that has taken place.

	Debit	Credit
Rent Expense	£48,325	
Cash		£48,325

This entry records rent payments to the landlord.

13 By looking at the following journal entry, describe the transaction that has taken place.

	Debit	Credit
Creditors	£19,250	
Cash		£19,250

This entry records the payment of amounts owed for previous purchases on credit.

14 For the day, a business makes £38,900 credit sales to other businesses. How should these credit sales be recorded?

	Debit	Credit
Debtors	£38,900	
Sales Revenue		£38,900

15 For the day, a business makes $48,000 credit card sales to individuals. It immediately sends the credit card information to its bank, which deducts 1.5 per cent on credit card charges and puts the remainder in the business's checking account. How should these credit card sales be recorded?

	Debit	Credit
Cash	$47,280	
Credit Card Discount Expense	$720	
Sales Revenue		$48,000

16 Over the course of a business day, a few customers return products to the business. For the day, the total of customer returns is $2,300, and the business refunds cash to these customers. How should the product returns be recorded?

	Debit	Credit
Sales Returns & Allowances	$2,300	
Cash		$2,300

In this scenario, the debit isn't in the sales revenue account but rather in sales returns and allowances account, which is the contra account to sales revenue. The balance in this account is deducted from sales revenue to determine net sales revenue, and the balance in sales returns and allowances is compared with the balance in sales revenue to gauge the returns against sales. (Also, we should mention that a second entry needs to be made to record the return of products to stock. The question doesn't give the cost of the goods returned by customers, and so you're not asked to include this entry.)

17 A business invests in a deposit account to earn income on excess cash that it doesn't need for its day-to-day operations. It just received $450 interest for interest earned over the last six months. None of this income has been recorded yet. How should this income be recorded? (Use the journal entry format shown in the preceding example answer.)

	Debit	Credit
Cash	$450	
Interest received		$450

18 The business's Cost of Goods Sold for its sales during the period is $938,450. The sales revenue for these sales has been recorded. What journal entry should be made for this expense?

	Debit	Credit
Cost of Goods Sold Expense	$938,450	
Stock		$938,450

19 The business just received a bill for $15,000 from the outside security firm that guards its warehouse and offices. No entry has been made for this expense yet, and the business normally waits several weeks to pay this bill. What journal entry should be made for this expense?

	Debit	Credit
Security Guard Expense	$15,000	
Creditors		$15,000

20 Its actuarial firm informs the business that the cost of its employees' retirement pension benefit for the period is $565,000. According to the contract with its employees, the business decides to transfer $300,000 to the trustee of the pension plan and to defer payment of the remainder until a later time (which it has the option to do). No entry has been made for this expense yet. What journal entry should be made for this expense?

	Debit	Credit
Employees' Benefit Expense	$565,000	
Cash		$300,000
Employees' Retirement Liability		$265,000

21 Unfortunately, one of the major customers of the business declares bankruptcy. This customer owes the business $35,000. The business has already recorded the credit sale to the customer and the Cost of Goods Sold for the sale. After careful analysis, the business comes to the conclusion that it won't be able to collect any money from this customer. The business doesn't record an expense caused by uncollectible debts until it actually writes off the debt. What journal entry should be made for this expense?

	Debit	Credit
Bad Debts Expense	$35,000	
Debtors		$35,000

 We deliberately made this bad debt that has to be written off as uncollectible a relatively large amount in order to call your attention to this problem. Basically, the business gave away its products for nothing. That really smarts! Of course, the business should shut off credit privileges to this customer and also consider reporting this incident to credit-rating agencies.

22 A business needs more capital to expand and grow, and so it issues additional stock shares for a total of $25,000,000. What journal entry should be made for this financing transaction?

	Debit	Credit
Cash	$25,000,000	
Owners' Capital – Invested Capital		$25,000,000

23 A business has a very good year; its $58,000,000 net income for the year is an all-time high. Being in a generous mood, its board of directors declares a whopping cash distribution of $30,000,000 based on the business's record-setting performance. What journal entry should be made for this financing transaction?

	Debit	Credit
Owners' Capital – Retained Earnings	$30,000,000	
Cash		$30,000,000

Instead of directly debiting (decreasing) the retained earnings account, as shown in the entry above, some accountants favour making two entries for dividends, as follows:

	Debit	Credit
Dividends	$30,000,000	
Cash		$30,000,000

	Debit	Credit
Owners' Capital – Retained Earnings	$30,000,000	
Dividends		$30,000,000

As you can see, the end result is the same: the retained earnings account is decreased by the amount of the dividends.

Chapter 4

The Bookkeeping Cycle: Adjusting and Closing Entries

*T*he end of a business's fiscal year is a very important time. Accountants prepare the business's Profit and Loss Statement and cash flow statement for the year as well as its balance sheet. The board of directors critically reviews these financial statements to assess the business's financial performance and position and to plan the future course of the business. The financial statements are sent to lenders and shareholders who make their lending and investment decisions based on these accounting reports.

In short, the annual financial statements of a business are extraordinarily important. Accordingly, the financial statements require extraordinarily good accounting; financial statements are no better than the quality of accounting behind them. As we explain in Chapter 3, good accounting demands a well-designed and reliable bookkeeping system, one that records the business's transactions during the period completely and accurately.

This chapter talks about the additional accounting procedures done at the end of the period. An accountant can't use a business's various accounts to prepare financial statements until these end-of-period accounting steps are completed. As the saying goes, 'It ain't over until the fat lady sings'.

Getting Accurate with Adjusting Entries

During an accounting period, certain expenses either aren't recorded or aren't fully recorded. The accountant waits until the end of the period and records adjusting entries for these expenses. In addition to expenses, revenue and income accounts may also need adjusting entries at the end of the period. Adjusting entries complete the profit accounting process for the period.

The term *adjusting* doesn't mean 'fiddling with'. Adjusting entries aren't made to manipulate profit, such as moving profit closer to the forecast target for the period. Instead, an accountant makes adjusting entries to make profit for the period as accurate as possible.

In other words, adjusting entries make revenue and expenses correct for the period, and without them, the bottom-line net income for the period would be wrong. Keep in mind that the managers, directors, lenders and shareholders of a business rely on the profit number more than any other figure in the business's financial statements.

Businesses prepare quarterly (three-month) financial statements. In this chapter, however, we focus on the annual (12-month) accounting period. In the business world (and for economic analysis in general), one year is the standard time unit. One year includes the complete cycle of seasonal variations that many businesses experience. The annual Profit and Loss Statement draws the most attention in business financial reporting, and everyone holds this statement to high standards of accounting.

In broad overview, year-end adjusting entries are needed for two reasons:

✔ To correct errors that may have crept into the bookkeeping process.

✔ To make final entries for the year in revenue, income, expense and loss accounts so that the profit or loss for the year is accurate (or as accurate as possible given the inherent accounting problems of measuring profit and loss).

An accounting system involves an enormous amount of data and detail, and so safeguards and procedures should be put in place to prevent bookkeeping errors. A business is well-advised to conduct a thorough search at the end of the year for bookkeeping errors that have gone undetected. In the section 'Instituting Internal Controls' later in the chapter, we discuss internal accounting controls that should be put in place to minimise bookkeeping errors. Despite their best efforts, most businesses find that errors sneak into their bookkeeping systems.

Q. At year-end, the business searches for bookkeeping errors that may have gone undetected. Based on its year-end review, the business discovers that some office and computer supplies were thrown away and no entry was made. (The supplies were thrown out because they were no longer of any use, but the bookkeeping department wasn't informed that the supplies had been discarded.) In general, at the time of purchase, the costs of office and computer supplies are entered (debited) in an Asset account called prepaid expenses. As these supplies are used, the appropriate amount of cost is removed from the Asset account and recorded to expenses. The cost of the discarded supplies is £4,800. What adjusting entry should be made?

A. The required adjusting entry is as follows:

	Debit	Credit
Office and Computer Supplies Expense	£4,800	
Prepaid Expenses		£4,800

You can argue that throwing away office and computer supplies causes a special type of loss that should be recorded in a separate loss account, but we think that most accountants would put the cost of discarded office and computer supplies in the regular Expense account.

1. In its year-end review for errors, a business discovers that the recent invoice from its law firm was entered as £6,500 instead of £5,600, which is the correct amount. The invoice hasn't been paid yet. What adjusting entry should be made to correct this error?

Solve It

2. In its year-end review for errors, a business discovers that an order of products was shipped to a customer, and the cost of the products was correctly charged to Cost of Goods Sold expenses. However, the paperwork for this particular sales order wasn't sent to the bookkeeping department on time. Therefore, the sale hasn't been recorded. The total price for this credit sale is £36,260. What adjusting entry should be made to correct this error?

Solve It

3. The £1,500 waste collection invoice for the last month of the fiscal year normally arrives before the end of the month. However, the waste management firm didn't get its invoices out on time, and so the expense hasn't been recorded. What adjusting entry should be made to correct this error?

Solve It

4. In the hustle and bustle of the end-of-year accounting activities, the bookkeeper simply forgot to record the business's PAYE/NI payments from its last payroll in the year. The amount is £29,600. What adjusting entry should be made to correct this error?

Solve It

Breaking Down the End-of-Year Adjusting Entries

The chief accountant of a business, often known as the Financial Controller, must know which end-of-year adjusting entries need to be made and should follow through to make sure that these critical entries are recorded correctly. In most businesses, the chief accountant takes a hands-on approach in recording adjusting entries at the end of the year.

Recording year-end adjusting entries marks a dividing line between bookkeeping and accounting. Bookkeeping consists of following established rules for accounting and recordkeeping, and the chief accountant makes and enforces the rules and takes charge of the year-end adjusting entries.

Recording the depreciation expense

The theory of depreciation isn't complicated. Businesses invest in long-term fixed assets such as land, buildings, machines, equipment, delivery vans and cars, fork lifts, office furniture, computers and so on. These items are called fixed assets because they're fixed in place, or stationary (well, vans and cars move around of course). The term *fixed* also implies that the assets aren't held for sale (that is, not until they reach the end of their useful lives to the business).

In a balance sheet, these assets typically are reported in categories such as Land and Buildings, Plant and Machinery, Fixtures and Fittings, Office Equipment and so on.

Charging the entire cost of fixed assets to expenses at the time they're bought or constructed wouldn't be very smart. The obvious thing to do is to allocate the cost of a fixed asset over the years of its useful life; this practice is called *depreciation*.

Ah, but here's the rub. Can you predict the future useful life of a fixed asset? Some machines don't really wear out; with proper maintenance and repair, they can last indefinitely. Another complicating factor is that businesses replace many fixed assets before the end of their useful lives – not because they wear out physically, but because they become obsolete and inefficient.

The business needs to determine over what period its assets should be depreciated. This accounting policy must be decided upon and then fixed.

A note is made in the accounts as to which method of depreciation and over what period the assets are being depreciated. For example, motor vehicles are quite often depreciated over a four-year period, even though they may be driven for more years. Furniture and fittings can be over three years and computers are often a lot less, sometimes over only one year. (The computer industry is always changing and newer, faster machines are being produced all the time, which means that computers become obsolete in a very short space of time.)

Depreciation also raises the question of whether each year of using a fixed asset should be charged with the same amount of depreciation. Or should some years be hit with more depreciation expense than others? Generally the answer to this question boils down to a choice between the straight-line depreciation method (an equal amount is charged to expenses each year) and the reducing balance method (earlier years are hit with more expenses than later years).

We explain depreciation in-depth in Chapter 9. Our purpose here is simply to illustrate the year-end adjusting entry for depreciation.

Q. A business buys a new van for £24,000 at the start of the year. The business decides to depreciate the van over four years and use the straight-line method (equal amounts per year). The business hasn't recorded any depreciation on this van during the year. How is the depreciation recorded?

A. The depreciation is recorded as follows:

	Debit	Credit
Depreciation Expense – Motor Vehicles	£6,000	
Accumulated Depreciation – Motor Vehicles		£6,000

In the entry, we debit a specific depreciation expense account, but this action doesn't mean that this depreciation account is disclosed separately in the business's Profit and Loss Statement. Most likely, it's grouped with other depreciation expense accounts, and only one total depreciation expense is reported in the Profit and Loss Statement. A full-year depreciation amount is recorded because the business has used the asset for the entire year. The calculation is £24,000 ÷ 4 years = £6,000 per year.

Instead of crediting (decreasing) the fixed Asset account, the standard accounting practice is to credit accumulated depreciation, which is the contra account to the fixed Asset account. In essence, the contra account is the credit side of the fixed Asset account, and it's maintained so that both the original cost of fixed assets and the cumulative depreciation amount on the fixed assets are available for reporting in the balance sheet.

5. Based on a business's depreciation schedules, the annual depreciation on its machinery is £32,000. The business uses the straight-line depreciation method. It records a machinery depreciation expense at the end of each quarter during the year, but no entry has been made for the fourth and final quarter. What adjusting entry for machinery depreciation should be recorded at year-end?

Solve It

6. A bookkeeper who was recently hired by a business recorded the depreciation expense on delivery vans for the year as follows:

	Debit	Credit
Depreciation Expense – Delivery Trucks	£215,000	
Delivery Trucks – cost		£215,000

Is this entry wrong?

Solve It

7. On the last day of the year, a particular piece of equipment that originally cost £87,500 many years ago is removed from the production line and put on the shipping dock. The equipment is of no further use to the business and will be hauled away to the junk heap in a few days. The asset is fully depreciated. What entry should be made for the disposal of the fixed asset?

Solve It

Recording the amortisation expense

In addition to tangible fixed assets, a business may invest in intangible assets, which can't be seen or touched. The value of an intangible asset is rooted in law. For example, a patent gives the owner the exclusive legal right to use the patent in the pursuit of profit. No one else can legally use the patent without being held liable for infringement. All sorts of intangible assets exist. For instance, a business may purchase a list consisting of thousands of names of potential customers or acquire the right to use an established trade name and logo.

 The acquisition of an intangible asset is recorded as a debit (increase) in an Asset account. The cost of an intangible asset usually is allocated over its predicted useful life to the business, much like depreciation (see the preceding section). Allocating the cost of an intangible asset to expenses over the years of its useful life is called *amortisation*.

Q. A business invests in a franchise, which gives it the right to operate under a well-known trade name and logo. The franchise contract is for ten years, and the business pays £250,000 to the franchisor. What adjusting entry should be made at the end of the first year concerning the cost of the franchise?

A. At the end of the first year, the business has used up one year of the ten-year franchise investment. Therefore, the following year-end adjusting entry is made:

	Debit	Credit
Franchise Amortisation Expense	£25,000	
Franchise		£25,000

Generally, the straight-line amortisation method is used, which means that an equal amount is charged to expenses each year. The Asset account is credited (decreased) in recording the amortisation expense. A contra account isn't used to accumulate amortisation.

8. A business pays the owner of a patent £500,000 for the right to use the patent for a period of five years.

    a. What entry should be made for the purchase of the patent right?

    b. What adjusting entry should be made one year later?

Solve It

9. The business signs a ten-year contract with the inventor of a secret process that it plans to use in its manufacturing operations. As an incentive to agree to the contract, the business immediately pays the inventor £1,000,000. In addition, the business agrees to pay the inventor a royalty equal to 5 per cent of its sales revenue from these products over the next ten years.

    a. What entry should be made for the initial payment to the inventor?

    b. What adjusting entry should be made one year later?

Solve It

Recording other adjusting entries

Depending on the business, year-end adjusting entries are made for the following items

- ✔ Bad debts expense (caused by uncollectible debtors).
- ✔ Buildup of liabilities for operating expenses that haven't been recorded.
- ✔ Increases in liability for unfunded employees' retirement benefits and for post-retirement medical and healthcare benefits.
- ✔ Investment income that has been earned but not recorded.
- ✔ Liability for product warranty and guarantee costs.
- ✔ Losses due to asset impairments.
- ✔ Stock losses due to shrinkage and write-downs required by the lower of cost or net realisable value accounting rule.
- ✔ Tax liability based on the final determination of income tax for the year.

This list is quite a dog's breakfast, isn't it? And we don't even list all possible adjusting entries made by businesses! This list should give you some idea of the burden on the chief accountant of a business to make sure that all its revenue and expenses are correctly recorded for the year.

Q. A business makes mostly credit sales. At the end of the year, its accountant does an aging analysis of its debtors, analysing the debtors according to their age. Generally, the older a debt is, the greater the risk of not collecting it or not collecting the entire amount owed by the customer. At the end of the year, the business has £4,538,600 total debtors. This ending balance doesn't include specific debts that were written off during the period. Based on its aging analysis, the business estimates that sooner or later customers aren't going to pay about £95,000 of the ending balance of its debtors. What year-end adjusting entry is made?

A. You can use two methods of accounting for the bad debts expense. In the direct write-off method, no expense is recorded until specific debtors are actually written off. Under this method, no adjusting entry is made at year-end because the business hasn't identified specific customers' accounts from its debtors at year-end that should be written off. During the year, the business did write off specific debtors, and the bad debts expense was debited (increased) in these entries. Only these write-offs are recorded in the bad debts expense account.

In the provision method, based on the estimated amount of debtors that will have to be written off in the future, the following entry is made:

	Debit	**Credit**
Bad Debts Expense	£95,000	
Provision for Doubtful Debts		£95,000

Provision for doubtful accounts is the contra account to the debtors account.

We don't discuss several bookkeeping procedures connected with the provision method for recording the bad debts expense because our goal simply is to illustrate that the bad debt expense can be recorded before specific debtors are actually identified and written off as uncollectible. The compelling theory of the provision method is that the expense is recorded in the same period as the credit sales that generates the bad debts. On the other hand, estimating the amount of future write-offs of debtors is very tricky and open to manipulation.

The following questions offer examples of common year-end adjusting entries made by businesses, but a particular business doesn't necessarily make every one of the following adjusting entries. For instance, consider a business that makes only cash sales and no credit sales. This business doesn't have a bad debts expense from uncollectible debtors, but it does have expenses from taking counterfeit currency, accepting bad cheques, making mistakes in giving change to customers and thefts from cash registers.

10. A business makes almost all credit sales. At the end of the year, the business has £485,000 total debtors. This ending balance doesn't include £28,500 specific debtors that were written off during the period. The business estimates that customers aren't going to pay £6,500 of the ending balance of its debtors. What year-end adjusting entry is made?

Solve It

11. At the end of the year, the business owes its employees £58,300 for accumulated holiday and sick pay. This amount will be paid when employees actually take their holidays and time off for sick leave. No entry has been made for this accrued liability. What adjusting entry is made at the end of the year?

Solve It

12. At the end of the year, the business counts and inspects its stock of products on hand, which is stored in its warehouse and retail sales areas. Usually, employees discover some damaged and spoiled products that can't be sold and this year is no exception. The cost of spoiled and damaged products that have to be thrown away is £26,300. What adjusting entry is made?

Solve It

Closing the Books on the Year

The annual Profit and Loss Statement of a business is prepared from its revenue, other income, expenses and loss accounts for the year. Indeed, where else can information for preparing the Profit and Loss Statement come from? Accountants use these accounts to determine the amount of profit or loss for the year. We needn't remind you how important the annual profit number is to the managers and directors of the business as well as to its lenders and shareholders.

Even a modest-size business may have 100 or so revenue accounts and 1,000 or so Expense accounts. Managers need a lot of detailed information to run their businesses, and so they depend on their accountants to generate regular reports that provide the detailed account information they need for decision-making and management control.

In sharp contrast, the external Profit and Loss Statement distributed to a business's lenders and shareholders includes relatively few lines of information. In this external statement, the business compresses its many revenue accounts into only one or two sales revenue lines and its many Expense accounts into relatively few expense lines. (We refer to the Profit and Loss Account in Chapter 5.)

After the business prepares its annual financial statements, the revenue and Expense accounts have served their dual purpose of providing information for preparing the Profit and Loss Statement and helping to determine profit or loss for the year.

What happens to these revenue and Expense accounts after the year is concluded? The traditional bookkeeping procedure is to make closing entries in the accounts. These special entries close, or shut down, the revenue and Expense accounts for the year just ended. Also, the amount of profit or loss for the year is recorded in the retained earnings account.

In the few pages we have here to illustrate closing entries, we can't show you 100 revenue accounts and a 1,000 Expense accounts. So in the following example, we use just one sales revenue account and only four Expense accounts. This scenario isn't realistic, but it gets the point across.

Q. At the end of the year, after all year-end adjusting entries have been made and posted, the balances in the revenue and Expense accounts of the business are as follows:

Cost of Goods Sold Expense		Sales Revenue	
2,725,000			4,526,500

Selling & Administrative Expenses	
1,228,500	

Interest Expense	
175,000	

Income Tax Expense	
138,000	

What is the journal entry to close the nominal accounts?

The journal entry to close the nominal accounts and enter the profit or loss for the year is as follows:

	Debit	Credit
Sales Revenue	$4,526,500	
Cost of Goods Sold Expense		$2,725,000
Selling and Administrative Expenses		$1,228,500
Interest Expense		$175,000
Income Tax Expense		$138,000
Owners' Capital – Retained Earnings	$260,000	

 The debit to sales revenue and the credits to expenses close out these accounts. The $260,000 profit for the year (sales revenue less all expenses) is recorded in the retained earnings account, where it belongs. Are the books still in balance? In other words, is the accounting equation still in balance after making this entry? Sure. The total credit in this closing entry equals the total debit and so this entry doesn't throw the accounting equation out of balance.

13. Refer to the closing entry in the answer to the example in this section. The T accounts before the closing entry is recorded are provided here. What are the balances in the revenue and Expense accounts after the closing entry is posted?

Solve It

Instituting Internal Controls

Have you ever made an error in your chequebook or forgot to pay a bill on time? Have you ever misplaced an important document that you desperately need but can't find? Have you started to fill out a loan application and realised that you don't keep records for the types of information the lender wants to know? (Trust us; you don't want to know our answers to these questions!)

Your individual bookkeeping system may have holes in it, but you can probably get by. In contrast, a business can't get by if its bookkeeping system is full of errors and doesn't provide the information accountants need. A good accounting system is a matter of life and death for a business.

A business accounting system has many components:

> ✔ **The forms and procedures used to facilitate business transactions and activities,** such as making purchases, paying bills, depositing cash receipts in the bank, preparing payroll cheques and so on.
>
> ✔ **The chart of accounts (refer to** Chapter 3).
>
> ✔ **The bookkeeping procedures used to record its transactions,** which should work perfectly if no errors are made.

Bookkeeping errors can happen, of course (as Murphy's Law says: 'If something can go wrong, it will'). To counteract bookkeeping errors, a layer of internal accounting controls is superimposed on the bookkeeping procedures of the business.

This layer of controls builds redundancy into the accounting system in that accountants take extra steps to double-check the data and information recorded in the original entries and accounts. Think of this action as looking at your speedometer not once but twice to make sure that your speed is acceptable. Businesses know that effective internal accounting controls reduce the incidence of bookkeeping errors to a minimum, and that's extremely important.

The accountant's function extends beyond establishing and policing internal accounting controls. The accounting department is assigned responsibility for designing and enforcing controls to guard against a broad range of threats facing the business. Businesses are at risk from all sorts of dishonesty, theft and fraud. They handle a lot of cash and have valuable assets, and so businesses are natural targets for people who steal and cheat. Everyone that a business deals with poses a potential risk.

Another serious problem to consider is that instead of being the victim, a business may be the perpetrator of wrongdoing. A business may cheat its employees and customers, knowingly violate laws or resort to accounting fraud to make its financial statements look better than the facts support. In other words, a business may cook its books. You may have heard about Enron and other high profile accounting fraud scandals

The chief accountant of a business has to make sure that basic internal accounting controls are in place and working effectively to minimise bookkeeping errors. In addition, this person is responsible for establishing effective controls that prevent employee theft and embezzlement as well as fraud against the business by its customers, suppliers and other outside parties it deals with. Furthermore, a business needs to adopt controls to prevent it from issuing fraudulent financial statements. All these responsibilities are a tall order, to say the least!

EXAMPLE

Q. A business establishes an internal control procedure that, for every cash disbursement of £2,500 or more, requires a second manager to countersign the cheque. The manager who has authority to initiate the disbursement signs the cheque and then sends the cheque with supporting documentation to the second manager for her signature. What is the logic of this control?

A. The theory behind this internal control procedure is that the second manager makes a careful review and judges whether the payment is for a legitimate purpose and is reasonable in amount. If two persons have to sign off on expenditures over a certain amount, they would have to collude to pull off a scam against the business. Even if someone is inclined to make a quick buck and doesn't care how, she is unlikely to be in cahoots with another untrustworthy crook.

14. The purchasing manager of the business has authority to issue purchase orders. She also inspects shipments as they arrive, approves suppliers' invoices for payment and posts cheques to the suppliers. Do you see any potential problems here?

Solve It

15. A business doesn't bother to reconcile its monthly bank statement balance and its cash account balance, claiming that its bookkeepers have more important things to do and, besides, the bank never makes a mistake. What do you think?

Solve It

Answers to Problems on the Bookkeeping Cycle

Here are the answers to the practice questions presented earlier in this chapter.

1 In its year-end review for errors, a business discovers that the recent invoice from its law firm was entered as £6,500 instead of £5,600, which is the correct amount. The invoice hasn't been paid yet. What adjusting entry should be made to correct this error?

	Debit	Credit
Creditors (Accounts Payable)	£900	
Legal Expenses		£900

This type of error is called a transposition error because two digits in the number are transposed, or switched. This error is common. Experienced bookkeepers and accountants know that this type of error is divisible by nine. (The difference caused by any two digits you transpose is always divisible by nine.)

2 In its year-end review for errors, a business discovers that an order of products was shipped to a customer, and the cost of the products was correctly charged to Cost of Goods Sold expense. However, the paperwork for this particular sales order wasn't sent to the bookkeeping department on time. Therefore, the sale hasn't been recorded. The total price for this credit sale is £36,260. What adjusting entry should be made to correct this error?

	Debit	Credit
Debtors	£36,260	
Sales Revenue		£36,260

The sales revenue for this sale should be recorded because the sale was completed, and the products were delivered to the customer. The sale should be recorded to match revenue and expenses. If this error isn't corrected, a mismatch occurs because the expense is in this year but the revenue will be in next year.

3 The £1,500 waste collection bill for the last month of the fiscal year normally arrives before the end of the month. However, the waste management firm didn't get its invoices out on time, and so the expense hasn't been recorded. What adjusting entry should be made to correct this error?

	Debit	Credit
Waste Collection Expense	£1,500	
Creditors (Accounts Payable)		£1,500

This entry records the 12th month of expense for the year. If this entry were not recorded, only 11 months of waste collection expense would be recorded for the year. Also, the amount owed to the waste collection firm is clearly a liability of the business and should be included in its creditor balance at the end of the year.

4 In the hustle and bustle of the end-of-year accounting activities, the bookkeeper simply forgot to record the business's PAYE/NI on its last payroll in the year. The amount is £29,600. What adjusting entry should be made to correct this error?

	Debit	Credit
PAYE/NI Expense	£29,600	
Accrued PAYE/NI		£29,600

5 Based on a business's depreciation schedules, the annual depreciation on its machinery is £32,000. The business uses the straight-line depreciation method. It records a machinery depreciation expense at the end of each quarter during the year, but no entry has been made for the fourth and final quarter. What adjusting entry for machinery depreciation should be recorded at year-end?

	Debit	Credit
Machinery Depreciation	£8,000	
Accumulated Depreciation – Machinery		£8,000

Note: by the end of the year, the business had already recorded three quarters of depreciation on its machinery. In the year-end adjusting entry, only the last quarter of the total annual depreciation expense is recorded.

6 A bookkeeper who was recently hired by a business recorded the depreciation expense on delivery vans for the year as follows:

	Debit	Credit
Depreciation Expense – Vans	£215,000	
Delivery Vans		£215,000

Is this entry wrong?

The debit to depreciation expense is correct, but the wrong account is credited. The credit should be made in the Accumulated Depreciation – Delivery Vans account, which is the contra account to the Delivery Vans Asset account.

Standard practice is to report the original cost of fixed assets in the balance sheet and to deduct the cumulative amount of depreciation from original cost. To have this information available for preparing the balance sheet, the accumulated depreciation account is credited when recording the depreciation expense.

7 On the last day of the year, a particular piece of equipment that originally cost £87,500 many years ago is removed from the production line and put on the shipping dock. The equipment is of no further use to the business and will be hauled away to the junk heap in a few days. The asset is fully depreciated. What entry should be made for the disposal of the fixed asset?

	Debit	Credit
Accumulated Depreciation – Equipment	£87,500	
Equipment		£87,500

When a fixed asset is disposed of and removed from service, its cost and accumulated depreciation should be removed from the accounts. The fixed asset is fully depreciated, and so the balance in the accumulated depreciation account is equal to the original cost of the fixed asset. Not making this entry would inflate the balances of the fixed Asset account and of its contra account.

8 A business pays the owner of a patent £500,000 for the right to use the patent for a period of five years.

a. What entry should be made for the purchase of the patent right?

The entry to record the purchase of the patent is:

	Debit	Credit
Patent	£500,000	
Cash		£500,000

b. What adjusting entry should be made one year later?

The entry to record the first year amortisation expense on the patent is:

	Debit	Credit
Patent Amortisation Expense	£100,000	
Patent		£100,000

The business has the right to use the patent for only five years. Therefore, it should amortise the cost of the patent right over the five-year period. Generally, the straight-line method of allocation is used for amortising the cost of an intangible asset. Therefore, £100,000 expense (⅕ of £500,000) is recorded each year. The amortisation is recorded as a direct reduction (credit) in the intangible Asset account.

9 The business signs a ten-year contract with the inventor of a secret process that it plans to use in its manufacturing operations. As an incentive to agree to the contract, the business immediately pays the inventor £1,000,000. In addition, the business agrees to pay the inventor a royalty equal to 5 per cent of its sales revenue from these products over the next ten years.

a. What entry should be made for the initial payment to the inventor?

The entry to record the purchase of the rights to the secret process is:

	Debit	Credit
Secret Process	£1,000,000	
Cash		£1,000,000

b. What adjusting entry should be made one year later?

The entry to record the first year amortisation expense on the cost of the secret process is:

	Debit	Credit
Secret Process Amortisation Expense	£100,000	
Secret Process		£100,000

The purpose of this question is to illustrate that the cost of the intangible asset should be amortised over the life of the contract to use the secret process. To be more accurate, however, this amount is a cost of production. The amortisation amount should be charged to the cost of the products that are manufactured using the secret process. When these products are sold, their costs are charged to the Cost of Goods Sold expense account. Therefore, the amortisation ends up in the Cost of Goods Sold expense account. Likewise, depreciation on fixed assets that are used in a business's manufacturing process is charged to the cost of products manufactured.

10 A business makes almost all credit sales. At the end of the year, the business has £485,000 total debtors. This ending balance doesn't include £28,500 specific debtors that were written off during the period. The business estimates that customers aren't going to pay £6,500 of the ending balance of its debtors. What year-end adjusting entry is made?

If the business uses the direct write-off method, no adjusting entry is made at the end of the year. Only the debtors actually written off during the year are included in the bad debts expense; so the bad debts expense for the year is £28,500.

If the business uses the allowance method, the following adjusting entry is made at the end of the year:

	Debit	*Credit*
Bad Debts Expense	£6,500	
Provision for Doubtful Accounts		£6,500

Its bad debts expense for the year is £35,000 (£28,500 specific accounts written off during the year + £6,500 recorded in this adjusting entry).

11 At the end of the year, the business owes its employees £58,300 for accumulated holiday and sick pay. This amount will be paid when employees actually take their holidays and time off for sick leave. No entry has been made for this accrued liability. What adjusting entry is made at the end of the year?

The year-end adjusting entry for the accumulation of holidays and sick pay is as follows.

	Debit	*Credit*
Wages and Salaries Expense	£58,300	
Accrued holiday and sick pay		£58,300

The titles of the accounts debited and credited in this year-end entry vary from business to business. For example, a separate Expense account for employees' benefits can be used instead of debiting all labour costs in one general wages and salaries Expense account. And the exact title of the Liability account credited may vary; separate accounts may be used for each specific liability.

12 At the end of the year, the business counts and inspects its ending stock of products on hand, which is stored in its warehouse and retail sales areas. Usually, employees discover some damaged and spoiled products that can't be sold and this year is no exception. The cost of spoiled and damaged products that have to be thrown away is £26,300. What adjusting entry is made?

The business should make the following year-end adjusting entry:

	Debit	*Credit*
Cost of Goods Sold Expense	£26,300	
Stock		£26,300

Some accountants may disagree about the account we debit in this adjusting entry. Some amount of spollage and damage from handling products is unavoidable and a normal cost of receiving, moving, storing and handling products. Therefore, we include this amount in the Cost of Goods Sold expense. On the other hand, an unusually high percentage of products can be thrown away – beyond what's normal for the business. In such a situation, we would record the excess cost as a special expense, such as loss from damaged products. Regardless of which Expense account is debited, accountants definitely agree that the cost of products thrown out should be recorded to expenses in the year.

13 Refer to the closing entry in the answer to the example in this section. The T accounts after the closing entry is posted are provided here. What are the balances in the revenue and Expense accounts after the closing entry is posted?

As you can see, the accounts have zero balances. They have served their purposes for the year and are shut down and made ready for next year.

14 The purchasing manager of the business has authority to issue purchase orders. She also inspects shipments as they arrive, approves suppliers' invoices for payment and posts cheques to the suppliers. Do you see any potential problems here?

This business is asking for trouble. Assigning all these different functions to the same person violates a fundamental tenet of internal control: the separation of duties. Giving the purchasing manager control over the procurement process from start to finish is dangerous; ideally, a different person should be in charge of each of the steps listed in the question. For example, someone other than the purchasing manager should inspect shipments as they arrive on the receiving dock to make sure that the items received match up with the items listed on the invoice from the supplier, and a different person should post cheques to suppliers. If we were the boss, we'd tell the purchasing manager that her time is too valuable to do all these things and that she should focus on getting better prices.

15 A business doesn't bother to reconcile its monthly bank statement balance and its cash account balance, claiming that its bookkeepers have more important things to do and, besides, the bank never makes a mistake. What do you think?

A business should routinely reconcile its monthly bank statement balance and its cash account balance. Even if the bank 'never' makes an error (hum!), the bookkeeper may make errors in recording cash receipts and payments. Also, keep in mind that the monthly bank statement reports cheques from customers that have bounced (for insufficient funds) and unusual charges by the bank that the business may not have recorded, as well as regular charges that the business may wait to record until it gets its monthly bank statement. In short, the bookkeeper should make time to do a monthly reconciliation.

Part II
Preparing Financial Statements

'Oh no! Not another bad company
financial report.'

In this part . . .

One of the main purposes of accounting is to prepare the financial statements of the business. This part explains the three primary financial statements of every business: the profit and loss statement that reports the profit-making activities of the business for the period, the balance sheet that summarises its financial condition at the end of the profit period, and the cash flow statement for the period.

One innovative feature in this part is Chapter 7, in which we explain the connections between sales revenue and expenses reported in the profit and loss statement with their corresponding assets and liabilities reported in the balance sheet. These couplings are very important to understand. The end result of making profit is not found in the profit and loss statement (even though profit is called the bottom line). As you discover, the final resulting place of profit is actually in the balance sheet.

Chapter 5

Reporting Profit

• •

In This Chapter

▶ Getting a grip on what profit is and isn't

▶ Designing the Profit and Loss statement

▶ Minding your p's and q's with revenue and expenses

▶ Seeing the effect of profit on assets and liabilities

• •

T his chapter explains the effects of profit or loss on financial condition and how profit and loss performance is reported outside the business in the Profit and Loss statement.

The job of accountants is to measure profit performance, not to pass judgement on a business's morality. Yet, accountants shouldn't behave like the three monkeys who see no evil, speak no evil and hear no evil. If a business is acting illegally, the last thing it wants to do is record a liability that may potentially highlight those illegal activities, ultimately leading to the likelihood of losing a major lawsuit or having to pay a huge fine. The chief accountant has to decide whether to be part of the conspiracy to conceal the illegal activities or to leave the business.

Understanding the Nature of Profit

Profit doesn't have a single, universal meaning or definition. One concept of profit is to buy low and sell high – which applies to investing in stocks and property but isn't a useful definition for business profit. Another concept of profit is an increase in the market value of an asset. Accounting for business profit ignores market value increases of operating assets; except for investment firms and hedge funds, businesses don't earn profit by holding assets that appreciate in value.

Most businesses earn profit through an ongoing process of selling products and services for prices that provide revenue higher than the expense of providing the products and services. Business profit is the *residual*, the amount remaining after deducting expenses from revenue.

To make profit, a business needs to raise capital (generally money) to invest in operating assets that are used in its profit-making activities. These assets aren't held for sale or for market value appreciation. The business's sources of capital expect a return on their capital, and interest is paid on money loaned to the business. The profit remaining after paying interest to lenders and income tax to HM Revenue and Customs (HMRC) accrues to the benefit of the shareholders of the business.

Of course, a business may pursue profit in many other directions – from trading in pork belly futures to property speculation. But this chapter focuses on generating profit the old-fashioned way – making sales and controlling expenses. The Profit and Loss statement we discuss in this chapter is for the standard model of a business that sells products and services.

The term *Profit and Loss statement* generally means the external Profit and Loss statement that a business reports to its shareholders and lenders. (In Part III of this book, we discuss internal profit reports used by a business's managers; internal management profit reports include much more detailed and confidential information than external Profit and Loss statements.)

Externally reported Profit and Loss statements are bound by authoritative financial reporting standards for measuring and reporting profit. These rules are called generally accepted accounting principles, or GAAP for short. Business profit measurement and reporting shouldn't deviate from these standards in any significant respect. Otherwise, the Profit and Loss statement can be judged as misleading and possibly fraudulent.

Profit is a calculated number equal to the difference between sales revenue and expenses. Sales revenue is on one side of the scale, expenses are on the other side, and profit is the measure of how much the revenue side outweighs the expense side. To locate profit, you must trace the effects of revenue and expenses.

Suppose a business collects cash for all its sales and pays cash for all its expenses during the year. You need to look at only one place – its cash account – to find the business's profit. However, a business may make credit sales and not collect cash from all its sales during the year. Furthermore, the typical business doesn't pay all its expenses during the year and pays some expenses before the start of the year. In summary, sales and expenses affect several assets, including cash and liabilities.

To follow the trail of profit, keep the following in mind:

✔ Sales Revenue = Asset Increase or Liability Decrease

✔ An Expense = Asset Decrease or Liability Increase

Q. During the year, Business A's assets increase £3,000,000 and its liabilities increase £400,000 as the result of its profit-making activities. During the year, Business B's assets increase £2,700,000 and its liabilities increase £100,000 as the result of its profit-making activities. During the year, Business C's assets increase £2,000,000 and its liabilities decrease £600,000 as the result of its profit-making activities. None of these three businesses distributes any part of its annual profit to shareholders during the year. What is the annual profit of each business?

A. All three businesses earn the same profit for the year: £2,600,000. The accounting equation can be stated as follows:

Assets – Liabilities = Owners' Capital

Profit increases the owners' capital of a business, which means that the changes in assets and liabilities have the effect of increasing owners' capital. For each business in this scenario, owners' capital improves £2,600,000, which is the amount of profit for the year.

1. A business reports £346,000 net income (profit) for the year just ended. How may assets and liabilities change as a result of this profit? Note two different scenarios.

Solve It

2. A business reports £3,800,000 loss for the year just ended. How may assets and liabilities change as a result of this loss? Note two different scenarios.

Solve It

3. A business reports £5,250,000 net income for the year just ended. In its cash flow statement for the year (we discuss this statement further in Chapter 8), the business reports that its cash flow from operating activities (from its profit for the year) is £4,650,000. In other words, its cash balance increased £4,650,000 from its profit-making activities for the year. Determine two valid scenarios for changes in assets other than cash and in liabilities that result from its profit for the year.

Solve It

4. A business reports £836,000 loss for the year just ended. In its cash flow statement for the year, the business reports that its cash flow from operating activities (from its loss for the year) is a *negative* £675,000. In other words, its cash balance decreased £675,000 from its profit-making activities for the year. Determine two valid scenarios for changes in assets other than cash and in liabilities resulting from its loss for the year.

Solve It

Profit and Loss Statement Format

The bottom line profit (or loss) in a Profit and Loss statement draws the most attention, but the statement is really about revenue and expenses. A business can't make profit without sales and expenses, and therefore the Profit and Loss statement reports sales revenue and expenses.

A Profit and Loss statement reports three basic items of information, in the following order:

✔ Sales Revenue

✔ Expenses

✔ Profit

Here we show you a simplified format for the Profit and Loss Statement.

Sales Revenue	£26,000,000
Less Cost of Goods Sold	£14,300,000
Gross Profit	£11,700,000
Selling and general expenses	£8,700,000
Operating Profit	£3,000,000
Interest payable	£400,000
Profit before tax	£2,600,000
Taxation	£910,000
Profit after tax	£1,690,000

This example is what you would probably expect to see in your year-end accounts, but it doesn't give you enough detail for management reports.

Below you find an example with more detail included (to make it look more realistic).

The Profit and Loss statement may look as follows with a little more detail added:

Revenues	
Sales	£20,000
Cost of Goods Sold	(£10,000)
Gross Profit	£10,000
Operating Expenses	
Advertising	£1,400
Salaries	£2,200
Supplies	£1,500
Interest Expenses	£800
Depreciation	£500
Total Operating Expenses	£6,400
Operating Profit	£3,600
Other Income	
Interest income	£200
Net Profit	£3,800

5. The sales revenue and expenses of a business for the year just ended are as follows:

Cost of Goods Sold expense	£6,358,000
Income tax expense	£458,000
Interest expense	£684,000
Selling and general expenses	£4,375,000
Sales Revenue	£13,125,000

Prepare the annual Profit and Loss statement of the business.

Solve It

6. The sales revenue and expenses of a business for the year just ended are as follows:

Cost of Goods Sold expense	£598,500
Income tax expense	none
Interest expense	£378,000
Selling and general expenses	£896,500
Sales Revenue	£1,698,000

Prepare the annual Profit and Loss statement for the business.

Solve It

Examining How Sales and Expenses Change Assets and Liabilities

In a financial report, the Profit and Loss statement may seem like a bath standing on its own feet, disconnected from the balance sheet and the cash flow statement. Nothing is further from the truth. The three financial statements are interdependent and interconnected. For example, if sales revenue or one of the expenses had been just £10 different to the amount reported in the Profit and Loss statement, a £10 difference would appear somewhere in the balance sheet and the cash flow statement.

 As you know, a Profit and Loss statement reports sales revenue, expenses and profit (or loss). But a Profit and Loss statement doesn't report how sales revenue and expenses change the financial condition of the business. For example, in the simplified Profit and Loss Statement shown earlier, £26,000,000 sales revenue is reported in the annual Profit and Loss statement of a business. The business also reports £24,310,000 total expenses for the year. How does the sales revenue and expenses change its financial condition? The Profit and Loss statement doesn't say.

Business managers rely on their accountants to explain how sales and expenses change the assets and liabilities of their businesses. Business lenders and shareholders also need to understand these effects in order to make sense of financial statements.

Suppose that you're the chief accountant of the business whose Profit and Loss statement is presented in the earlier simplified Profit and Loss Statement. The CEO asks you to explain the financial effects of sales revenue and expenses reported in the latest annual Profit and Loss statement at the next meeting of its board of directors. To help organise your thoughts for the presentation, you decide to prepare summary sales revenue and expense journal entries for the year. Based on your analysis, you prepare the following summary journal entries for sales revenue and for each of the four expenses reported in the Profit and Loss statement.

Sales Revenue:

	Debit	Credit
Cash	£25,000,000	
Debtors	£1,000,000	
Sales Revenue		£26,000,000

The business makes credit sales. When recording a credit sale, the Asset account debtors is debited. When the customer pays, debtors is credited. The business collects £25,000,000 from customers. Therefore, its debtors balance increases £1,000,000.

Cost of Goods Sold Expense:

	Debit	Credit
Cost of Goods Sold Expense	£14,300,000	
Stock	£2,000,000	
Cash		£14,500,000
Creditors		£1,800,000

The business purchases £16,300,000 of products during the year, and its Cost of Goods Sold is £14,300,000. So, its stock increases £2,000,000. It doesn't pay for all its £16,300,000 of purchases. Its creditors for stock purchases increases £1,800,000. Therefore, cash outlay for products during the year is £14,500,000.

Selling and General Expenses:

	Debit	Credit
Selling and General Expenses	£8,700,000	
Prepaid Expenses	£300,000	
Cash		£6,900,000
Creditors		£850,000
Accrued Expenses Payable		£725,000
Accumulated Depreciation		£525,000

Selling and general expenses is a somewhat complicated entry because operating expenses involve several balance sheet accounts. The business adds £300,000 to its prepaid expenses balance during the year. It records £525,000 depreciation expense for the year, as you see in the credit to accumulated depreciation. (Depreciation expense is included in the selling and general expenses amount reported in its Profit and Loss statement.) Not all expenses are paid for by the end of the year; unpaid expenses cause a £850,000 increase in creditors and a £725,000 increase in accrued expenses payable.

Interest Expense:

	Debit	Credit
Interest Expense	£400,000	
Cash		£350,000
Accrued Expense Payable		£50,000

The business pays £350,000 interest during the year. The amount of unpaid interest at year-end increases £50,000. A general Liability account for accrued expenses is shown in this entry. (The business may credit a more specific account, such as accrued interest payable.)

Income Tax Expense:

	Debit	Credit
Income Tax Expense	£910,000	
Cash		£910,000

The five summary entries aren't actual journal entries recorded by a business; they simply help summarise the effects of sales and expenses on the assets and liabilities of the business. Also, to develop the information for these entries, the accountant has to analyse the balance sheet accounts affected by sales and expenses, which takes time.

Q. From the five summary journal entries for sales revenue and expenses for the year listed in this section, determine the cash flow from profit (that is, the net cash increase or decrease from its profit-making activities for the year).

A. Each of the summary entries involves a debit (increase) or credit (decrease) to the cash account. The net effect on cash from its sales revenue and expenses for the year is summarised as follows:

Sales Revenue	£25,000,000
Cost of Goods Sold Expense	(£14,500,000)
Selling and General Expenses	(£6,900,000)
Interest Expense	(£350,000)
Income Tax Expense	(£910,000)
Net Cash Increase	£2,340,000

Note that the £2,340,000 net cash increase is labelled 'cash flow from operating activities' in the cash flow statement. (For more on this financial statement, check out Chapter 8.)

7. Using the journal entries shown earlier in this chapter, look at the following entry:

	Debit	Credit
Cash	£25,000,000	
Debtors	£1,000,000	
Sales Revenue		£26,000,000

Assume that debtors increases £500,000 instead of the £1,000,000 shown. Prepare the summary journal entry for sales revenue.

Solve It

8. Using the journal entries, look at the following entry:

	Debit	Credit
Cost of Goods Sold	£14,300,000	
Stock	£2,000,000	
Cash		£14,500,000
Creditors		£1,800,000

Assume that stock *decreases* by £500,000 (not the £2,000,000 increase shown) during the year because the business sells more products than it purchases. And assume that creditors *decreases* £250,000 during the year because the business pays more of its purchase liabilities than it buys on credit. Prepare the summary journal entry for Cost of Goods Sold expense.

Solve It

9. Using the journal entries, look at the following entry:

	Debit	Credit
Selling and general expenses	£8,700,000	
Prepaid expenses	£300,000	
Cash		£6,900,000
Creditors		£850,000
Accrued expenses payable		£725,000
Accumulated depreciation		£525,000

Assume that no prepaid expenses exist during the year. The amounts for depreciation expense and the increases in creditors and accrued expenses payable are the same as in the summary journal entry. Selling and general expenses are £8,700,000, the same as in the example. Prepare the summary journal entry for selling and general expenses.

Solve It

Summing Up the Manifold Effects of Profit

Making sales and incurring expenses cause a multitude of effects on the assets and liabilities of a business. In other words, making profit causes many changes in the financial condition of a business. It would be convenient if a £1 profit caused a £1 cash increase and nothing more, but the effects of making profit are much broader and reach throughout the balance sheet.

The journal entries in the preceding section summarise the effects of sales and expenses on a business's assets and liabilities. The following figure shows these changes in T accounts for the assets and liabilities. As you probably know, *T accounts* aren't the official, formal accounts of a business. Rather, T accounts are like scratch paper that accountants use to analyse and 'think out' the effects of transactions. A T account has two columns: debits are always put in the left column and credits in the right column. The rules for debits and credits are explained in Chapter 3.

Cash			Trade Creditors	
25,000,000	14,500,000			1,800,000
	6,900,000			850,000
	350,000			
	830,000		Accrued Expenses Payable	
				725,000
Trade Debtors				50,000
1,000,000				80,000
Stock			Accumulated Depreciation	
2,000,000				525,000
Prepaid Expenses				
300,000				

We use seven Asset and Liability accounts to illustrate the recording of sales revenue and expenses for the year. In reality even a relatively small business keeps 100 or more Asset and Liability accounts, but these seven accounts are sufficient to illustrate the effects of sales revenue and expenses on the financial condition of a business.

In order to help you understand what profit consists of, we collapse the changes in assets and liabilities caused by sales and expenses shown in the summary entries into one comprehensive journal entry, which shows the diverse effects of making profit. In this entry, the £1,690,000 profit for the year is shown as an increase in the retained earnings owners' Capital account.

Comprehensive Journal Entry that Summarises Changes in Assets and Liabilities from Profit-Making Activities During the Year

	Debit	Credit
Cash	£2,420,000	
Debtors	£1,000,000	
Stock	£2,000,000	
Prepaid Expenses	£300,000	
Creditors		£2,650,000
Accrued Expenses Payable		£855,000
Accumulated Depreciation		£525,000
Owners' Capital – Retained Earnings		£1,690,000

Q. This comprehensive journal entry for the asset and liability effects of making profit 'speaks' to an accountant, who's familiar with journal entries and debits and credits. Translate this journal entry into plain English, giving an explanation that non-accounting business managers, lenders and investors can understand.

A. A good way of explaining the diverse effects of profit on assets and liabilities is to prepare a summary of the changes in balance sheet accounts affected.

Summary of Asset and Liability Changes from Making Profit

Cash	£2,420,000
Debtors	£1,000,000
Stock	£2,000,000
Prepaid Expenses	£300,000
Fixed Assets (Depreciation)	(£525,000)
Net Increase of Assets	£5,195,000
Creditors	£2,650,000
Accrued Expenses Payable	£855,000
Increase of Liabilities	£3,505,000
Net Worth Increase from Profit	£1,690,000

Profit improves the net worth of a business, and net worth, another name for the owners' capital, equals total assets minus total liabilities. In this example, the business makes a profit, and the effect on the balance sheet is that assets increase more than liabilities, which is the typical profit effect. On the other hand, assets can remain relatively flat and liabilities can decrease. (Although unlikely, profit can consist of a decrease in liabilities more than the decrease in assets.)

10. The effects from sales and expenses for the year just ended for a business are as follows: sales revenue is £15,700,000; the business collects £13,900,000 cash from customers; and debtors increases £1,800,000.

The Cost of Goods Sold during the year is £9,800,000, and the business adds £500,000 of products to stock. It doesn't pay for all £10,300,000 in purchases. Its creditors for stock purchases increases £250,000.

Selling and general expenses are £4,860,000. The business adds £125,000 to its prepaid expenses balance during the year. It records a £145,000 depreciation expense for the year. (Depreciation is included in the selling and general expenses amount reported in its Profit and Loss statement.) Not all expenses are paid for by the end of the year; unpaid expenses cause a £150,000 increase in creditors and a £225,000 increase in accrued expenses payable.

The business pays £200,000 interest during the year. The amount of unpaid interest at year-end increases £25,000. (Use the general Liability account *accrued expenses payable*.)

a. Prepare the annual Profit and Loss statement for the business.

b. Prepare a summary journal entry for the sales and for each expense of the business for the year.

c. Prepare a comprehensive entry showing the changes in assets and liabilities from profit for the year.

Solve It

11. The comprehensive entry for this business summarising the changes in assets and liabilities from its sales and expenses for the year is as follows:

	Debit	*Credit*
Cash		£280,000
Debtors	£825,000	
Stock	£375,000	
Prepaid Expenses	£25,000	
Creditors		£955,000
Accrued Expenses Payable		£475,000
Accumulated Depreciation		£390,000
Owners' Capital – Retained Earning	£875,000	

For the business's board of directors, prepare a schedule of changes in assets and liabilities that summarises the effects on the business's financial condition from its profit for the year.

Solve It

Answers to Problems on the Effects and Reporting of Profit

Here are the answers to the questions presented earlier in this chapter.

1 A business reports $346,000 net income (profit) for the year just ended. How may assets and liabilities change as a result of this profit? Note below two different scenarios.

The simplest scenario is that assets increase $346,000 and liabilities remain the same (zero change). Another valid scenario is a situation in which assets increase $346,000 more than liabilities increase; for example, assets increase $846,000 and liabilities increase $500,000. An unusual but valid scenario is that assets remain the same (zero change) and liabilities decrease $346,000. The key point is that if profit is $346,000, *net worth* (assets minus liabilities) increases $346,000.

2 A business reports $3,800,000 loss for the year just ended. How may assets and liabilities change as a result of this loss? Note below two different scenarios

The simplest scenario is that assets decrease $3,800,000 and liabilities remain the same (zero change). Another valid scenario is a situation in which assets decrease $3,800,000 more than liabilities decrease; for example, assets decrease $6,800,000 and liabilities decrease $3,000,000. An unusual but valid scenario is that assets remain the same (zero change) and liabilities increase $3,800,000. The key point is that if loss is $3,800,000, *net worth* (assets minus liabilities) decreases $3,800,000.

3 A business reports $5,250,000 net income for the year just ended. In its cash flow statement for the year, the business reports that its cash flow from operating activities (from its profit for the year) is $4,650,000. In other words, its cash balance increased $4,650,000 from its profit-making activities for the year. Determine two valid scenarios for changes in assets other than cash and in liabilities that result from its profit for the year.

$5,250,000 profit less the $4,650,000 cash increase from profit leaves $600,000 to be explained. One asset (cash) increased $4,650,000, and so you have to figure out what happened to other assets and to liabilities. One valid scenario is that assets other than cash increased $1,600,000 and liabilities increased $1,000,000. If liabilities remained the same (zero change), assets other than cash would have increased $600,000. Possibly assets other than cash remained the same (zero change) and liabilities decreased $600,000, although this scenario is unlikely.

4 A business reports $836,000 loss for the year just ended. In its cash flow statement for the year, the business reports that its cash flow from operating activities (from its loss for the year) is a *negative* $675,000. In other words, its cash balance decreased $675,000 from its profit-making activities for the year. Determine two valid scenarios for changes in assets other than cash and in liabilities resulting from its loss for the year.

Not all the loss is accounted for by the cash decrease. The $836,000 loss compared with the $675,000 cash decrease leaves $161,000 to be explained. The simplest scenario is that liabilities remained the same (zero change) and assets other than cash decreased $161,000. The reverse of this scenario is that assets other than cash remained the same (zero change) and liabilities increased $161,000. Possibly assets other than cash increased even though the business suffered a loss for the year, in which case liabilities would have increased $161,000 more than assets other than cash.

5 The sales revenue and expenses of a business for the year just ended are as follows:

Cost of Goods Sold expense	$6,358,000
Income tax expense	$458,000
Interest expense	$684,000
Selling and general expenses	$4,375,000
Sales revenue	$13,125,000

Prepare the annual Profit and Loss statement of the business.

The annual Profit and Loss statement is shown as follows:

Sales revenue	$13,125,000
Less Cost of Goods Sold	$6,358,000
Gross Profit	$6,767,000
Selling and general expenses	$4,375,000
Operating profit	$2,392,000
Interest expenses	$684,000
Earnings before interest and tax	$1,708,000
Income tax expense	$458,000
Net Profit	$1,250,000

6 The sales revenue and expenses of a business for the year just ended are as follows:

Cost of goods sold expense	$598,500
Income tax expense	none
Interest expense	$378,000
Selling and general expenses	$896,500
Sales revenue	$1,698,000

Prepare the annual Profit and Loss statement of the business.

The annual Profit and Loss statement for the business is:

Sales revenue	$1,698,000
Less Cost of Goods Sold	$598,500
Gross Profit	$1,099,500
Selling and general expenses	$896,500
Operating profit	$203,000
Interest expenses	$378,000
Earnings before interest and tax	$(175,000)
Income tax expense	$Nil
Net Loss	$(175,000)

7 Look at the following entry:

	Debit	Credit
Cash	£25,000,000	
Debtors	£1,000,000	
Sales Revenue		£26,000,000

Assume that debtors increases £500,000 instead of the £1,000,000 increase shown. Prepare the summary journal entry for sales revenue.

The summary sales revenue entry for this scenario is:

	Debit	Credit
Cash	£25,500,000	
Debtors	£500,000	
Sales Revenue		£26,000,000

8 Look at the following entry:

	Debit	Credit
Cost of Goods Sold	£14,300,000	
Stock	£2,000,000	
Cash		£14,500,000
Creditors		£1,800,000

Assume that stock *decreased* £500,000 during the year because the business sold more products than it purchased during the year. And assume that creditors *decreased* £250,000 during the year because the business paid more of its purchase liabilities than it bought on credit. Prepare the summary journal entry for Cost of Goods Sold expense.

The summary Cost of Goods Sold expense entry for this scenario is:

	Debit	Credit
Cost of Goods Sold Expense	£14,300,000	
Stock		£500,000
Cash		£14,050,000
Creditors	£250,000	

In the summary entry for Cost of Goods Sold expense in the example, cash decreases £14,500,000, whereas in this scenario cash decreases £14,050,000, which is a £450,000 smaller cash outlay for the year. Why? Instead of adding to stock, which requires more purchases of goods than the goods that were sold, the business allows its stock to fall, which means that its purchases are less than the goods sold and produces a £2,500,000 reduction in cash outlay. In the example, creditors increases £1,800,000, but in this scenario, this liability decreases £250,000. This difference means additional cash outlay of £2,050,000. The net cash difference, therefore, is £450,000. The stock difference reduces cash outlay £2,500,000, and the creditors difference increases cash outlay £2,050,000.

9   Using the journal entries shown earlier in this chapter, look at the following entry:

	Debit	**Credit**
Selling and general expenses	£8,700,000	
Prepaid expenses	£300,000	
Cash		£6,900,000
Creditors		£850,000
Accrued expenses payable		£725,000
Accumulated depreciation		£525,000

Assume that no prepaid expenses exist during the year. The amounts for depreciation expense and the increases in creditors and accrued expenses payable are the same as in the summary journal entry. Selling and general expenses are £8,700,000, the same as in the example. Prepare the summary journal entry for selling and general expenses.

The summary selling and general expenses entry for this scenario is:

	Debit	**Credit**
Selling and General Expenses	£8,700,000	
Cash		£6,600,000
Creditors		£850,000
Accrued Expenses Payable		£725,000
Accumulated Depreciation		£525,000

This entry doesn't have any debit or credit to prepaid expenses (an Asset account) because its balance doesn't change in this scenario. In the example, the business increases its prepaid expenses £300,000, and so in this scenario, cash outlay is £300,000 lower because the business doesn't increase its prepaid expenses.

10   The effects from sales and expenses for the year just ended of a business are as follows: sales revenue is £15,700,000; the business collects £13,900,000 cash from customers, and debtors increases £1,800,000.

The cost of products sold during the year is £9,800,000, and the business adds £500,000 of products to stock. It doesn't pay for £10,300,000 in purchases. Its creditors for stock purchases increases £250,000.

Selling and general expenses are £4,860,000. The business adds £125,000 to its prepaid expenses balance during the year. It records a £145,000 depreciation expense for the year. (Depreciation is included in the selling and general expenses amount reported in its Profit and Loss statement.) Not all expenses are paid for by the end of the year. Unpaid expenses cause a £150,000 increase in creditors and a £225,000 increase in accrued expenses payable.

The business pays £200,000 interest during the year. The amount of unpaid interest at year-end increases £25,000. (Use the general Liability account accrued expenses payable.)

a. Prepare the annual Profit and Loss statement for the business.

The Profit and Loss statement is as follows:

Sales Revenue	£15,700,000
Less Cost of Goods Sold	£9,800,000
Gross Profit	£5,900,000
Selling and general expenses	£4,860,000
Operating Profit	£1,040,000
Interest payable	£225,000
Profit before tax	£815,000

b. Prepare a summary journal entry for the sales and for each expense of the business for the year.

The summary entries are as follows:

Sales Revenue:

	Debit	Credit
Cash	£13,900,000	
Debtors	£1,800,000	
Sales Revenue		£15,700,000

Cost of Goods Sold Expense:

	Debit	Credit
Cost of Goods Sold Expense	£9,800,000	
Stock	£500,000	
Cash		£10,050,000
Creditors		£250,000

Selling and General Expenses:

	Debit	Credit
Selling and General Expenses	£4,860,000	
Prepaid Expenses	£125,000	
Cash		£4,465,000
Creditors		£150,000
Accrued Expenses Payable		£225,000
Accumulated Depreciation		£145,000

Interest Expense:

	Debit	Credit
Interest Expense	£225,000	
Cash		£200,000
Accrued Expenses Payable		£25,000

c. Prepare a comprehensive entry showing the changes in assets and liabilities from profit for the year.

The comprehensive entry summarising the changes in assets and liabilities caused by sales and expenses during the year is as follows:

	Debit	Credit
Cash		$815,000
Debtors	$1,800,000	
Stock	$500,000	
Prepaid Expenses	$125,000	
Creditors		$400,000
Accrued Expenses Payable		$250,000
Accumulated Depreciation		$145,000
Owners' Capital – Retained Earnings		$815,000

You may notice that cash decreases in this scenario. In other words, the sales and expenses of the business result in an $815,000 cash decrease even though the business earns $815,000. The fact that the cash decrease and profit are the same amounts is purely coincidental.

11 The comprehensive entry for this business summarising the changes in assets and liabilities from its sales and expenses for the year is as follows:

	Debit	Credit
Cash		$280,000
Debtors	$825,000	
Stock	$375,000	
Prepaid Expenses	$25,000	
Creditors		$955,000
Accrued Expenses Payable		$475,000
Accumulated Depreciation		$390,000
Owners' Capital – Retained Earnings	$875,000	

Prepare a schedule of changes in assets and liabilities for its board of directors that summarises the effects on the business's financial condition from its profit for the year.

Summary of Asset and Liability Changes From Making Profit

Cash	($280,000)
Debtors	$825,000
Stock	$375,000
Prepaid Expenses	$25,000
Fixed Assets (Depreciation)	($390,000)
Net Increase of Assets	$555,000
Creditors	$955,000
Accrued Expenses Payable	$475,000
Increase of Liabilities	$1,430,000
Net Worth Decrease From Loss$	875,000

In this scenario, net worth decreases $875,000 because liabilities increases $1,430,000 and assets increase only $555,000. This unfavorable difference is the essence of a loss. Notice that even though the business suffers a loss for the year, its cash balance decreases far less than the amount of loss. The cash decrease is relatively low because the business avoids cash payments due to the relatively large increases in its creditors and accrued expenses payable.

Chapter 6

Reporting Financial Condition in the Balance Sheet

. . . .

In This Chapter

▶ Breaking down the balance sheet

▶ Building and filling out a balance sheet

▶ Valuing assets in balance sheets

. . . .

*I*magine that your rich aunt just left you a small fortune, and you've always wanted to own and manage a business. Well, wouldn't you know? The owners of a reputable business in your hometown want to sell. The firm is privately owned, and the shareholders offer to sell all their shares to you.

You ask to see the business's latest annual financial report, but before the present owners hand over this information, they ask you to sign a confidentiality agreement. This contract requires that if you decide not to buy the business, you must keep confidential all the information in the financial report. You may not divulge anything you discover from the financial report. You concur and sign the agreement.

The annual financial report of a business includes four essential elements:

✔ **Profit and Loss statement** for the year just ended.

✔ **Balance sheet** at the close of business on the last day of the year.

✔ **Cash flow statement** for the year just ended.

✔ **Footnotes** that supplement and are an integral part of the financial statements.

So you study the annual Profit and Loss statement of the business you're interested in purchasing. All the examples and questions in this chapter are based on the following information for this firm: the business reports £12,000,000 sales revenue and £11,400,000 total expenses for the year, which equal 95 per cent of sales revenue. So net income is £600,000 for the year, or 5 per cent of sales revenue. In your opinion, the profit performance is satisfactory for a firm in this line of business.

You now turn your attention to its balance sheet, which is a summary of the business's assets and liabilities and, as such, provides a comprehensive picture of its financial condition.

Getting Started on the Balance Sheet

Satisfactory profit performance doesn't guarantee that the financial condition of the business is satisfactory. In fact, the business may have serious financial problems despite earning profit. It may have too little cash and assets that can be converted into cash soon enough to pay its short-term liabilities. It may be operating at the mercy of its creditors. Conversely, the business may be sitting on a hoard of cash. You have to look in the balance sheet to find out what's really going on financially.

The balance sheet is also called the statement of financial condition, which better indicates its nature and purposes. This financial statement presents a summary of the assets and the liabilities of a business. Liabilities are claims against the assets of the business; they arise from unpaid purchases and expenses and from borrowing money. The readers of a balance sheet compare the liabilities of the business against its assets and judge whether the business will be able to pay its liabilities on time.

The total assets of a business should equal more than its total liabilities, of course. The excess of assets over liabilities equals the owners' capital of the business. Liabilities have definite due dates for payment, but owners have no such claims on the business. Owners' capital is in the business for the long haul. By majority vote, the owners can decide to dissolve the business, liquidate all its assets, pay off all liabilities and return what's left to the owners. But individual owners can't call up the business and ask for some of their capital to be paid out to them. In short, owners' capital is the permanent capital base of the business.

A business reports two sources of owners' capital:

✔ The total amount of capital its owners invested in the business.

✔ The accumulated amount of profit earned and retained by the business.

Assets, liabilities and owners' Capital accounts aren't intermingled in the balance sheet. Assets are presented in one grouping, liabilities in another and owners' capital in a third group. The following shows the different groupings of assets and liabilities:

✔ **Fixed Assets accounts:** Assets that you expect to own for more than 12 months.

✔ **Current Assets accounts:** Assets that you expect to use in the next 12 months.

✔ **Current Liabilities accounts:** Liabilities that you expect to pay in the next 12 months.

✔ **Long-term Liabilities accounts:** Liabilities that you will pay over more than 12 months.

✔ **Capital accounts:** Accounts that reflect the claims owners have against the business.

The preceding groupings of assets, liabilities and Capital accounts are presented in one of two different formats as follows:

✔ **Horizontal format:** A two-column format with assets on one side and liabilities and capital on the other side.

✔ **Vertical format:** A one column layout with assets listed first, and then liabilities and finally equities.

The balance sheet of the business you're thinking of buying reports these three basic groups: total assets equal $8,000,000, total liabilities equal $4,800,000 and total owners' capital equals $3,200,000 at the end of its most recent year.

Here's the balance sheet shown in horizontal format:

Assets	8,000,000	Liabilities	$4,800,000
		Owner's Capital	$3,200,000
Total Assets	$8,000,000	Total Liabilities and Capital	$8,000,000

Many businesses use the vertical format rather than the horizontal format. One advantage of the vertical format is that it allows a business to keep its balance sheet on one page in its financial report, whereas the horizontal format may require a business to put its balance sheet on two facing pages in its annual financial report. Here's the firm's balance sheet presented in the vertical format:

Assets	8,000,000
Less Liabilities	4,800,000
	3,200,000
Owners' capital	3,200,000

---

1. A business has $2,500,000 total assets and $1,000,000 total liabilities. Present the balance sheet in the horizontal format for the business.

Solve It

2. A business has $4,800,000 total liabilities and $6,500,000 total owners' capital. Present the balance sheet in the vertical format for the business.

Solve It

---

3. A business has $725,000 total assets and $425,000 total owners' capital. Present the balance sheet in both the horizontal and the vertical formats for the business.

Solve It

Building a Balance Sheet

A brand-spanking-new business starts with a blank balance sheet. It builds up its balance sheet over time with three basic types of transactions:

- **Financing activities:** Includes the investment of capital in the business by its owners, the return of some capital to owners (which may happen from time to time) and distributions from profit (if the business decides to make such distributions).

- **Investing activities:** Includes the purchase and construction of long-lived (fixed) assets used in the operations of the business, the purchase of intangible assets used in manufacturing and making sales, and the disposal of operating assets when they're no longer needed or are replaced.

- **Operating activities:** Includes the profit-making activities of the business, including sales, expenses and other income and losses.

In Chapter 5, we explain how sales and expenses change the financial condition of the business. In fact, the profit-making transactions of a business drive a good part of its balance sheet. Before a business begins its profit-making activities, it needs to raise capital and invest capital in long-term operating assets. These financing and investing activities are the place to start in building a balance sheet.

Q. Several investors come together to start a new business. They raise £1,000,000 and invest this sum in the business. The business issues 10,000 shares to the owners of the business. The business borrows £1,500,000 from a bank, and also purchases various long-term operating assets (fixed assets) for a total cost of £2,000,000. The firm is now ready to begin hiring employees, manufacturing products and making sales. Prepare the company's Balance Sheet after these initial financing and investing activities using the horizontal format.

A. The business's balance sheet after its initial financing and investing activities is as follows:

Assets		Liabilities and Owners' Capital	
Fixed Assets		Long-term Liabilities	
Plant and machinery	£2,000,000	Bank Loan	£1,500,000
Current Assets		Capital	
Cash	£500,000	Opening capital	£1,000,000
	£2,500,000		£2,500,000

The business hasn't started manufacturing products, making sales and incurring expenses. Therefore, its balance sheet doesn't yet include certain other assets and liabilities that are generated by the profit-making process.

Q. After its initial financing and investing activities, the business manufactures its first batch of products. The total cost of this production run is £800,000. No sales have been made yet, but the business is poised to send out its sales force to call on customers. Prepare the balance sheet (in horizontal format) after the first production run.

A.

Fixed Assets		*Current Liabilities*	
Plant and machinery	£2,000,000	Trade Creditors	£225,000
Accumulated Depreciation	(£15,000)	Bank Overdraft	£500,000
	£1,985,000		
Current Assets		*Long-term Liabilities*	
Stock	£800,000	Bank Loan	£1,500,000
Cash	£440,000		
		Capital	
		Opening capital	£1,000,000
Total Assets	£3,225,000	**Total liabilities and capital**	£3,225,000

Below we explain the changes in the business's balance sheet, starting with its balance sheet immediately after its initial financing and investing transactions (see the preceding example question).

The changes in its balance sheet caused by manufacturing the first batch of products are summarised in the following journal entry:

Balance Sheet Changes Caused By Manufacturing First Batch of Products

	Debit	Credit
Cash		£60,000
Stock	£800,000	
Creditors		£225,000
Bank Overdraft		£500,000
Accumulated Depreciation		£15,000

You read this entry as follows. The £800,000 cost of manufacturing the first batch of products was provided by borrowing £500,000, via a bank overdraft and by purchasing £225,000 raw materials on credit, by £15,000 depreciation and by spending cash £60,000.

The business realises that it doesn't have enough cash to pay for its first production run, and so it borrows an additional £500,000 from its bank. Because it makes purchases on credit for the raw materials needed for manufacturing products, creditors has a balance of £225,000. The cash balance is £60,000 lower compared with its balance immediately after the initial financing and investing transactions (£500,000 balance before – £440,000 balance after = £60,000 decrease).

To have products available for sale, the business has first to manufacture those products. The cost of manufacturing its first batch of products is £800,000, which is in the stock Asset account. The business records depreciation on its fixed assets (plant and machinery) because these resources are used in the manufacturing process. The business records £15,000 depreciation, which is included in the cost of products manufactured.

4. Instead of the initial financing and investing transactions presented in the preceding example questions, assume that the business issues 100,000 shares for £1,500,000, borrows £2,000,000 from the bank and invests £2,800,000 in fixed assets. Using the horizontal format, prepare its balance sheet after these initial financing and investing transactions.

Solve It

5. Following its initial financing and investing transactions in Question 4, the business manufactures its first batch of products. The cost of products manufactured is £650,000, depreciation is £20,000 and creditors increases £185,000. To provide additional cash, the business gains an overdraft facility for £250,000. Using the horizontal format, prepare its balance sheet after its first production run. Start with the balance sheet after the initial financing and investing transactions in your answer to Question 4.

Solve It

6. A new business has just been organised. A group of investors puts £5,000,000 in the business and the business issues 5,000,000 shares to the owners. The business borrows £2,500,000 from a local bank and negotiates the purchase of land and buildings costing £1,250,000. It also pays £5,250,000 for machinery, production equipment, delivery vehicles and office equipment and furniture. Using the horizontal format, prepare the balance sheet of the business immediately after these initial financing and investing activities.

Solve It

7. The business introduced in Question 6 manufactures its first batch of products. It hasn't yet sold any of these products. The balance sheet changes that are caused by the first production run are summarised in the following journal entry:

	Debit	Credit
Cash		£665,000
Stock	£2,000,000	
Creditors		£550,000
Overdraft facility		£750,000
Accumulated Depreciation		£35,000

Using the vertical format, prepare its balance sheet after giving effect to the first production run. Start with your balance sheet answer to Question 6.

Solve It

Fleshing Out the Balance Sheet

The most recent balance sheet of the business you're considering buying is presented in Table 6-1. The first few transactions of the business that we explain in the earlier section 'Building a Balance Sheet') took place some years ago. Since then, the business has grown and prospered.

Table 6-1	The Most Recent Balance Sheet of the Business		
Fixed Assets		**Current Liabilities**	
Plant and machinery	£4,800,000	Trade Creditors	£700,000
Accumulated Depreciation	(£1,400,000)	Accrued Expenses	£600,000
	£3,400,000	Bank Overdraft	£1,500,000
			£2,800,000
Current Assets		**Long-term Liabilities**	
Stock	£1,800,000	Bank Loan	£2,000,000
Debtors	£1,000,000		
Cash	£1,500,000	**Capital**	
Prepaid expenses	£300,000	Opening capital	£1,000,000
	£4,600,000	Retained earnings	£2,200,000
Total Assets	£8,000,000	**Total liabilities and capital**	£8,000,000

What does the balance sheet in Table 6-1 tell you about the business? Well, quite a lot. You know that the business sells on credit because it reports on debtors and you know that it sells products, the cost of which is reported in the stock. Because it reports prepaid expenses, you know that the business pays some of its expenses in advance, and the report of accrued expenses payable liability indicates that it delays paying some expenses. Also, you can tell that the business buys on credit because it reports on creditors.

The balance sheet reveals that the business borrows money, which is evident in its bank overdraft and long-term loan liabilities. It invested £4,800,000 in long-term fixed assets, and over the years depreciated £1,400,000 of the cost of these assets. According to the balance sheet, the owners invested £1,000,000 in the business for which they received 10,000 shares. And the business retained £2,200,000 of its cumulative net income over the years. Did you get all that from reading the balance sheet? If not, read it again!

Q. Does the balance sheet shown in Table 6-1 report the current replacement costs of the business's fixed assets (which are labelled 'Plant and machinery' in the balance sheet)? Also, does the balance sheet indicate which depreciation methods the business uses to depreciate its fixed assets?

A. The short answer to the first question is no, balance sheets don't report current replacement cost values of fixed assets. Indeed, the business probably hasn't taken the time and trouble to estimate these replacement costs because it isn't planning to replace its fixed assets. The answer to the second question is a little more involved. This business, like most businesses, doesn't disclose its depreciation methods in the balance sheet itself, but it discloses depreciation methods in the footnotes to the financial statements. (You have to take our word for it because this example doesn't present the footnotes to the business's financial statements.)

The following questions are based on the balance sheet details outlined earlier in this section.

8. Suppose that the business doesn't make credit sales and makes only cash sales. Which account(s) would you expect not to see in its balance sheet?

Solve It

9. Suppose that the business is very conservative and doesn't borrow money. Which account(s) would you expect not to see in its balance sheet?

Solve It

10. Suppose that the business sells only services and not products. Which account(s) would you expect not to see in its balance sheet?

Solve It

Classifying assets and liabilities

The balance sheet in Table 6-1 separates current assets from other assets and separates current liabilities from other liabilities. Financial reporting standards require this classification of assets and liabilities:

- ✔ **Current assets** are cash and assets that are going to be converted into cash *within 12 months*. This is the time taken to manufacture products, hold the products until they're sold and collect the debtors from sales. (Prepaid expenses are also included in current assets because the business uses cash to prepay these costs.)

- ✔ **Current liabilities** include those that are going to be paid within 12 months, which are mainly creditors and accrued expenses payable. Also, bank overdrafts and any other liabilities that will be paid within one year from the balance sheet date are included in current liabilities. The subtotals of current assets and current liabilities appear in a balance sheet so that the reader can compare these two amounts. Dividing current assets by current liabilities gives the *current ratio*.

Traditionally, businesspeople assume that the current ratio needs to be at least 2.00 to 1.00, although this minimum has never become a hard-and-fast rule. But if the current ratio dips below 1.00 to 1.00, alarm bells are certain to go off. In fact, many people argue that the ratio of cash and cash equivalents divided by current liabilities should be at least 1.00 to 1.00. This figure is called the quick ratio.

Q. Referring to the balance sheet in Table 6-1, how would you assess the business's *short-run solvency* (the ability of a firm to pay its liabilities on time?)

A. The current ratio of the business is 1.64 to 1.00 (£4,600,000 current assets ÷ £2,800,000 current liabilities = 1.64). In other words, for £1.00 of current liabilities, the business has £1.64 of current assets. The question is whether this ratio is high enough to 'guarantee' the short-run solvency of the business, or whether a serious risk exists that the business may not be able to pay its short-term (current) liabilities when they come due for payment.

We doubt that the business's bank or shareholders would be upset about its 1.64 to 1.00 current ratio. The business's quick ratio is only 0.54 to 1.00 (£1,500,000 cash ÷ £2,800,000 current liabilities = 0.54 to 1.00). The business's lender (its bank) decides whether or not this ratio is a major impediment when the time comes to renew its bank overdraft with the business. Although the business's 'credit score' (as measured by its current and quick ratios) isn't on the high side, we think that its creditors wouldn't be worried about the solvency of the business. On the other hand, the creditors would probably keep a close eye on the business to make sure that things don't take a turn for the worse.

11. Based on the business whose balance sheet appears in Table 6-1, suppose that just before the end of the year, the business pays an additional £400,000 of its creditors. Normally, it wouldn't accelerate payments of creditors, but the order to do so came down from 'on high', and the payments are made. Why do you think the business may have done this?

Solve It

12. Suppose that the business holds its books open for several days into the next year. It records an additional £200,000 of payments from customers as if they have been received on 31 December (the last day of its fiscal year) even though the money isn't actually received and deposited in its bank account until after the end of the year. Why do you think that the business may have done this?

Solve It

Comparing revenue with asset size

This chapter focuses on the balance sheet of a business that sells products (see Table 6-1). We make only a fleeting comment early in the chapter about the annual sales revenue and profit of the business, which, as you know, are reported in its Profit and Loss statement. To recap, its sales revenue for the year just ended is £12,000,000, and the business earns £600,000 bottom-line profit for the year. At this point, you can compare the revenue size of the business with its asset size.

The ratio of annual sales revenue to total assets, called the *asset turnover ratio*, varies from industry to industry. Many businesses are capital intensive, which means that they need a lot of assets to make sales. For example, companies that sell electricity make huge investments in electric power generating plants. Similarly, airlines make large investments in aircraft and car manufacturers invest heavily in production plants and equipment. These types of businesses have relatively low asset turnover ratios. Many other retailers have high asset turnover ratios because they don't need to make large investments in long-lived operating assets.

Q. Referring to Table 6-1, we now determine whether the size of the business's balance sheet is consistent with the size of its Profit and Loss statement. The business has $8,000,000 total assets and its annual sales revenue is $12,000,000; therefore, its annual sales revenue is 1.5 times total assets (this figure is its asset turnover ratio). Is this ratio consistent with the average asset turnover for industry or not?

A. You need to understand that businesses in most industries join trade associations. One of the functions of these trade groups is to collect information from their members and publish norms for the industry. So we look at the trade association information to judge whether the business is significantly above or below the norm for the industry. Generally speaking, an asset turnover ratio of 1.5 to 1.00 is on the low side. On the other hand, the business is fairly capital-intensive (meaning that its fixed assets represent a relatively large percentage of its total assets). Therefore, its 1.5 to 1.00 asset turnover ratio may be reasonable.

13. Suppose that the average asset turnover ratio for businesses in the industry is 2.0 to 1.0. The asset turnover ratio of the business you're considering buying is 1.5 to 1.0 ($12,000,000 annual sales revenue ÷ $8,000,000 total assets = 1.5). What may explain the deviation of the business's asset turnover ratio from the average ratio for the industry?

Solve It

14. Does the balance sheet presented in Table 6-1 give any indication of how old the business is, or how many years it has been in business? Do any particular accounts or other items in the balance sheet indicate whether the business is fairly new or has been around for many years?

Solve It

Clarifying the Values of Assets in Balance Sheets

The evidence is pretty strong that readers of financial reports aren't entirely clear about the sterling amounts reported for assets in a balance sheet. Other than cash – the value of which is clear enough – the amounts reported for assets in a balance sheet aren't at all obvious to non-accountants. Balance sheets don't include reminders or annotations for the valuation basis of each asset. Accountants presume that balance sheet readers understand, or should understand, the asset values that are reported. Accountants are presumptuous, in our opinion.

Of course, accountants should be certain about the valuation of every asset reported in the balance sheet. In preparing a year-end balance sheet, an accountant needs to do a valuation check on every asset. However, using generally accepted accounting principles, the values can be very different for each type of asset. Book values are the amounts recorded during the accounting process and they don't necessarily equate to the current market value. Obviously cash, current liabilities and current assets, such as debtors, are very close to current market values, but items such as stock and other fixed assets may have been purchased a while ago, and their values in the balance sheet may be very different to the replacement cost of the same asset.

The recorded values of assets aren't written up to recognise appreciation in the replacement or market values of the assets. For example, the current market value of the land and buildings owned by a business may be considerably higher than the cost paid for the land and property many years ago. Or the current replacement value of machinery and equipment owned by a business can be more than the depreciated book value of the assets. These assets are used in the operations of the business and aren't held for sale. Moreover the assets may not be replaced for many years. Therefore, appreciation in the market and replacement values of these assets aren't recorded. The business makes profit not by holding these assets for sale but by using them in the selling of products and services.

The sterling amounts reported for assets in a balance sheet are the amounts that were recorded in the original journal entries made when recording the asset transactions. These journal entries may have been recorded last week, last month, last year or 20 years ago for some assets. For example:

- The balance of the asset debtors is from amounts entered in the Asset account when credit sales were recorded. These sales are recent, probably within the few weeks before the end of the year.

- The stock balance is from the costs of manufacturing or purchasing products. These costs can be from the last two or three months.

- The costs of fixed assets reported in the property, plant and equipment Asset account in the balance sheet may go back five, ten or more years – these economic resources are used a long time.

Accountants have devised different ways to record several expenses. The choice of accounting methods affects the balances of several assets, including debtors, stock and accumulated depreciation. (We explain these expense accounting methods in Chapter 9.) The reported values of these assets depend on which accounting methods a business adopts to record its expenses. The differences between accounting methods create yet another maddening factor in understanding the sterling amounts reported for assets. No wonder financial report readers are confused about the values reported for assets in balance sheets!

Although we don't discuss accounting fraud in this chapter (although we do mention more in Chapter 1), we should point out that, when reading a financial report, you need to be alert for any red flags that indicate something may not be right in the financial statements. This vigilance is especially important when you're considering buying or making a major investment in a business. Not to cast aspersions on the present shareholders of the business, but they know you're considering buying the business, and they may just have 'suggested' that the chief accountant massage the numbers or even to cook the books to make the financial statements look as good as possible.

15. Refer to the business's most recent balance sheet in Table 6-1. In the following scenario, the business decides to use different accounting methods (check out Chapter 9 for more on this subject) to arrive at the following figures:

- Debtors balance becomes £50,000 higher
- Stock becomes £225,000 higher
- Accumulated depreciation becomes £300,000 lower

Using the horizontal format, prepare a revised balance sheet for the business giving effect to these differences. (Ignore income tax effects.)

Solve It

16. Do you see anything suspicious in the balance sheet in Table 6-1 that may indicate accounting fraud?

Solve It

Using the Balance Sheet in Business Valuation

How much would you pay for a business? Frankly, no accountant can tell you what a business is worth because the question isn't really an accounting one. Accountants prepare financial statements; they don't put a value on the business and report this value in its financial report. Not in their wildest dreams would accountants think of doing so.

Some argument surrounds the question of whether determining the market value of a going business is rocket science or not. One school of thought is that business valuation should be based on a complicated, multi-factor, formula-driven model. The opposite camp argues that in buying a business you're buying a future stream of earnings but forecasting future earnings is notoriously difficult and unreliable. Their argument is that you're just as well off using a simple method.

What does this debate have to do with a balance sheet? Well, both sides agree on one thing: the profit performance track record of the business (reported in its recent

Profit and Loss statements) and its present financial condition (reported in its latest balance sheet) are absolutely critical information for the valuation of a business. The debate concerns how you should analyse and use that information.

The owners' capital amount of a business is roughly like you telling us how much you paid for your house some years ago and how much additional money you spent over the years on home improvements. This cost isn't very relevant to the current market value of your home. When have you ever seen a home for sale advertisement that mentions the cost paid by its present owners? In a similar manner, the 'cost' of the owners' capital reported in a balance sheet usually isn't very relevant in putting a value on the business.

Although not a dominant factor in setting the market value of a business, the owners' capital reported in the balance sheet isn't completely irrelevant. Owners' capital equals the book (recorded) value of assets less the liabilities of the business, and a business rarely sells for less than its owners' capital amount, which tends to be a floor, or minimum value.

Q. In reading the business's latest balance sheet (Table 6-1), you see that £3,200,000 is reported for owners' capital. Is this book value of owners' capital a good guide for putting a value on the business?

A. In answering this question, the first thing to mention is that its balance sheet is the historical financial record of the business, meaning that it looks backward. In contrast, putting a value on a business is forward-looking. The £3,200,000 balance in owners' capital is a measure of the financial sacrifice the owners have made to get the business to its present point. From Table 6-1, you discover that the shareholders invested £1,000,000 in the business some years ago and that the business retained £2,200,000 of its profits over the year instead of paying cash dividends to its shareholders. This amount of cumulative profit has been 'ploughed back' into the business.

The book value (historical-based) of owners' capital isn't a bad point of departure for putting a current value on a business. However, business valuation looks at other factors as well, including the current replacement values of the business's assets, its future earnings and cash flow prospects, and so on. Taking into account these other factors in a business valuation equation often yields a current market value that's considerably higher than the book value of owners' capital reported in the business's balance sheet.

17. One simple business valuation approach doesn't look at the balance sheet, at least not in putting a numerical value on the business. (The potential buyer of a business would scour the balance sheet to see whether any solvency problems exist.) This business valuation approach is called the *earnings multiple method*. For example, the £600,000 annual income of the business can be multiplied by 8 to get £4,800,000 value for the business. Suppose that you and the present shareholders agree to this price, and you buy all the shares for this price. What happens to the difference between the £4,800,000 price you paid and the £3,200,000 owners' capital reported in the balance sheet?

Solve It

18. Suppose that you agree to pay £4,800,000 for all the shares of the business. At the last moment, the owners ask you to make one concession: they want to take out £500,000 from the business as a cash dividend but are still asking £4,800,000 for their shares. Would this action make a difference in the price you're willing to pay for the business?

Solve It

Answers to Problems on Reporting Financial Condition in the Balance Sheet

Here are the answers to the questions presented earlier in this chapter.

1 A business has $2,500,000 total assets and $1,000,000 total liabilities. Present the balance sheet in the horizontal format for the business.

Assets	$2,500,000	Liabilities	$1,000,000
		Owner's Capital	$1,500,000
Total Assets	$2,500,000	Total Liabilities and Capital	$2,500,000

2 A business has $4,800,000 total liabilities and $6,500,000 total owners' capital. Present the balance sheet in the vertical format for the business.

Assets	$11,300,000
Less Liabilities	$4,800,000
	$6,500,000
Owners' capital	$6,500,000

3 A business has $725,000 total assets and $425,000 total owners' capital. Present the balance sheet in both the vertical and horizontal format for the business.

Vertical Format

Assets	$725,000
Less Liabilities	$300,000
	$425,000
Owners' capital	$425,000

Horizontal Format

Assets	$725,000	Liabilities	$300,000
		Owner's Capital	$425,000
Total Assets	$725,000	Total Liabilities and Capital	$725,000

4 Instead of the initial financing and investing transactions presented in the preceding example questions, assume that the business issues 100,000 shares for $1,500,000, borrows $2,000,000 from the bank using a long-term loan and invests $2,800,000 in fixed assets. Using the horizontal format, prepare its balance sheet after these initial financing and investing transactions.

Horizontal Format

Fixed Assets	$2,800,000	Liabilities	$2,000,000
Cash	$700,000	Owner's Capital	$1,500,000
Total Assets	$3,500,000	Total Liabilities and Capital	$3,500,000

You would assume that no other transactions have taken place, and after raising $3,500,000 cash and then spending $2,800,000 on fixed assets, $700,000 cash is left over.

5 Following its initial financing and investing transactions in Question 4, the business manufactures its first batch of products. The cost of products manufactured is $650,000, depreciation is $20,000 and creditors increases $185,000. To provide additional cash, the business borrows

£250,000 and arranges a short-term overdraft. Using the horizontal format, prepare its balance sheet after its first production run. Start with the balance sheet after the initial financing and investing transactions in your answer to Question 4.

Horizontal Format

Fixed Assets	£2,800,000	Creditors	£185,000
Accumulated Depreciation	(£20,000)	Overdraft	£250,000
	£2,780,000		
Stock	£650,000	Long-term Loan	£2,000,000
Cash	£505,000	Owner's Capital	£1,500,000
Total Assets	£3,935,000	Total Liabilities and Capital	£3,935,000

6 A new business has just been organised. A group of investors puts £5,000,000 in the business and the business issues 5,000,000 shares to them. The business borrows £2,500,000 from a local bank on the basis of a long-term loan and negotiates the purchase of land and buildings costing £1,250,000. It also pays £5,250,000 for machinery, production equipment, delivery vehicles and office equipment and furniture. Using the horizontal format, prepare the balance sheet of the business immediately after these initial financing and investing activities.

Horizontal Format

Fixed Assets		Liabilities	
Land and Buildings	£1,250,000	Long-term Loan	£2,500,000
Plant and Machinery	£5,250,000		
Cash	£1,000,000	Owner's Capital	£5,000,000
Total Assets	£7,500,000	Total Liabilities and Capital	£7,500,000

7 The business introduced in Question 6 manufactures its first batch of products. It hasn't yet sold any of these products. The balance sheet changes that are caused by the first production run are summarised in the following journal entry:

	Debit	Credit
Cash		£665,000
Stock	£2,000,000	
Creditors		£550,000
Bank Overdraft		£750,000
Accumulated Depreciation		£35,000

Using the horizontal format, prepare its balance sheet after giving effect to the first production run. Start with your balance sheet answer to Question 6.

Fixed Assets		Liabilities	
Land and Buildings	£1,250,000	Creditors	£550,000
Plant and Machinery	£5,250,000	Overdraft	£750,000
Less Depreciation	(£35,000)	Long-term Loan	£2,500,000
	£6,465,000		
Stock	£2,000,000		
Cash	£335,000	Owner's Capital	£5,000,000
Total Assets	£8,800,000	Total Liabilities and Capital	£8,800,000

8 Suppose that the business doesn't make credit sales and makes only cash sales. Which account(s) would you expect not to see in its balance sheet?

The business wouldn't have a debtors account because the balance in this Asset account comes from credit sales, which the business doesn't make. Also, the business wouldn't have a bad debts Expense account. This expense comes from uncollectible debts that are written off; however, a business that sells only for cash has other frustrating expenses, including accepting bad cheques from customers, giving the wrong change to customers and accepting counterfeit currency.

9 Suppose that the business is very conservative and doesn't borrow money. Which account(s) would you expect not to see in its balance sheet?

In this unusual situation, the business wouldn't have interest-bearing Liability accounts, such as long-term loans, or an interest Expense account. The business would have normal operating Liability accounts, such as creditors and accrued expenses payable, because these operating liabilities don't bear interest.

10 Suppose that the business sells only services and not products. Which account(s) would you expect not to see in its balance sheet?

The business wouldn't have a stock account or a Cost of Goods Sold Expense account. Also, its creditors liability balance would be relatively low compared with a business that sells products. For a business that sells products, a good part of its creditors balance consists of products purchased on credit (or raw materials used in the manufacturing process that are purchased on credit). In contrast, a business that sells only services doesn't buy products or raw materials on credit.

11 Suppose that just before the end of the year, the business pays an additional £400,000 of its creditors. Normally, it wouldn't accelerate creditor payments, but the order to do so came down from 'on high', and the payments were made. Why do you think that the business may have done this?

In order to answer this question, you need to look at the business's year-end balance sheet:

Fixed Assets		Liabilities	
Plant and Machinery	£4,800,000	Creditors	£300,000
Less Depreciation	£1,400,000	Overdraft	£1,500,000
	£3,400,000	Accrued Expenses	£600,000
Stock	£1,800,000	**Total current liabilities**	£2,400,000
Debtors	£1,000,000	Long-term Loan	£2,000,000
Cash	£1,100,000	**Owner's Capital**	
Prepaid expenses	£300,000	Ordinary shares	£1,000,000
Total current assets	£4,200,000	Retained earnings	£2,200,000
		Total owners' capital	£3,200,000
Total Assets	£7,600,000	**Total Liabilities and Capital**	£7,600,000

Pay attention to the current ratio: £4,200,000 current assets ÷ £2,400,000 current liabilities = 1.75 current ratio. By making pay downs on creditors very late in the year (perhaps on the very last day of the year), the business improves its current ratio to 1.75 from the 1.64 current ratio in the original scenario (see Table 6-1). In many cases, a business is under pressure to keep its current ratio as high as possible. What the business in this question did isn't illegal, but the payment should arouse some uneasiness in the accountant. The accountant needs to make a judgement on the materiality of this action that improves the current ratio from 1.64 to 1.75. Is this a material difference, that is, is it one that may mislead the balance sheet readers? This question is a tough one to answer.

If the effect on the current ratio isn't material, nothing would be said about it in the financial statements of the business. If the effect is judged to be material, the accountant should consider calling it to the attention of the audit committee of the business or another high-level financial officer in the business. The business's financial statements may be audited by an independent accounting firm. The auditors should catch this manipulation of the current ratio, and if they judge it to be material, the auditing firm should bring it to the attention of the board of directors.

12 Suppose that the business holds its books open for several days into the next year. It records an additional £200,000 of payments from customers as if they have been received on 31 December (the last day of its fiscal year) even though the money isn't actually received and deposited in its bank account until after the end of the year. Why do you think the business may have done this?

This manoeuvre is called *window dressing*; it's done to improve the cash balance reported in the balance sheet and to improve the quick ratio. In order to answer this question, you need to look at the business's year-end balance sheet:

Fixed Assets		*Liabilities*	
Plant and Machinery	£4,800,000	Creditors	£700,000
Less Depreciation	(£1,400,000)	Overdraft	£1,500,000
	£3,400,000	Accrued Expenses	£600,000
Stock	£1,800,000	**Total current liabilities**	£2,800,000
Debtors	£800,000	Long-term Loan	£2,000,000
Cash	£1,700,000	**Owner's Capital**	
Prepaid expenses	£300,000	Ordinary shares	£1,000,000
Total current assets	£4,600,000	Retained earnings	£2,200,000
		Total owners' capital	£3,200,000
Total Assets	£8,000,000	**Total Liabilities and Capital**	£8,000,000

In the original scenario, the quick ratio is 0.54 to 1.00, which is lower than the manipulated ratio (£1,700,000 cash ÷ £2,800,000 current liabilities = 0.61 to 1.00 quick ratio). When we worked in public accounting years ago, many of our audit clients employed window dressing. Some auditors may tolerate holding the books open for a few days in order to allow the business to report a higher cash balance and a better quick ratio. Current assets and current liabilities don't change, and so holding the books open doesn't change the current ratio.

13 Suppose that the average asset turnover ratio for businesses in the industry is 2.0 to 1.0. The asset turnover ratio of the business you're considering buying is 1.5 to 1.0 (£12,000,000 annual sales revenue ÷ £8,000,000 total assets = 1.5). What may explain the deviation of the business's asset turnover ratio from the average ratio for the industry?

The business's total assets are too high relative to its annual sales revenue; looking at it another way, its annual sales revenue is too low relative to its total assets. One reason may be that the business has *excess capacity*, meaning that it may be over-invested in its fixed assets. For example, its building may be too large or it may have more vehicles than it needs to make deliveries. Excess capacity is a good place to start, but fixed assets may not be the main reason for a below-normal asset turnover ratio. You should examine all assets to see whether their balances are too big.

The business may have allowed the size of its stock to get out of control. Perhaps its debtor balance is too high because of lax collection efforts, or the business has too much cash relative to its day-to-day operating needs. Maybe the business had a sudden and unexpected dip in sales towards the end of the year, or it hasn't had time to downsize its assets and adjust to the lower sales level. The business may think that the drop in sales is only temporary and, therefore, it wants to keep its assets at their present levels to support the predicted bounce back in sales next year.

14 Does the balance sheet presented in Table 6-1 give any indication of how old the business is, or how many years it has been in business? Do any particular accounts or other items in the balance sheet indicate whether the business is fairly new or has been around for many years?

One clue regarding the age of the business is the balance in its accumulated depreciation account as a percentage of the cost of the fixed assets being depreciated. The higher the percentage, the older the business is likely to be. But this conclusion is really just guesswork. Financial statements don't report the age of a business. However, financial reports may include a historical summary of key data (such as annual sales, annual net income, total assets and so on), which often go back to the first year of business.

15 Refer to the business's most recent balance sheet in Table 6-1. In the following scenario, the business decides to use different accounting methods (check out Chapter 9 for more on this subject) to arrive at the following figures:

- Debtors balance becomes £50,000 higher
- Stock becomes £225,000 higher
- Accumulated depreciation becomes £300,000 lower

Using the horizontal format, prepare a revised balance sheet for the business giving effect to these differences. (Ignore income tax effects.)

The year-end balance sheet of the business becomes:

Fixed Assets		Current Liabilities	
Plant and machinery	£4,800,000	Trade Creditors	£700,000
Accumulated Depreciation	(£1,100,000)	Accrued Expenses	£600,000
	£3,700,000	Bank Overdraft	£1,500,000
			£2,800,000
Current Assets		**Long-term Liabilities**	
Stock	£2,025,000	Bank Loan	£2,000,000
Debtors	£1,050,000		
Cash	£1,500,000	**Capital**	
Prepaid expenses	£300,000	Opening capital	£1,000,000
	£4,875,000	Retained earnings	£2,775,000
		Total owners' capital	£3,775,000
Total Assets	£8,575,000	**Total liabilities and capital**	£8,575,000

The expenses of the business over the years would have been £575,000 lower; (£50,000 lower bad debts expense + £225,000 lower Cost of Goods Sold expense + £300,000 lower depreciation expense = £575,000 lower expenses in total). Therefore, cumulative net income becomes £575,000 higher (before income tax), and the balance of retained earnings becomes £575,000 higher. (Adding the £575,000 increase in cumulative net income to the £2,200,000 retained earnings balance in Table 6-1 equals the £2,775,000 retained earnings balance shown in this answer.)

16 Do you see anything suspicious in the balance sheet in Table 6-1 that may indicate accounting fraud?

We don't see anything suspicious in the balance sheet that may indicate that some accounting hanky-panky is going on, but you never know. A good con artist tries to make everything look right. So, who knows for sure? The first rule of an auditor is to be sceptical. We're 'old auditors' at heart, and we've seen too many fraudulent financial statements in our time. As they say in politics, 'Trust, but verify'. The problem is that financial report users may not be able to verify the information presented in financial statements. Furthermore, auditors don't necessarily catch accounting fraud in financial statements. Unfortunately, the risk of accounting fraud is always present.

17 One simple business valuation approach doesn't look at the balance sheet, at least not in putting a numerical value on the business. (The potential buyer of a business would scour the balance sheet to see whether any solvency problems exist.) This business valuation approach is called the *earnings multiple method*. For example, the £600,000 annual profit of the business can be multiplied by 8 to get £4,800,000 value for the business. Suppose that you and the present shareholders agree to this price, and you buy all the shares for this price. What happens to the difference between the £4,800,000 price you paid and the £3,200,000 owners' capital reported in the balance sheet?

This question relates directly to a point we mention in Chapter 1: the starting point in accounting is to identify the *entity* being accounted for. The business is one entity and your investment in the business is another entity. They're two distinct entities. Accounting for the financial activities of a business doesn't involve keeping track of the investment activities of its individual shareholders.

One shareowner may sell her capital stock shares to another person, but this exchange of shares isn't a transaction of the business. The business didn't receive the £4,800,000 you paid for the shares you bought; the individuals that sold their shares to you received the £4,800,000. The same number of shares remains in the hands of shareholders, and the business makes no accounting entry for the exchange of shares among its shareholders. In the accounting for your individual investment, you should record the £4,800,000 cost of your investment, but this record is your private affair and as such isn't recorded by the business.

18 Suppose that you agree to pay £4,800,000 for all the shares of the business. At the last moment, the owners ask you to make one concession: they want to take out £500,000 from the business as a cash dividend but are still asking £4,800,000 for their shares. Would this action make a difference in the price you're willing to pay for the business?

The market valuation of a business usually doesn't consist of adding up the market values of every asset and deducting the liabilities of the business. In most cases, the forecast of its future earnings is the dominant factor in setting a value on a business. The fact that the business would have £500,000 less cash may not affect its future earnings performance; the business would still have £1,000,000 cash to operate with, and this balance may be adequate. Yet, this last-minute tactic by the present owners isn't good because it takes £500,000 out of the business, which means that you (the new owner) have £500,000 less cash to work with for growth and expansion of the business.

Chapter 7

Coupling the Profit and Loss Statement and Balance Sheet

In This Chapter

▶ Connecting the two financial statements

▶ Placing vital elements into the balance sheet puzzle using ratios

▶ Adding assets to the balance sheet

▶ Examining debt versus capital on the balance sheet

*E*very time accountants record a sale or expense entry using double-entry accounting, they see the interconnections between the Profit and Loss statement and balance sheet. (We explain the rules for debits and credits in Chapter 3.) A sale increases an asset or decreases a liability, and an expense decreases an asset or increases a liability. Therefore, one side of every sales and expense entry is in the Profit and Loss statement, and the other side is in the balance sheet. You can't record a sale or an expense without affecting the balance sheet. The Profit and Loss statement and balance sheet are inseparable, but they aren't reported this way!

To interpret financial statements properly – the Profit and Loss statement, the balance sheet and the cash flow statement – you need to understand the links between the statements, but unfortunately, these links aren't easy to see. Each financial statement appears on a separate page in the annual financial report, and the threads of connection between the financial statements aren't referred to. In reading financial reports, non-accountants – and even accountants – usually don't spot these connections.

We discuss the Profit and Loss statement in Chapter 5 and the balance sheet in Chapter 6. In this chapter, we stitch these two financial statements together and mark the trails of connections between sales revenue and expenses (in the Profit and Loss statement) and their corresponding assets and liabilities (in the balance sheet). In Chapter 8, we explain the connections between the amounts reported in the cash flow statement and the other two financial statements.

Rejoining the Profit and Loss Statement and Balance Sheet

Figure 7-1 shows the lines of connection between Profit and Loss statement accounts and balance sheet accounts. When reading financial statements, in your mind's eye you should 'see' these lines of connection. Because financial reports don't offer a clue about these connections, you may find that drawing the lines of connection is helpful, as if you were highlighting lines in a textbook.

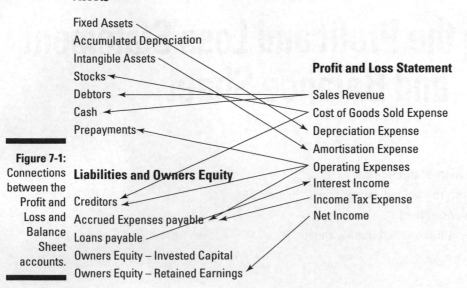

Figure 7-1:
Connections
between the
Profit and
Loss and
Balance
Sheet
accounts.

Here's a quick summary explaining the lines of connection in Figure 7-1, starting from the top and working down to the bottom:

- ✔ Making sales (and incurring expenses for making sales) requires a business to maintain a working cash balance.

- ✔ Making sales on credit generates debtors.

- ✔ Selling products requires the business to carry a stock of products.

- ✔ Acquiring products involves purchases on credit that generate creditors.

- ✔ Depreciation expense is recorded for the use of fixed assets (long-term operating resources).

- ✔ Depreciation is recorded in the accumulated depreciation account (instead of decreasing the fixed asset cost account).

- ✔ Amortisation expense is recorded for limited-life intangible assets.

- ✔ Operating expenses is a broad category of costs encompassing selling, administrative and general expenses. Some of these operating costs:

  - • are prepaid before the expense is recorded, and until that time the cost stays in the prepaid expenses Asset account.

  - • involve purchases on credit that generate creditors.

  - • are from recording unpaid expenses in the accrued expenses payable liability.

- ✔ Borrowing money causes interest expense.

- ✔ A portion (usually relatively small) of income tax expense for the year is unpaid at year-end, which is recorded in the accrued expenses payable liability.

- ✔ Earning net income increases retained earnings.

EXAMPLE

Q. For the year just ended, a business reports £5,200,000 sales revenue. All its sales are made on credit (to other businesses). Historically, its year-end debtors balance equals about five weeks of annual sales revenue; in other words, an amount equal to five weeks of annual sales revenue isn't yet collected at the end of the year. Sales are level throughout the year. How do you calculate the amount of debtors that you would expect in the business's year-end balance sheet?

A. First, you need to divide £5,200,000 annual sales revenue by 52 weeks, which gives £100,000 average sales per week. Based on its past experience, the ending balance of debtors should be about £500,000, which equals five weeks of annual sales revenue.

1. The business in the example question has an annual Cost of Goods Sold expense of £3,120,000. Historically, its ending stock balance equals about 13 weeks of annual sales. What amount of stock would you expect in its year-end balance sheet?

Solve It

2. The business in the example question has an annual Cost of Goods Sold expense of £3,120,000. Historically, the business's creditors for stock purchases equals about four weeks of annual Cost of Goods Sold. What amount of creditors for stock purchases would you expect in its year-end balance sheet? (Note that the creditors balance also includes an amount from purchases of supplies and services on credit; this question concerns only the amount of creditors from stock purchases.)

Solve It

3. The business in the example question has an annual operating expenses amount of £1,378,000 (which excludes depreciation, amortisation, interest and income tax expenses). Historically, its year-end balance of accrued expenses payable equals about six weeks of its annual operating expenses. Ignoring accrued interest payable and income tax payable, what amount of accrued expenses payable would you expect in its year-end balance sheet?

Solve It

4. For the business in the example question, the average amount borrowed during the year was £1,500,000. The average annual interest rate on this loan was 6.5 per cent. What amount of interest expense would you find in the business's Profit and Loss statement for the year?

Solve It

Filling in Key Pieces of the Balance Sheet from the Profit and Loss Statement

Ratios can be used to express the size of an asset or liability on the basis of sales revenue or an expense in the annual Profit and Loss statement. The ratio that is calculated can be used as a benchmark against the industry average to see how well the business is performing. A business should be 'turning over' assets to make sales. The higher the turnover, the more times the assets are used and replaced the better. The 'asset turnover' ratio compares annual sales revenue with total assets as follows:

>   annual sales revenue ÷ total assets = asset turnover ratio

For example, using the information from Figure 7-1, if total assets are £14,080 and the sales revenue is £25,000, the asset turnover ratio would be:

>   £25,000 ÷ £14,080 = 1.8

Therefore, the total assets are being turned over 1.8 times.

Unfortunately this information isn't hugely helpful and takes into account only how well the business is using its assets to generate sales: the ratio doesn't evaluate profitability.

Sales revenue and debtors

You can take other elements of the balance sheet, such as debtors, and compare these to sales revenue. For example, suppose a business, Firm X, makes all its sales on credit and offers its customers one month to pay. Very few customers pay early, and some customers are chronic late-payers. To encourage repeat sales, the business tolerates these late-payers, and as a result, its debtors equals five weeks of annual sales revenue.

If we assume that sales revenue is £25,000, the debtor balance is:

>   £25,000 ÷ 52 × 5 = £2,404

Another way of looking at debtors is to calculate the debtor days. Using the same information as above, the following calculation proves the number of days that debtors are taking to pay:

>   debtors ÷ sales revenue × 365

Therefore, we can calculate the debtor days for our example as follows:

>   £2,404 ÷ £25,000 × 365 = 35 days (or five weeks)

On average, our debtors are taking 35 days to pay their invoices. This information is useful and should be monitored, because it tells you the probable time taken to get the cash in. If this figure begins to deviate wildly from the norm, you need to take action and be more aggressive on the credit control.

5. The business has debtors of £2,375,000 and a turnover of £25,000,000. Calculate the number of debtor days?

Solve It

Cost of Goods Sold and stock

Businesses need to have some sort of benchmark for stock. They don't want to carry too much stock because it is money tied up in the business, but too little and they can't service orders.

The following calculation helps you determine the average number of days that your stock is held within the business:

average stock holding period = stock ÷ Cost of Goods Sold × 365 days

Using the information from Figure 7-1, the stock holding period can be calculated as follows:

£3,575,000 ÷ £15,000,000 × 365 = 87 days

This result tells us that the stock is being held for an average of 87 days. Of course, some stock may stay in the business for a lot longer and some may be sold much more quickly; this figure is only an average.

The average for each industry can vary. Some industries have a very long stock holding period (for example, heavy manufacturing industries), whereas that of others is relatively short (supermarkets have a very quick turnaround of stock.)

6. A business has stock of £5,757,000 with Cost of Goods Sold of £12,000,000. Calculate the average stock holding period. What comments would you make?

Solve It

Connections between selling, admin and general expenses and the balance sheet

Figure 7-1 demonstrates that four connections exist between selling, admin and general expenses (SA&G) and the balance sheet: cash, prepaid expenses, creditors and accrued expenses.

Cash is paid out when recording payroll, certain expenses and petty cash items. On the other hand, insurance, or maybe an advertising plan, may be prepaid and then released as an expense over time. In this case, cash is paid before receipt of all the service. Alternatively, expenses may not be paid until weeks after the goods have been received. These delayed payments (liabilities) must be recorded as accrued expenses.

Businesses may want to adopt benchmarks for each of these accounts that are associated with the operating expenses of the business. For example, Figure 7-1 shows that the accrued expenses payable is £1,200,000, which is 20 per cent of SA&G expenses. You don't know whether this figure is high in comparison to previous years unless you've been monitoring the figure for a period of time.

Practical action

Have a look at your recent balance sheet and calculate some ratios such as debtor days. Also, check out your stock holding period and perhaps calculate some benchmark ratios for your own business.

Note: you can calculate your creditor days, which is how long you're taking to pay your suppliers. This information, however, is probably less important than knowing how long your debtors are taking to pay you.

If you want to do this calculation, carry out the following:

$$\text{creditors} \div \text{purchases} \times 365$$

Fixed assets and depreciation expense

The ratio of annual depreciation expense to the original cost of fixed assets can't be benchmarked, because different fixed assets are depreciated over different estimated useful life spans. Some fixed assets are depreciated according to the straight-line method and others according to the reducing balance depreciation method (we explain these depreciation methods in Chapter 9).

The annual depreciation expense needs to be a reasonable fraction of original cost. A depreciation expense of more than 15 per cent or so of the total original cost of fixed assets would be unusual, and in fact even suspicious.

Putting Fixed Assets in the Picture

Virtually every business needs fixed assets (long-lived economic resources) to carry out its profit-making activities. Types of fixed assets include land and buildings, plant and machinery, office equipment and so on.

The cost and accumulated depreciation of a business's fixed assets depends on when the assets were bought (recently or many years ago), the sort of long-term operating assets the business needs and whether the business leases or owns these assets. We can't offer you a ratio for the original cost of fixed assets and annual sales revenue, because generalising about the cost of fixed assets relative to annual sales revenue is very difficult. As a rough estimate for this ratio, annual sales revenue of a business is generally between two to four times the total cost of its fixed assets. But please take this estimation with a grain of salt. The ratio varies widely from industry to industry, and even within the same industry, the ratio can vary from business to business. Generally speaking, retailers have a higher ratio of sales to fixed assets than heavy equipment manufacturers and transportation businesses (airlines, haulage firms and so on).

The partial balance sheet shown below tells an interesting story: Firm X has £3,855,000 total assets, but where did it get that £3,855,000? Its two current liabilities provide £515,000 of the total assets; (£350,000 Creditors + £165,000 accrued expenses payable = £515,000), but what about the remaining £3,340,000?

£3,855,000 total assets – £515,000 short-term operating liabilities = £3,340,000 needed from sources of business capital. We look at the ways a business can be financed in the 'Completing the Balance Sheet with Debt and Capital' section that follows the next two questions.

Firm X's Balance Sheet below includes assets and Short term liabilities.

Fixed Assets		**Current Liabilities**	
Plant and Machinery	£2,450,000	Creditors	£350,000
Accumulated Depreciation	(£685,000)	Accrued Expenses	£165,000
Cost less depreciation	£1,765,000		£515,000

Current Assets	
Stock	£780,000
Debtors	£500,000
Cash	£700,000
Prepaid Expenses	£110,000
Total current assets	£2,090,000
Total Assets	**£3,855,000**

Note: This Balance Sheet is only partial as it does not show the owners equity. You can calculate the owners equity by deducting the current liabilities from the total assets. (£3,855,000 - £515,000 = £3,340,000). The Owners equity would thus be £3,340,000.

7. Instead of the amounts shown in Firm X's Balance Sheet, suppose that the cost of Firm X's fixed assets is £3,850,000 and that accumulated depreciation is £958,000. Determine the amount of capital the business would have to raise in this scenario.

Solve It

8. Assume that the balances of assets, creditors and accrued expenses payable are the same as shown in Firm X's Balance Sheet. However, the balance of accumulated depreciation is £400,000. In this scenario, would Firm X have to raise more capital?

Solve It

Completing the Balance Sheet with Debt and Capital

Imagine that you own Firm X, whose balance sheet is depicted in the previous section; how would you raise the £3,340,000 capital? You can debate this question until the cows come home because no right or best answer exists. The two basic sources of business capital are interest-bearing debt and capital (more precisely, owners' capital). Where to secure capital is really a business financial management question, not an accounting question. As a practical matter, many businesses borrow as much as they can and use owners' capital for the rest of the capital they need.

Most businesses use debt for part of their capital needs, and this practice makes sense as long as the business doesn't overextend its debt obligations. Because this book isn't concerned with business finance, a debate concerning debt versus capital is beyond its scope. Instead, we move on to the complete balance sheet of the business.

Here's the complete balance sheet for Firm X, including its debt and owners' Capital accounts. The business has borrowed £500,000 as an overdraft facility (which is shown in the balance sheets as being due in one year or less) and £1,000,000 on a long-term bank loan.

Fixed Assets		Current Liabilities	
Plant and Machinery	£2,450,000	Creditors	£350,000
Accumulated Depreciation	(£685,000)	Accrued Expenses	£165,000
Cost less depreciation	£1,765,000	Overdraft	£500,000
		Total Current Liabilities	£1,015,000
Current Assets		**Long Term Liabilities**	
Stock	£780,000	Bank loan	£1,000,000
Debtors	£500,000		
Cash	£700,000	**Owners Equity**	
Prepaid Expenses	£110,000	Capital	£750,000
		Retained Earnings	£1,090,000
Total current assets	£2,090,000	Total Equity	£1,840,000
Total Assets	**£3,855,000**	**Total Liabilities & Equity**	**£3,855,000**

The shareholders in Firm X invest £750,000, for which they receive 10,000 shares. Even relatively simple-looking business ownership structures can be more complex than they appear. Typically, a footnote is necessary to explain fully the ownership structure of a business. (If you don't believe us, read the shareholders' capital footnotes of any business.) As a general rule, private firms don't have to disclose who owns how many of their shares in their financial statements. In contrast, public companies are subject to many disclosure rules regarding the share ownership of the business.

Over the years, the business in this scenario retains £1,090,000 of its yearly profits (see retained earnings in the balance sheet). You can't tell from the balance sheet how much of this cumulative total is from any one year. Nor can you tell from the Profit and Loss statement or the balance sheet how much of its current year profit is distributed as a cash dividend to shareholders during the year just ended. One purpose of the statement of cash flows (which we explain in Chapter 8) is to report the cash dividends paid from net income to shareholders during the year.

The next two questions are based on the Profit and Loss statement and balance sheet shown in Figure 7-2.

Company Z's Profit and Loss Statement

Sales Revenue	£23,530,000
Cost of goods sold	(£14,118,000)
Gross margin	£9,412,000
Selling and general expenses	(£7,722,000)
Depreciation Expense	(£826,500)
Operating Profit	£863,500
Interest expense	(£245,000)
Profit before tax	£618,500
Tax	£185,550
Net Profit	£432,950

Company Z's Balance Sheet

Figure 7-2: Firm Z's Profit and Loss Statement and Balance Sheet

Fixed Assets

Plant and Machinery	£4,575,000
Accumulated Depreciation	(£1,385,000)
Cost less depreciation	£3,190,000

Current Assets

Stock	£2,172,000
Debtors	£2,715,000
Cash	£1,357,500
Prepaid Expenses	£519,750
Total current assets	£6,764,250
Total Assets	**£9,954,250**

Current Liabilities

Creditors	£2,100,000
Accrued Expenses	£742,500
Overdraft	£750,000
Total Current Liabilities	£3,592,500

Long Term Liabilities

Bank Loan	£2,000,000

Owners Equity

Capital	£1,500,000
Retained Earnings	£2,861,750
Total Equity	£4,361,750
Total Liabilities and Equity	**£9,954,250**

9. Based on Firm Z's Profit and Loss statement and balance sheet, determine the business's debtors days.

Solve It

10. Based on Firm Z's Profit and Loss statement and balance sheet, determine the business's average stockholding period.

Solve It

Answers to Problems on Coupling the Profit and Loss Statement and Balance Sheet

Here are the answers to the questions presented earlier in this chapter.

1 The business in the example question has an annual Cost of Goods Sold expense of £3,120,000. Historically, its ending stock balance equals about 13 weeks of annual sales. What amount of stock would you expect in its year-end balance sheet?

£3,120,000 ÷ 52 weeks = £60,000 average Cost of Goods Sold per week × 13 weeks = £780,000 stock balance in its year-end balance sheet

2 The business in the example question has an annual Cost of Goods Sold expense of £3,120,000. Historically, the business's creditors for stock purchases equals about four weeks of annual Cost of Goods Sold. What amount of creditors for stock purchases would you expect in its year-end balance sheet? (**Note that t**he creditors balance also includes an amount from purchases of supplies and services on credit; this question concerns only the amount of creditors from stock purchases.)

£3,120,000 ÷ 52 weeks = £60,000 average Cost of Goods Sold per week × 4 weeks = £240,000 creditors for stock purchases balance in its year-end balance sheet

3 The business in the example question has an annual operating expenses amount of £1,378,000 (which excludes depreciation, amortisation, interest and income tax expenses). Historically, its year-end balance of accrued expenses payable equals about six weeks of its annual operating expenses. Ignoring accrued interest payable and income tax payable, what amount of accrued expenses payable would you expect in its year-end balance sheet?

£1,378,000 ÷ 52 weeks = £26,500 average operating expenses per week × 6 weeks = £159,000 accrued expenses payable balance in its year-end balance sheet

4 For the business in the example question, the average amount borrowed using a bank loan during the year was £1,500,000. The average annual interest rate on these notes was 6.5 per cent. What amount of interest expense would you find in the business's Profit and Loss statement for the year?

£1,500,000 bank loan ÷ 6.5 per cent interest rate = £97,500 annual interest expense

5 The business has debtors of £2,375,000 and a turnover of £25,000,000. Calculate the number of debtor days?

Debtors days calculation is as follows:

Debtors ÷ turnover × 365 days

2,375,000 ÷ 25,000,000 × 365 = 35 days (or five weeks)

This result is pretty good because most debtors are paying just after the 30 days. Everyone wants customers like that!

6 A business has stock of £5,757,000 with Cost of Goods Sold of £12,000,000. Calculate the average stock holding period. What comments would you make?

To calculate the average number of days that the stock has been held, you need to perform the following calculation:

stock ÷ Cost of Goods Sold × 365 days

5,757,000 ÷ 12,000,000 × 365 days = 175 days

You can see that stock on average for this firm is held for quite a long period of time, almost six months before being sold. This may be indicative of the type of industry that the business is in or prove that perhaps too much stock is being bought to meet current demand. The business shouldn't be investing in stock if it's simply just going to sit on shelves and deteriorate. Stock control and production methods should perhaps be investigated to ensure that less money is tied up unnecessarily. The investment of money may be better spent on purchasing more efficient equipment (assuming a manufacturing business) rather than masses of raw materials.

7 Instead of the amounts shown in Firm X's Balance Sheet, suppose that the cost of Firm X's fixed assets is £3,850,000 and that accumulated depreciation is £958,000. Determine the amount of capital the business would have to raise in this scenario.

Based on the higher amount invested in fixed assets, and taking into account the larger amount of accumulated depreciation, Firm X would have to raise £4,467,000 total capital (see the following balance sheet for the business). This amount is £1,127,000 more compared to the example in Firm X's Balance Sheet (£4,467,000 capital raised in this scenario ÷ £3,340,000 capital raised in the following figure = £1,127,000 additional capital).

Fixed Assets		Current Liabilities	
Plant and Machinery	£3,850,000	Creditors	£350,000
Accumulated Depreciation	(£958,000)	Accrued Expenses	£165,000
Cost less depreciation	£2,892,000		£515,000

Current Assets	
Stock	£780,000
Debtors	£500,000
Cash	£700,000
Prepaid Expenses	£110,000
Total current assets	£2,090,000
Total Assets	**£4,982,000**

Note: This Balance Sheet is only partial as it does not show the owners equity. You can calculate the owners equity by deducting the current liabilities from the total assets. (£4,982,000 - £515,000 = £4,467,000). The Owners equity would thus be £4,467,000.

8 Assume that the balances of assets, creditors and accrued expenses payable are the same as shown in Firm X's Balance Sheet. However, the balance of accumulated depreciation is £400,000. In this scenario, would Firm X have to raise more capital?

Based on the smaller balance of accumulated depreciation, Firm X would have to raise £3,625,000 total capital (see the following balance sheet for the business). This figure is £285,000 more compared to the example in Figure 7-2 (£3,625,000 capital raised in this scenario – £3,340,000 capital raised in Figure 7-2 = £285,000 additional capital).

Firm X records £285,000 less depreciation in this scenario than in Firm X's Balance Sheet (£685,000 accumulated depreciation in the following figure – £400,000 accumulated depreciation in this scenario = £285,000 less accumulated depreciation). Therefore, the retained earnings balance of the business is £285,000 higher (before income tax). Retained earnings is part of owners' capital, and so the owners' capital source of capital is £285,000 higher in this scenario than in the scenario depicted in Firm X's Balance Sheet.

Fixed Assets		**Current Liabilities**	
Plant and Machinery	£2,450,000	Creditors	£350,000
Accumulated Depreciation	(£400,000)	Accrued Expenses	£165,000
Cost less depreciation	£2,050,000		£515,000

Current Assets	
Stock	£780,000
Debtors	£500,000
Cash	£700,000
Prepaid Expenses	£110,000
Total current assets	£2,090,000
Total Assets	**£4,140,000**

Note: This Balance Sheet is only partial as it does not show the owners equity. You can calculate the owner's equity by deducting the current liabilities from the total assets. (£4,140,000 - £515,000 = £3,625,000). The Owners equity would thus be £3,625,000.

In the original Firm X's Balance Sheet the capital introduced was calculated as £3,340,000. With the changes made to the above Balance Sheet, the capital introduced has been calculated as £3,625,000 an increase of £285,000 (£3,625,000 - £3,340,000).

9 Based on Firm Z's Profit and Loss statement and balance sheet, determine the business's debtors days.

debtors ÷ turnover × 365 = debtor days

£2,715,000 ÷ £23,530,000 × 365 = 42 days (or 6 weeks)

10 Based on Firm Z's Profit and Loss statement and balance sheet, determine the business's average stock holding period.

stock ÷ Cost of Goods Sold × 365 days

£2,172,000 ÷ £14,118,000 × 365 days = 56 days (or 8 weeks)

Chapter 8

Reporting Cash Flows and Changes in Owners' Capital

In This Chapter
▶ Revisiting the determination of profit
▶ Addressing changes in owners' capital
▶ Looking at profit from the cash flow point of view
▶ Preparing the cash flow report

*T*he history of the cash flow statement is complex; despite repeated calls from the investment community for cash flow information in financial reports – and after a rather inept experiment with reporting a funds flow statement – in 1987 the accounting profession finally required that a cash flow statement be included in financial reports. Therefore, the cash flow statement has been included in financial reports for about two decades and is likely to remain a permanent fixture in business financial reporting.

In our opinion, the cash flow statement is the most difficult of the three financial statements to understand and interpret. This statement reports a business's sources and uses of cash, and that seems pretty straightforward. However, many cash flow statements present tangled cash flow threads that are very difficult to follow. We think that accountants are partly to blame for this mess; if we were a paranoid investor, we may think that businesses deliberately make their cash flow statements difficult to read.

This chapter carries a disclaimer: the following discussion doesn't adhere to the party line. Our approach isn't the standard textbook approach to understanding cash flows; we think it's better. Of course, we may be a tiny bit biased.

Figuring Profit from the Balance Sheet

Suppose that you're the accountant for a business that suffers a terrible fire that destroys virtually everything, including its accounting records. (In hindsight, the business should have stored back-up accounting records off-premises, but it didn't.) When escaping the burning building, the bookkeeper manages to grab one piece of smoldering paper. The bottom part of the page had already burned away, but the bookkeeper thinks (rightly) that this scrap of paper may be helpful. The paper contains the business's balance sheets at the end of its two most recent years, minus the last few lines that burned away.

Figure 8-1 presents the balance sheets of the business at the end of its two most recent years. The changes between the year-end balances are included, and the balance sheet is presented in the portrait, or vertical format. Accountants like to see the changes between two balance sheet periods. This is sometimes also shown as *movement* as it explains the movements of balances between periods.

Assets	2008	2009	Changes
Fixed Assets			
Plant & Machinery	£2,450,000	£2,875,000	£425,000
Accumulated Depreciation	(£685,000)	(£876,000)	(£191,000)
Cost less depreciation	£1,765,000	£1,999,000	
Current Assets			
Stock	£780,000	£825,000	£45,000
Debtors	£500,000	£535,000	£35,000
Cash	£700,000	£901,000	£201,000
Prepaid expenses	£110,000	£125,000	£15,000
Total current assets	£2,090,000	£2,386,000	
Liabilities & Owners Equity			
Current Liabilities			
Creditors	£350,000	£385,000	£35,000
Accrued expenses	£165,000	£205,000	£40,000
Bank Overdraft	£500,000	£625,000	£125,000
Total current liabilities	£1,015,000	£1,215,000	
Long term loans	£1,000,000	£1,125,000	£125,000
Owners Equity			
Capital			

Figure 8-1: The Incomplete comparative Balance Sheet at Year ends 2008 and 2009.

Unfortunately, the 2009 Profit and Loss statement was lost in the fire. The CEO wants to know the net income for the year and asks whether you can determine profit from the information in Figure 8-1. Yes, you can determine profit by comparing the net worth of the business at year-end 2009 against its net worth at the end of 2008.

The net worth of a business equals its total assets minus its total liabilities. Earning net income increases the net worth of the business. The net worth of the business in this example increases £205,000 from year-end 2008 to year-end 2009, and so the net income of the business for 2009 is £205,000. Well, maybe net income is £205,000 or maybe not.

The net income amount for this business depends on two other factors, and you need to answer the following questions before you can reach a final answer regarding net income:

- ✔ **Did the shareholders invest additional capital in the business?** An infusion of new ownership capital in the business increases the net worth of the business. Any amount of net worth increase from owners putting additional capital into the business is deducted from the change in net worth when determining net income for the year.

- ✔ **Did the business distribute cash dividends to its shareholders during the year?** Cash dividends from profit decrease the net worth of the business. Therefore, the amount of cash dividends is added to the change in net worth when determining net income for the year.

Q. The CEO of the business also serves as the chair of its board of directors. After you determine the net income for 2009 based on the balance sheet in Figure 8-1, the CEO tells you that she thinks that £200,000 cash dividends were paid to shareholders during 2009. Based on this additional information about cash dividends, what amount of net income does the business earn in 2009?

A. The net worth of the business increases £205,000 during the year, as explained earlier in this section. The £200,000 amount of cash dividends to shareholders decreases net worth because £200,000 of owners' capital is taken out of the business. The £200,000 amount of cash dividends is added to the £205,000 net worth increase to get £405,000 net income for the year. In other words, even after the £200,000 cash dividends, net worth still increases £205,000. Net income had to increase £405,000 for this result to happen.

1. After you revise your net income answer (see the earlier example question), the CEO tells you that she's talked with other directors of the business and realises that she was wrong about the cash dividends. Now she's fairly certain that £250,000 cash dividends were paid to shareholders during 2009 and that the business issued additional shares for £50,000. Based on this additional information, what amount of net income does the business earn in 2009?

Solve It

2. A business reports £500,000 net loss for the year just ended. It doesn't issue any shares during the year or pay cash dividends because of its loss in the year. Does its net worth decrease £500,000 during the year? Does its cash balance decrease £500,000 during the year because of its loss?

Solve It

3. Can the net worth of a business go negative? If so, explain briefly how this situation may happen and whether it means that the business would have a negative cash balance.

Solve It

Reporting the Statement of Changes in Shareholders' Capital

From information about the business's annual profit performance, dividends and capital invested by or returned to shareholders, the accountant prepares a statement of changes in shareholders' capital. This statement is included in the annual financial report of the business. Despite being called a 'statement', it's really more of a schedule of changes in the owners' Capital accounts. Because the primary audience of the financial report is the business's shareholders, they're very interested in the changes in their accounts.

Figure 8-2 presents the basic structure of a statement of changes in shareholders' capital for the business example introduced in Figure 8-1. Note that the statement covers two years. The statement of changes in shareholders' capital illustrated in Figure 8-2 is actually a fairly simple example. A business may have a complicated capital structure, in which case this schedule includes much more detail than shown in Figure 8-2; the number of shares for each class of share issued by the business would usually be reported, but that number isn't important for the task at hand, which is why we don't include this data in Figure 8-2.

	Capital Stock	Retained Earnings	Total Owners Equity
Balance at end of 2007	£750,000	£922,000	£1,672,000
Net Income 2008		£318,000	
Cash Dividends – 2008	_____	(£150,000)	
Balance at end of 2008	£750,000	£1,090,000	£1,840,000
Issued Share Capital	£50,000		
Net Income 2009		£405,000	
Cash Dividends 2009		(£250,000)	
Balance at end of 2009	£800,000	£1,245,000	£2,045,000

Figure 8-2: The Statement of Changes in Shareholders Equity.

In Figure 8-2, total owners' capital equals £1,840,000 at the end of 2008 (£750,000 share capital + £1,090,000 retained earnings = £1,840,000). And at the end of 2009, total owners' capital equals £2,045,000 (£800,000 share capital + £1,245,000 retained earnings = £2,045,000). These two owners' capital amounts are the same as the net worth amounts used in determining profit by the comparative net worth method (see the preceding section). In short, net worth equals owners' capital and net income increases owners' capital.

4. Please refer to Figure 8-1, which presents the comparative balance sheet of the business, and to Figure 8-2, which presents its statement of changes in shareholders' capital. Suppose that the business pays £175,000 cash dividends (instead of £250,000) to shareholders in 2009. In this scenario, which sterling amounts in the business's comparative balance sheet would be different as the result of this one change?

Solve It

5. Suppose that the business in the example (shown in Figure 8-2) doesn't issue additional shares in 2009 and doesn't distribute dividends to its shareholders in 2008 or 2009. In this scenario, is the statement of changes in shareholders' capital necessary? Should it be presented in the business's 2009 annual financial report?

Solve It

Determining Cash Effect from Making Profit

Someone has to be in charge of managing the cash flows and cash balance of a business. In mid-size and large businesses, the person with this heavy responsibility is probably the Financial Controller, or Finance Director. In smaller businesses, the Managing Director may manage cash flows in addition to all her other functions. Simply put, if cash isn't managed carefully, the business can run out of it, which would be a disaster. (One major consequence is that employees wouldn't be paid on time.) Managing cash flow is a top priority of every business, and this management starts with cash flow from profit.

Borrowing money and gaining owner investments in the business increase its cash balance. But cash flow from profit doesn't refer to these two sources of cash. The term refers to the net cash result from the sales and expenses of the business during the relevant period.

Sales and expenses are also called operating activities or profit-making activities. In the cash flow statement the increase or decrease of cash during the period from the business's profit-making activities is called cash flow from operating activities. This term is rather technical term and in our opinion not all that clear. For brevity and clarity we prefer the term cash flow from profit, which is used throughout this chapter – except where we have to use the formal term cash flow from operating activities in the cash flow statement.

Q. Continuing the example scenario created earlier in this chapter, the CEO asks you to determine cash flow from profit (net income) in 2009. In other words, she wants to know how much the business's cash balance increased from making profit in the year. Based on the information in its comparative balance sheet (Figure 8-1) and its statement of changes in shareholders capital (Figure 8-2), determine the business's cash flow from profit for 2009. Does its cash balance increase £405,000, the same amount as net income? Or, does cash increase a different amount? Does cash *decrease* as the result of the business's profit-making activities (which is possible)?

A. During the year, the business increases its cash £250,000 from borrowing (see the increases in short-term and long-term debt in Figure 8-1). The business issues additional shares for £50,000 and pays £250,000 cash dividends to shareholders during the year (see Figure 8-2). Therefore, the net cash increase from its *financing activities* is £50,000 (£250,000 increase in debt + £50,000 issue of stock shares – £250,000 dividends = £50,000 cash increase). The business spends £425,000 cash for additions and replacements to its plant and machinery (see the increase in this fixed Asset account in Figure 8-1). These cash outlays are classified as *investing activities*. Finally, note that the business's cash balance increases £201,000 during the year (see Figure 8-1).

This question asks you to determine the business's cash flow from operating activities (cash flow from profit) for the year; it doesn't ask you to prepare the formal cash flow statement for the year (which we explain in the following section). The objective is to get cash flow from profit, and so we favour the method explained in Chapter 1. The four components of cash

flow from profit are assembled in the following summary for the business example:

Summary of Cash Flows For the Year

Cash flow from operating activities	????
Cash flow from investing activities	(£425,000)
Cash flow from financing activities	£50,000
Increase in cash during the year	£201,000

Solving for the unknown factor, cash flow from profit is £576,000 for the year. The £576,000 cash flow from profit plus the £50,000 net cash increase from financing activities provides the business with £626,000 cash. It uses £425,000 for capital expenditures, and so its cash balance increases by £201,000.

This analysis method (solving for the unknown factor) is a 'backdoor' approach for determining cash flow from profit. First, you determine the net change in cash that the investing and financing activities cause. Then you compare this amount to the change in cash during the year. The rest of the change in cash during the year must equal the cash flow from profit. This method is an expedient and practical way to answer the question.

If all you need to know is the final amount of cash flow from profit for the period, this analysis method gives you the correct answer. But we should remind you that the cash flow statement provides information about several determinants of cash flow from operating activities, as well as the final amount. These determinants of cash flow from profit are explained in the following section.

6. Figure 8-3 presents a business's comparative balance sheet that's missing the information for owners' capital. Assume that the business doesn't issue additional shares during the year and doesn't pay cash dividends to its shareholders during the year. Determine its net income for the year 2009.

Solve It

Assets	2008	2009	Changes
Fixed Assets			
Plant and Machinery	£897,000	£1,060,000	£163,000
Accumulated depreciation	(£257,000)	(£318,000)	(£61,000)
Net Book Value	£640,000	£742,000	
Current Assets			
Stock	£518,000	£576,000	£58,000
Debtors	£386,000	£340,000	(£46,000)
Cash	£456,000	£425,000	(£31,000)
Prepaid Expenses	£46,000	£52,000	£6,000
	£1,406,000	£1,393,000	
Current Liabilities			
Creditors	£246,000	£230,000	(£16,000)
Bank Overdraft	£350,000	£300,000	(£50,000)
Accrued Expenses	£204,000	£215,000	£11,000
	£800,000	£745,000	
Long Term Liabilities			
Long term loan	£400,000	£525,000	£125,000

Figure 8-3: Comparative Balance Sheet which is missing the owners' equity accounts.

7. From the information presented in Figure 8-3, determine the business's cash flow from profit (operating activities) for 2009.

Solve It

8. A business's net worth decreases £425,000 during the year just ended. It doesn't pay cash dividends during the year or issue share capital during the year. Determine its profit or loss for the year.

Solve It

9. A business's net worth decreases £585,000 during the year just ended. It doesn't pay cash dividends during the year, but it does issue additional shares during the year for £150,000. Determine its profit or loss for the year.

Solve It

Presenting the Cash Flow Statement

A business's accountant prepares the Profit and Loss statement from its sales revenue and Expense accounts and prepares the balance sheet from its Asset, Liability and owners' Capital accounts. However, no cash flow accounts are available from which to prepare the cash flow statement.

How does an accountant prepare the cash flow statement without ready-made accounts with cash flow balances? This question is interesting – to accountants anyway! (We doubt that non-accountants care a fig about how the accountants do their work in preparing financial statements.)

Accountants use different techniques for gathering and analysing the necessary information for preparing the cash flow statement. Theoretically, an accountant can analyse and classify all the entries in the cash account during the year to collect the information to prepare the cash flow statement. However, going back and looking at the large number of entries in the cash account during the year isn't a very practical method for pulling together the information.

Despite the fact that businesses use computers in their accounting systems, very few are able to design their data entry procedures and computer programs so that at the end of the year the computer spits out exactly the information needed to prepare the cash flow statement. In most businesses this financial statement is assembled the old fashion way – the accountant sits down and organises the information pretty much by hand. The information can be put into a spreadsheet program to do the tedious computations and groupings.

Reporting Cash Flows

Regardless of how the accountant goes about organising the information needed to prepare it, the cash flow statement is fundamentally the same for every business. Figure 8-4 presents a business's cash flow statement for 2009. The format of this financial statement is in accordance with the official standard governing reporting cash flows. Figure 8-4 presents cash flows for only one year, but most public businesses present a two- or three-year comparative cash flow statement.

In the cash flow statement, transactions are grouped into three types (see Figure 8-4):

- **Operating activities:** The section reports the determinants of the cash increase or decrease attributable to the profit-making operations of the business during the period, and the final amount of cash flow from operating activities for the period – a positive £576,000 in the example.

- **Investing activities:** This section includes expenditures for fixed assets and proceeds from the disposal of these assets (if any), and the net cash increase or decrease from these activities for the period – a negative £425,000 in the example.

- **Financing activities:** This section includes the cash flows from borrowing and paying debt, owners investing capital in the business and return of capital to them, and cash dividends to owners, and the net cash increase or decrease from these activities for the period – a positive £50,000 in the example.

Cash Flow Statement for 2009

Cash Flow from Operating Activities

Net Income	£405,000	
Stock increase	(£45,000)	
Debtors increase	(£35,000)	
Prepaid Expenses increase	(£15,000)	
Depreciation Expense	£191,000	
Creditors increase	£35,000	
Accrued Expenses increase	£40,000	£576,000

Cash Flow from Investing Activities

Capital expenditure		(£425,000)

Cash Flow from Financing Activities

Bank overdraft increase	£125,000	
Long term Loan increase	£125,000	
Issue of shares	(£50,000)	
Cash dividends to shareholders	(£250,000)	£50,000

Increase in cash during year	£201,000
Beginning cash balance	£700,000
Ending cash balance	£901,000

Figure 8-4:
How to present a Cash Flow Statement.

The 'bottom line' of the statement is the net cash increase or decrease from the three types of activities reported in the statement – a positive £201,000 in the example. As you can see in Figure 8-4, this £201,000 increase isn't the bottom line in the literal sense, because the beginning cash balance is added to the net cash increase during the year to arrive at the ending balance of cash. The £201,000 increase in cash during the year is the bottom line in the sense that the three main types of activities cause cash to increase this amount during the year.

Financial statement readers definitely want to know whether the business's cash balance increases or decreases during the year, and they want to know the main reasons for the increase or decrease. Hence the need for reporting the cash flow statement.

Many investment analysts and financial reporters – who should know better – take an inadvisable shortcut to calculate a number they call cash flow from profit: depreciation is added to net income to produce cash flow from profit. However, singling out depreciation as if it were the only factor that affects cash flow from profit is misleading. The depreciation expense should be put in the broader context of all the asset and liability changes that affect cash flow from profit. This purpose is exactly why the first section of the cash flow statement reports the cash flow from operating activities (see Figure 8-4).

Often, depreciation is the largest factor for the difference between cash flow and net income, as is the case in the example in Figure 8-4. But changes in other assets and liabilities also affect cash flow from profit. In some situations, these other changes overwhelm depreciation and are the main reasons for the difference between cash flow and profit. For instance, a business may lease all its fixed assets and have no depreciation expense.

A business needs to generate sufficient cash flow from profit to pay cash dividends to shareholders. In Figure 8-4, the business generates £576,000 cash flow from profit for the year and pays out £250,000 cash dividends to its shareholders. This comparison is one of many readers of the cash flow statement can make to judge the cash flow policies and decisions of the business. Given that the business needed £425,000 for investments in fixed assets during the year, should it have paid out such a large portion of its cash flow from profit? This important issue is just one of many that creditors and shareholders should ponder when reading a cash flow statement.

Connecting Balance Sheet Changes with Cash Flows

As we have said more than once in this book, the three primary financial statements of a business are intertwined and interdependent. The numbers in the cash flow statement derive from the changes in the business's balance sheet accounts during the year. Changes in the balance sheet accounts drive the amounts reported in the cash flow statement.

Figure 8-5 shows the lines of connection between changes in the business's balance sheet accounts during the year and the information reported in the cash flow statement. Note that the £155,000 net increase in retained earnings is separated between the £405,000 net income for the year and the £250,000 cash dividends for the year (£405,000 net income – £250,000 dividends = £155,000 net increase in retained earnings).

Balance sheet account changes, such as those shown in Figure 8-5, are the basic building blocks for preparing a cash flow statement. These changes in assets, liabilities and owners' Capital accounts are the amounts reported in the cash flow statement (as shown in Figure 8-5), or the changes are used to determine the cash flow amounts (as in the case of the change in retained earnings, which is separated into its net income component and its dividends component).

Note that in the cash flow from operating activities section in Figure 8-5, net income is listed first, and then several adjustments are made to determine the amount of cash flow from operating activities. The assets and liabilities included in this section are those that are part and parcel of the profit-making activity of a business. For example, debtors is increased (debited) when sales are made on credit. Stock is decreased (credited) when recording Cost of Goods Sold expense. The creditors account is increased (credited) when recording expenses that haven't been paid. And so on.

The rules for cash flow adjustments to net income are:

- An asset increase during the period decreases cash flow from profit.
- A liability decrease during the period decreases cash flow from profit.
- An asset decrease during the period increases cash flow from profit.
- A liability increase during the period increases cash flow from profit.

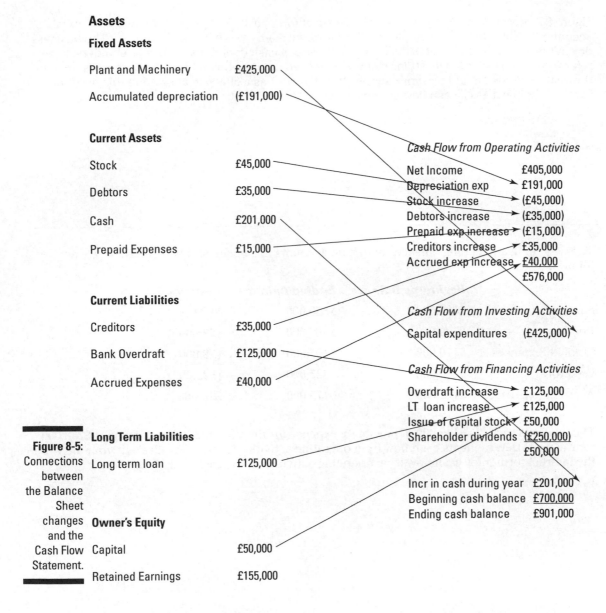

Figure 8-5: Connections between the Balance Sheet changes and the Cash Flow Statement.

Following the third listed rule, the £191,000 depreciation expense for the year is a positive adjustment, or add-back to net income – see Figure 8-4. Recording the depreciation expense reduces the book value of the fixed assets being depreciated. Well, to be more precise, recording depreciation increases the balance of the accumulated depreciation contra account that's deducted from the original cost of fixed assets. Recording depreciation doesn't involve a cash outlay. The cash outlay occurred when the business bought the assets being depreciated, which may be years ago.

The format of the cash flow from operating activities section shown in Figure 8-4 is referred to as the indirect method (a rather technical term). The large majority of public businesses use this method to report their cash flow from operating activities. However, the authoritative accounting standard on this matter permits an alternative method for reporting cash flow from operating activities, which is called the direct method (not that this term is any clearer). Very few businesses elect this alternative format, and we don't explain it here. But you should know that a business has this option for reporting cash flow from operating activities.

10. Figure 8-3 presents the comparative balance sheet for a business (without its owners' Capital accounts). (Note that this example is different to the main example in the chapter.) The business doesn't issue additional shares during the year or pay cash dividends to its shareholders. Please refer to your answers to Questions 6 and 7. You need to know the net income of the business for the year, and you should use your answer to Question 7 as a check in answering this question. Prepare the business's cash flow statement for 2009.

Solve It

11. The beginning and ending balances of certain accounts in a business's balance sheet are as follows:

	Beginning Balance	Ending Balance	Changes
Stock	$780,000	$860,000	$80,000
Debtors	$500,000	$465,000	($35,000)
Prepaid Expenses	$110,000	$105,000	($5,000)
Creditors	$350,000	$325,000	($25,000)
Accrued Expenses	$165,000	$175,000	$10,000

The business records $145,000 depreciation expense for the year and its net income is $258,000 for the year. Determine its cash flow from operating activities for the year. Present your answer in the indirect format for cash flow from operating activities in the cash flow statement.

Solve It

12. Referring to the scenario in Question 11, assume that the facts remain the same except that the business doesn't record depreciation expense in the year. Instead, it leases all its fixed assets and pays rent. The rent expense for the year is $145,000. (Note that the rent expense is the same amount as the depreciation expense in Question 11.) Determine its cash flow from operating activities for the year. Present your answer for reporting cash flow from operating activities according to the indirect format (as illustrated in Figure 8-4).

Solve It

Answers for Problems on Reporting Cash Flows and Changes in Owners' Capital

Here are the answers to the questions presented earlier in this chapter.

1 After you revise your net income answer (see the earlier example question), the CEO tells you that she's talked with other directors of the business and realises that she was wrong about the cash dividends. Now she's fairly certain that £250,000 cash dividends were paid to shareholders during 2009 and that the business issued additional shares for £50,000. Based on this additional information, what amount of net income does the business earn in 2009?

Net income is £405,000. The net effect on owners' capital is the same as in the example question; the share issue increases net worth £50,000 and the cash dividend decreases net worth £250,000.

2 A business reports £500,000 net loss for the year just ended. It doesn't issue any shares during the year or pay cash dividends because of its loss in the year. Does its net worth decrease £500,000 during the year? Does its cash balance decrease £500,000 during the year because of its loss?

Yes, net loss decreases net worth (owners' capital) £500,000. No other transactions affect owners' capital during the year (no share issue and no cash dividends).

To determine whether its cash balance decreases £500,000 because of the business's loss, you need to know the changes in the assets and liabilities of the business that sales and expenses affect. You can't answer this cash flow question without this information. Only if the business doesn't record any depreciation expense in the year, and the balances of the various assets and liabilities affected by sales and expenses remain absolutely flat during the year, would the loss decrease cash £500,000 during the year. But this scenario is highly unlikely for the business.

3 Can the net worth of a business go negative? If so, explain briefly how this situation may happen and whether it means that the business would have a negative cash balance.

Yes, the net worth of a business can go negative. A large enough loss in the year can wipe out all owners' capital and more, or repeated losses year after year can drive owners' capital into the negative column. Remember that a loss decreases the retained earnings balance of a business. The loss for the year or cumulative losses over time can push retained earnings into a large negative balance. The negative balance of retained earnings can become more than the balance in the owners' capital invested Capital account. In this case, owners' capital would be negative.

Regarding the second question, you have to put your finger on what a negative cash balance is. Usually, a negative cash balance refers to an overdrawn bank account balance in which the business has written cheques for more than exists in its account. Unless an overdraft facility is in place, banks don't typically allow overdraws to happen and refuse to honour cheques after the bank account balance is drawn down to zero. Although a bank may tolerate a temporary negative balance for a good customer, a business with a negative owners' capital hardly qualifies as a good customer.

4 Please refer to Figure 8-1, which presents the comparative balance sheet of the business, and to Figure 8-2, which presents its statement of changes in shareholders' capital. Suppose that the business pays £175,000 cash dividends (instead of £250,000) to shareholders in 2009. In this scenario, which sterling amounts in the business's comparative balance sheet would be different as the result of this one change?

One relatively small difference, like the one in this problem, causes several changes in the balance sheet. In the following answer, the amounts that are different are shaded so that you can easily identify them.

Assets	2008	2009	Changes
Fixed Assets			
Plant & Machinery	£2,450,000	£2,875,000	£425,000
Accumulated Depreciation	(£685,000)	(£876,000)	(£191,000)
Cost less depreciation	£1,765,000	£1,999,000	
Current Assets			
Stock	£780,000	£825,000	£45,000
Debtors	£500,000	£535,000	£35,000
Cash	£700,000	£976,000	£276,000
Prepaid expenses	£110,000	£125,000	£15,000
Total current assets	£2,090,000	£2,461,000	
Total assets	£3,855,000	£4,460,000	
Liabilities & Owners Equity			
Current Liabilities			
Creditors	£350,000	£385,000	£35,000
Accrued expenses	£165,000	£205,000	£40,000
Bank Overdraft	£500,000	£625,000	£125,000
Total current liabilities	£1,015,000	£1,215,000	
Long term loans	£1,000,000	£1,125,000	£125,000
Owners Equity			
Capital			

Figure 8-6:
The amounts that are different are shaded so that you can easily identify them.

5   Suppose that the business in the example (shown in Figure 8-2) doesn't issue additional shares in 2009 and doesn't distribute dividends to its shareholders in 2008 or 2009. In this scenario, is the statement of changes in shareholders' capital necessary? Should it be presented in the business's 2009 annual financial report?

Well, if the business did prepare and report this statement, it would look as follows:

	Capital Stock	Retained Earnings	Total Owners Equity
Balance at end of 2007	£750,000	£922,000	£1,672,000
Net Income 2008		£318,000	
Cash Dividends – 2008	_____	£Nil	
Balance at end of 2008	£750,000	£1,240,000	£1,990,000
Issued Share Capital	£Nil		
Net Income 2009		£405,000	
Cash Dividends 2009		£Nil	
Balance at end of 2009	£750,000	£1,645,000	£2,395,000

Figure 8-7: Statement of Changes in Shareholders equity.

You can make a good case that presenting the statement of changes in shareholders' capital in the business's annual report is unnecessary, because it contains so little information in addition to what's already in the comparative balance sheet. The statement does report that net income is added to the retained earnings balance each year, but most financial statement readers should understand this point.

 On the other hand, you can argue that showing no dividends and no issue of capital stock either year sends a message that the business is conserving its cash and presumably has a need for that cash. On balance, therefore, most businesses would go ahead and report a statement of changes in shareholders' capital. If readers aren't interested enough to read the statement, they can skip it. You never know; some business investors and creditors read every financial statement and every footnote, and these people expect to see the statement of changes in shareholders' capital in the financial report.

6 Figure 8-3 presents a business's comparative balance sheet that's missing the information for owners' capital. Assume that the business doesn't issue additional shares during the year and doesn't pay cash dividends to its shareholders during the year. Determine its net income for the year 2009.

The business's net income for 2009 is determined as follows:

	2008	2009
Total assets	£2,046,000	£2,135,000
Current Liabilities	(£800,000)	(£745,000)
Long term Loan	(£400,000)	(£525,000)
Net Worth at yearend	£846,000	£865,000
		(£846,000)
Net Income for 2009		£19,000

Figure 8-8: The business's net income.

The business doesn't issue shares or pay dividends during the year, and so £19,000 is its net income. In other words, the increase in net worth consists entirely of the increase in retained earnings caused by net income for the year.

If you think that the net income in this scenario is a rather paltry amount, you're right. Generally, a business expects to earn annual net income equal to 10 to 15 per cent or more of its owners' capital. Owners' capital is the investment by the owners in the business, and the owners expect to earn a return on their investment. Based on the £846,000 balance of owners' capital at the start of 2007, a 15 per cent return on investment would require about £127,000 net income. The business had better improve its profit performance, or else.

7 From the information presented in Figure 8-3, determine the business's cash flow from profit (operating activities) for 2009.

Using the method of solving for the unknown factor you set up the problem as follows:

Summary of Cash Flows For the Year

Cash flow from operating activities	????
Cash flow from investing activities	(£163,000)
Cash flow from financing activities	£75,000
Decrease in cash during the year	(£31,000)

Solving for the unknown factor, cash flow from profit is £57,000 for the year. In Figure 8-3, you can see that the business increases cash £75,000 from its loan and overdraft transactions during the year (£125,000 increase in long-term loans – £50,000 pay down on the overdraft = £75,000 net increase). The business doesn't raise money by issuing shares during the year and doesn't pay cash dividends during the year. Therefore, the net cash increase from its financing activities is £75,000. The firm spends £163,000 on plant and machinery (see Figure 8-3). Therefore, cash flow from profit must have increased cash £57,000: £57,000 cash increase from profit – £163,000 capital expenditures + £75,000 cash from financing activities = £31,000 decrease in cash during year. We hope that you follow all this: cash flow analysis isn't for the faint-hearted, is it?

8 A business's net worth decreases £425,000 during the year just ended. It doesn't pay cash dividends during the year or issue share capital during the year. Determine its profit or loss for the year.

All the decrease in net worth in this scenario must be due to the loss for the year. So, the bottom-line is that the business suffered a £425,000 loss for the year.

 Does this loss mean that bankruptcy is just around the corner? A loss doesn't necessarily mean that the business is out of cash and unable to pay its debts on time. The business may have plenty of cash to buy enough time to correct its problems and move into the black. Then again, if this result is the tenth straight year of losses, the business may be hanging on by a thread and may have to declare bankruptcy.

9 A business's net worth decreases £585,000 during the year just ended. It doesn't pay cash dividends during the year, but it does issue additional shares during the year for £150,000. Determine its profit or loss for the year.

The business's net worth increases £150,000 from the issue of additional shares. If the business had experienced a break-even year (sales revenue – expenses = zero), its net worth would have increased £150,000. But net worth actually decreased £585,000 during the year. Therefore, the business must have reported a £735,000 loss for the year.

10 Figure 8-3 presents the comparative balance sheet for a business (without its owners' Capital accounts). (Note that this example is different to the main example in the chapter.) The business doesn't issue additional shares during the year or cash dividends to its shareholders. Please refer to your answers to Questions 6 and 7. You need to know the net income of the business for the year, and you should use your answer to Question 7 as a check in answering this question. Prepare the business's cash flow statement for 2009.

Cash Flow Statement for 2009

Cash Flow from Operating Activities

Net Income	£19,000	
Stock increase	(£58,000)	
Debtors decrease	£46,000	
Prepaid Expenses increase	(£6,000)	
Depreciation Expense	£61,000	
Creditors decrease	(£16,000)	
Accrued Expenses increase	£11,000	£57,000

Cash Flow from Investing Activities

Capital expenditure	(£163,000)

Cash Flow from Financing Activities

Bank overdraft decrease	(£50,000)	
Long term Loan increase	£125,000	£75,000
Decrease in cash during year		(£31,000)
Beginning cash balance		£456,000
Ending cash balance		£425,000

11 The beginning and ending balances of certain accounts in a business's balance sheet are as follows:

Cash Flow from Operating Activities

Net Income	£258,000	
Stock increase	(£80,000)	
Debtors decrease	£35,000	
Prepaid Expenses decrease	£5,000	
Depreciation Expense	£145,000	
Creditors decrease	(£25,000)	
Accrued Expenses increase	£10,000	£348,000

The business records £145,000 depreciation expense for the year and its net income is £258,000 for the year. Determine its cash flow from operating activities for the year. Present your answer in the indirect format for cash flow from operating activities in the cash flow statement.

12 Referring to the scenario in Question 11, assume that the facts remain the same except that the business doesn't record depreciation expense in the year. Instead, it leases all its fixed assets and pays rent. The rent expense for the year is £145,000. (Note that the rent expense is the same amount as the depreciation expense in Question 11.) Determine its cash flow from operating activities for the year. Present your answer for reporting cash flow from operating activities according to the indirect format (as illustrated in Figure 8-4).

Cash Flow from Operating Activities

Net Income	£258,000	
Stock increase	(£80,000)	
Debtors decrease	£35,000	
Prepaid Expenses decrease	£5,000	
Creditors decrease	(£25,000)	
Accrued Expenses increase	£10,000	£203,000

For added insight, compare this answer with the answer to Question 11. Cash flow from profit in this situation is £145,000 less than for the scenario for Question 11, because the business doesn't record the depreciation expense. Instead, it pays £145,000 rent expense during the year.

Chapter 9

Choosing Accounting Methods

. . . .

In This Chapter

▶ Selecting the best Cost of Goods Sold expense method for the business

▶ Deciding on depreciation methods

▶ Biting the bad-debts bullet

. . . .

*Y*ou may think that two businesses that are identical in every financial respect and have identical transactions during the year would report identical financial statements. Well, you'd be wrong. The two businesses would have identical financial statements only if they make identical accounting choices, which is very unlikely: different businesses make different accounting decisions.

Accounting is more than just reading the facts or interpreting the financial outcomes of business transactions; it also requires accountants to choose between alternative accounting methods.

Accounting methods must stay within the boundaries of generally accepted accounting principles (GAAP). In the UK, accounting standards are issued by the Accounting Standards Board (ASB) and recognised as such under the Companies Act 1985. The ASB also collaborates with the International Accounting Standards Board (IASB) in order to ensure that its standards are progressed with regard to international developments (see www.asb.co.uk).

A business can't conjure up accounting methods out of thin air. GAAP isn't a straitjacket; it leaves plenty of wiggle room, but the one fundamental constraint is that a business must stick with its accounting method when it makes a choice. Consistency is the rule; the same accounting methods must be used year after year.

Getting Off to a Good Start

A new business with no accounting history needs to make its accounting decisions for the first time. If the business sells products, it has to select which Cost of Goods Sold expense method to use. If it owns fixed assets, it has to select which depreciation method to use. If it makes sales on credit, it has to decide which bad debts expense method to use. These accounting decisions are just three of the many that a business has to make.

The choices of accounting methods for these three expenses – Cost of Goods Sold, depreciation and bad debts – can make a sizable difference in the amount of profit or loss recorded for the year. For example, using a higher rate of depreciation has the effect of charging more depreciation expenses against business profit and therefore reduces the taxable profit for that business; the result is that the business pays less tax. The comprehensive exercises and questions in throughout this chapter demonstrate this point.

To explain these expense accounting methods, we use a start-up business example. This new business has no accounting history and so must make these expense accounting decisions for the first time. Assume that the business puts off making these accounting choices until the end of its first year. Everyone is very busy during the year getting the venture off the ground. In addition, waiting until the end of the year gives management and the chief accountant a year to find out more about the operating environment of the business and the kinds of problems the business faces.

The end of the first year of business arrives. One of the things a business does at this time is to prepare a listing of all its accounts, which serves as the main source of information for preparing its financial statements. Table 9-1 presents the accounts of the business at the end of its first year of business. Note that the total of accounts with debit balances equals the total of accounts with credit balances. (Chapter 3 explains all about debits and credits.) Therefore, no bookkeeping errors are present (or, at least, none that would cause these totals to be out of balance).

Table 9-1	Listing of Accounts of the Business at the End of its First Year	
	Debit (£)	Credit (£)
Cash	559,750	
Debtors	645,000	
Allowance for doubtful debts		0
Stock	3,725,000	
Prepaid Expenses	185,000	
Plant and Machinery	1,150,000	
Accumulated depreciation – Plant and Machinery		0
Trade Creditors		309,500
Accrued Expenses Payable		108,500
Bank Overdraft		350,000
Long-term Loans		500,000
Share Capital		1,500,000
Owners' Capital – Retained Earnings		0
Sales Revenue		4,585,000
Cost of Goods Sold	0	
Depreciation Expense	0	
Bad Debts Expense	0	
Selling and General Expenses	1,033,000	
Interest Expense	55,250	
Totals	**7,353,000**	**7,353,000**

At this point, the chief accountant sits down with top management to decide which accounting methods the business should use to record the Cost of Goods Sold expense, depreciation expense and bad debts expense. The financial statements for the first year can't be prepared until these accounting choices are made and the three expenses are recorded.

Q. Review the business's year-end listing of accounts' balances shown in Table 9-1. How can you tell from this listing of accounts that the business hasn't recorded its following three expenses for the year?

- **Bad debts expense:** Caused by uncollectible debtors.

- **Cost of Goods Sold expense:** For the cost of products sold; the revenue from these sales has been recorded in the sales revenue account.

- **Depreciation expense:** For the use of fixed assets (property, plant and machinery, and so on) during the year.

A. Taking the expenses in the order listed:

- The ending balances in the bad debts Expense account and in the allowance for doubtful account are both zero. Therefore, no bad debts expense has been recorded.

- The balance in the Cost of Goods Sold Expense account is zero; also, the balance in the stock account is very large compared with the balance in the sales revenue account. Therefore, no Cost of Goods Sold expense has been recorded.

- The balance in the accumulated depreciation account is zero, and the balance in the depreciation account is zero. Therefore, no depreciation expense has been recorded.

---

1. In Table 9-1, the Owners' Capital – Retained Earnings account has a zero balance. Why?

Solve It

---

2. In Table 9-1, note the Prepaid Expenses Asset account at the end of the year. What are three examples of such prepaid costs? Are the methods for allocating these costs to expenses fairly objective and noncontroversial?

Solve It

---

3. In Table 9-1, note the Accrued Expenses Payable Liability account at the end of the year. What are two or three examples of such accrued costs? Are the methods for allocating these costs to expenses fairly objective and noncontroversial?

Solve It

Cost of Goods Sold Expense Methods

Over the years, the accounting profession hasn't managed to settle on just one method for recording the Cost of Goods Sold expense and stock. Different methods have been permitted for many years. A business is entirely at liberty to choose which-ever method it desires from among the following generally approved methods:

  ✔ **Average cost method:** The costs of different batches of products are averaged to determine the Cost of Goods Sold Expense and ending stock cost.

  ✔ **First-in, first-out (FIFO) method:** The costs of batches are charged to Cost of Goods Sold in the order the batches are acquired, and the cost of ending stock is from the most recent batch(es) acquired.

  ✔ **Last-in, first-out (LIFO) method:** The costs of batches are charged to Cost of Goods Sold in the reverse order that the batches were acquired, and the cost of ending stock is from the oldest batch(es) acquired.

From the listing of accounts in Table 9-1, you can see that the business's stock account has a relatively large balance. Product purchases during the year were debited in this account, but no credits have been made for the Cost of Goods Sold during the year. Clearly, the appropriate amount should be removed from the stock Asset account and charged to the Cost of Goods Sold Expense account.

Q. Suppose that the business makes five purchases during the year. It buys 100,000 units of the one product it sells. Suppose, further, that the cost per unit in all five purchases is the same. In other words, no change exists in the purchase cost per unit during the year. (This scenario is unlikely but provides a good jumping off point for explaining the Cost of Goods Sold expense.) During the year, the business sells 80,000 units of product. The revenue from these sales is £4,585,000 (see the sales revenue account in Table 9-1). What amount of Gross Profit (margin) does the business earn from sales of products during the year?

A. To determine Gross Profit, you must first determine the cost of the 80,000 units sold during the year. In this scenario the purchase cost per unit of the products sold by the business remains constant during the year. So, only one method exists to determine Cost of Goods Sold: 80,000 units sold ÷ 100,000 units purchased × £3,725,000 cost of purchases = £2,980,000 Cost of Goods Sold. In other words, 80 per cent of the goods purchased and available for sale are sold during the year and, therefore, 80 per cent of the total cost of purchases should be charged to Cost of Goods Sold. The following journal entry is made:

	Debit	Credit
Cost of Goods Sold expense	£2,980,000	
Stock		£2,980,000

Therefore, the gross margin for the year is:

Sales revenue	£4,585,000
Cost of Goods Sold expense	£2,980,000
Gross margin	£1,605,000

The cost per unit of products purchased (or manufactured) usually doesn't stay the same from batch to batch; it fluctuates from batch to batch, which creates an accounting problem. We explain in the following three sections the three different methods used to deal with the fluctuation of cost per unit from batch to batch: average cost, FIFO and LIFO.

Table 9-2 presents the history of products purchased by the business during its first year. The business makes five purchases, and the costs per unit (purchase prices) drift upwards from purchase to purchase. The business sells only one product, which minimises the number crunching. (Of course, most businesses sell a variety of products.) We use the information in Table 9-2 to illustrate the three methods of accounting for Cost of Goods Sold and the cost of stock.

Table 9-2	History of Stock Acquisitions During the First Year		
	Quantity (Units)	**Cost Per Unit**	**Total Cost**
First purchase	24,000	£35.40	£849,600
Second purchase	22,500	£35.44	£797,400
Third purchase	20,000	£37.65	£753,000
Fourth purchase	10,000	£38.50	£385,000
Fifth purchase	23,500	£40.00	£940,000
Totals	100,000		£3,725,000

Averaging things out

Many accountants argue that when the acquisition cost per unit fluctuates, the thing to do is to use the average cost of products to determine the Cost of Goods Sold expense. The logic of the average cost method goes like this: five batches of products are purchased at different prices, and so lump together all five purchases and determine the average cost per unit. From the data in Table 9-2, the average cost per unit purchased during the year is calculated as follows:

£3,725,000 total cost of purchases ÷ 100,000 units = £37.25 average cost per unit

The Cost of Goods Sold expense for the products sold during the year is calculated as follows:

80,000 units sold during year × £37.25 average cost per unit = £2,980,000 Cost of Goods Sold expense

Alternatively, if you know that the business sells 80,000 of the 100,000 units available during the year, you can calculate the Cost of Goods Sold expense the following way:

(80,000 ÷ 100,000) × £3,725,000 total cost of purchases = £2,980,000 Cost of Goods Sold expense

Unless you've been asleep at the wheel, you should have noticed that the average cost method gives the same answer for the Cost of Goods Sold expense as in the earlier scenario in which we assume that the purchase cost per unit remains the same during the year. That's the effect of calculating an average. The five different costs per unit amounts (see Table 9-2) are condensed to one average number, as if this number equals the cost per unit during the year.

Using the average cost method, the £37.25 average cost per unit is used for the business's 20,000 units of ending stock (100,000 units acquired – 80,000 units sold):

> 20,000 units of stock × £37.25 average cost per unit = £745,000 cost of ending stock

Summing up, the £3,725,000 total cost of products purchased during the first year of business is divided between £2,980,000 Cost of Goods Sold expense and £745,000 cost of ending stock.

The average cost method isn't as easy to use in practice as this example may suggest. With this method, you face questions such as how often you determine the average cost per unit, and whether you calculate the average just once a year, once each quarter or once each month. Before computers came along, calculating an average cost per unit was a pain in the posterior.

4. During its first year, a business makes seven acquisitions of a product that it sells. Table 9-3 presents the history of these purchases. Compare the purchases history in Table 9-3 with the one in Table 9-2. Does the average cost method make more sense or seem more persuasive in one case over the other?

Solve It

5. Refer to the purchase history in Table 9-3. The bookkeeper says that he used the average cost method. He calculated the average of the seven purchase costs per unit and multiplied this average unit cost by the 158,100 units sold during the year. His average cost per unit is £24.76 (rounded). Is this the correct way to apply the average cost method? If not, what is the correct answer for the Cost of Goods Sold expense for the year?

Solve It

Table 9-3	History of Stock Acquisitions During the First Year		
	Quantity (Units)	*Cost Per Unit*	*Total Cost*
First purchase	14,200	£25.75	£365,650
Second purchase	42,500	£23.85	£1,013,625
Third purchase	16,500	£24.85	£410,025
Fourth purchase	36,500	£23.05	£841,325
Fifth purchase	6,100	£26.15	£159,515
Sixth purchase	52,000	£23.65	£1,229,800
Seventh purchase	18,200	£26.00	£473,200
Totals	186,000		£4,493,140

Going with the flow: The FIFO method

When asked how to calculate Cost of Goods Sold, people working on the receiving and shipping docks of businesses point out that the first goods into stock are the first to be delivered to customers when products are sold. In other words, the sequence follows a first-in, first-out order. Businesses don't buy an initial stock of products, put them away in a dark corner and then take a long time to deliver these products to customers (although wineries may be an exception to this general rule). The first-in, first-out flow of products delivered to customers means that the business's stock of products at the end of the year comes from its most recent purchase(s).

Businesses dealing with perishable goods are the most likely to use the FIFO method. For example, a shop puts all new deliveries of milk to the back of the shelf and sells the 'older' milk first.

Using FIFO, the most recently purchased stock is what still shows in stock. Therefore, the balance sheet shows the value of stock at its closest to current cost. Additionally, where product costs are steadily increasing, a business can sell its lower cost stock first and not have to pass on the increase in price to customers until they start using the higher purchase cost stock. This approach helps to keep selling prices down for a little longer.

The FIFO method of determining the Cost of Goods Sold expense follows the flow of products taken out of stock for delivery to customers. In this example, 80,000 units of product are sold to customers. Table 9-4 shows the calculation of the £2,925,000 total cost assigned to these products by the FIFO method. The first 24,000 units sold are assigned a cost of £35.40 per unit, or £849,600; the next 22,500 units sold are assigned a cost of £35.44 per unit, or £797,400; and so on.

Table 9-4	Cost of Goods Sold Expense Calculation by the FIFO Method		
	Quantity (Units)	*Cost Per Unit*	*Total Cost*
First purchase	24,000	£35.40	£849,600
Second purchase	22,500	£35.44	£797,400
Third purchase	20,000	£37.65	£753,000
Fourth purchase	10,000	£38.50	£385,000
Fifth purchase	3,500	£40.00	£140,000
Totals	80,000		£2,925,000

The entry to record the Cost of Goods Sold expense for the year using the FIFO method is:

	Debit	Credit
Cost of Goods Sold expense	£2,925,000	
Stock		£2,925,000

In internal accounting reports to managers, the accountant presents the cost per unit sold and compares it with the sales price during the year to determine the profit margin per unit. Using the FIFO method, the cost per unit sold is:

£2,925,000 Cost of Goods Sold ÷ 80,000 units sold = £36.5625, or £36.56 rounded cost per unit sold during year

This cost per unit sold doesn't equal any of the five acquisition costs or the average cost per unit purchased during the year, which is £37.25. Business managers are used to dealing with averages, and so this discrepancy shouldn't be a problem – although, whenever dealing with an average, remember to note and take into account how the average is determined.

What about ending stock? By the FIFO method, the cost of ending stock equals the cost of the most recent acquisition(s) – because the cost of earlier acquisitions are charged to the Cost of Goods Sold expense for the year. In the example, £2,925,000 is charged to Cost of Goods Sold, which leaves a remainder of £800,000 in the stock account: £3,725,000 cost of purchases during the year – £2,925,000 to Cost of Goods Sold = £800,000 cost of stock. The cost of ending stock is based on the cost of the last, or fifth, purchase and consists of 20,000 units at £40.00 cost per unit for the total cost of £800,000 (data from Table 9-2). The total quantity of the last (fifth) purchase is 23,500 units (3,500 units are charged to the Cost of Goods Sold expense, and the other 20,000 units remain in ending stock).

---

6. Table 9-3 presents the stock acquisition history of a business for its first year. The business sells 158,100 units during the year. By the FIFO method, determine its Cost of Goods Sold expense for the year and its cost of ending stock.

Solve It

7. In the example shown in Table 9-3, the purchase cost per unit bounces up and down over successive acquisitions, and the quantities purchased each time vary quite a bit. Do these two factors play a role in the choice of a Cost of Goods Sold method?

Solve It

Investigating the LIFO method

The FIFO method (which we discuss in the preceding section) has a lot going for it: it follows the actual sequence of products delivered out of stock to customers and is relatively straightforward to apply. Another method also exists, however, called LIFO (Last-In. First-Out). The method reverses the sequence in which products sold are removed from stock and charged to the Cost of Goods Sold. Essentially, this method assumes that the last items you put on the front of the shelf, are the first ones to sell. This system works well when the items aren't perishable. For example, a hardware shop selling hammers isn't too worried about the order in which the hammers are sold, because they probably all look the same.

When using LIFO, you're assigning the most recent costs of stock to the Cost of Goods Sold calculation. This system is great from a tax point of view, because you're maximising your Costs of Goods Sold and effectively minimising the taxable profit. However, the stock value in your balance sheet is reflected at the initial stock purchase costs, which may not necessarily reflect the current costs of replacing that stock.

Table 9-5 shows how the LIFO method calculates the cost of 80,000 units sold. In accordance with the reverse sequence basis of LIFO, the purchases batches are listed in reverse chronological order. The logic behind the LIFO method is that products sold must be replaced in order to stay in business. The closest approximations to replacement costs are the costs of the most recent purchases.

Table 9-5	Cost of Goods Sold Expense Calculation by the LIFO Method		
	Quantity (Units)	*Cost Per Unit*	*Total Cost*
Fifth purchase	23,500	£40.00	£940,000
Fourth purchase	10,000	£38.50	£385,000
Third purchase	20,000	£37.65	£753,000
Second purchase	22,500	£35.44	£797,400
First purchase	4,000	£35.40	£141,600
Totals	80,000		£3,017,000

The entry to record Cost of Goods Sold expense for the year using the LIFO method is:

	Debit	Credit
Cost of Goods Sold expense	£3,017,000	
Stock		£3,017,000

Using the LIFO method in internal reports to managers, the cost per unit sold for the year is:

£3,017,000 Cost of Goods Sold ÷ 80,000 units sold = £37.7125, or £37.71 rounded cost per unit sold during year

As with the FIFO method, the LIFO average cost per unit sold doesn't equal any of the five acquisition costs or the average cost per unit purchased during the year, which is £37.25. Averages and discrepancies like this one shouldn't be a problem for business managers; whenever dealing with an average, however, bear in mind how the average is determined and take that information into account.

What about ending stock? The cost of ending stock by the LIFO method depends on whether the business increases the number of products held in stock during the year.

Assume that the business does in fact increase its quantity of stock (acquiring more units than it sells during the year). In this case, the cost of ending stock equals the cost of its beginning stock and the cost of the additional units, which is based on the per unit costs from the earliest acquisitions during the year. On the other hand, when a business decreases its stock during the year its ending stock cost is based on the cost(s) per unit in its beginning stock.

In the example, the cost of ending stock is £708,000: £3,725,000 cost of purchases during the year – £3,017,000 to Cost of Goods Sold = £708,000 cost of stock. In other words, the cost of its ending stock comes from the oldest purchase and consists of 20,000 units at £35.40 cost per unit for a total cost of £708,000.

In this example, the ending balance sheet reports stock at £708,000 cost value by the LIFO method versus £800,000 cost value by the FIFO method, which is a fairly sizable difference. FIFO gives a more up-to-date stock cost in the balance sheet. But, nevertheless, many businesses use LIFO because it minimises taxable income and thus their tax liability overall.

Whether using LIFO to try and minimise your tax liability is right or not is open to question, but all businesses have to come to their own decisions on what stock valuation method is right for them. This choice may be easy depending on the type of stock they carry – for example, perishable goods need to be valued on a FIFO basis and LIFO would be totally inappropriate.

Assume that a business has been using LIFO for 40 years. Therefore, some part of its stock cost goes back to costs it paid 40 years ago. If the difference between the current cost value of stock (as measured by FIFO) and the LIFO cost is significant, the business discloses this discrepancy in a footnote to its financial statements.

8. Table 9-3 presents the stock acquisition history of a business for its first year. The business sells 158,100 units during the year. By the LIFO method, determine its Cost of Goods Sold expense for the year and its cost of ending stock.

Solve It

9. Suppose the business whose stock acquisition history appears in Table 9-3 sells all 186,000 units that it has available for sale during the year. In this situation, does the business's choice of Cost of Goods Sold expense method make any difference?

Solve It

Appreciating Depreciation Methods

The basic theory of depreciation accounting is unarguable: the cost of each fixed asset is divided over the assets estimated useful life to the business. In other words, instead of having a huge lump sum expense in the year that the asset is purchased, you charge a percentage of the cost each year, spread over the useful life of each asset.

A fixed asset's cost shouldn't be charged entirely to expenses in the year in which the asset's acquired. Doing so heavily penalises the year of acquisition and relieves future years from any share of the cost. But the opposite approach is equally bad: the business shouldn't wait until a fixed asset is eventually disposed of to record the expense of using the asset. Doing so heavily penalises the final year and relieves earlier years from any share of the fixed asset's cost.

You can choose from at least two depreciation methods (we talk more about these options in the next section, 'Evaluating your depreciation options'), but which one do you choose? What rate of depreciation should you use? How do you determine the estimated useful life of your asset? The subject is a bit of a minefield, but you need to determine a depreciation policy and then stick to it.

HM Revenue and Customs (HMRC) refers to SSAP 12 (an old accounting standard for depreciation) as being the appropriate reference for depreciation methods. In 2000, SSAP12 was replaced with FRS (Financial Reporting Standard) 15. The principles contained within SSAP 12 are however maintained within FRS 15 with no major changes.

The government also has a hand in the rules surrounding capital spending by businesses. If it wants to stimulate capital expenditure, the government can do so by varying 'writing down allowances', which is technical speak for tax relief on the depreciation expense. It sometimes sets 100 per cent writing down allowance on the first year's life of certain assets (computers are a favourite one!). You need to speak to your friendly tax accountant to get advice in this area.

Evaluating your depreciation options

When calculating your depreciation for the year, you have a choice of two methods. You can split the cost of the asset evenly over its useful life (straight line depreciation) or choose to depreciate a higher amount each month at the start of an asset's useful life and gradually reduce the amount of depreciation as the asset gets older (the reducing balance method). Both methods are suitable in the eyes of HMRC, as long as you stick with the same method each year.

Using the straight line depreciation method

You need to know the estimated useful life and the cost of the asset before you can calculate the annual depreciation using this method as follows:

Cost of fixed asset ÷ estimated useful life = annual depreciation expense

John buys a piece of machinery that he estimates will have a useful life of ten years. The asset costs £100,000 and he plans to depreciate using the straight line method:

£100,000 ÷ 10 years = £10,000 annual depreciation expense

Using the reducing balance method

The reducing balance method is the closest to matching the HMRC method of calculating capital allowances, which is their version of depreciation.

You're not allowed to treat the depreciation expense as a taxable expense. Instead you have to add back depreciation to your taxable profit and deduct capital allowances.

The peculiarity with the reducing balance method is that the annual depreciation expense varies, and in theory the asset is never fully depreciated. Each year, depreciation is calculated by applying the appropriate depreciation rate to the net book value (balance) of the asset. Effectively you're taking the previous years value and deducting the current year depreciation value to create the new brought forward figure. As time passes, the annual depreciation figure gets smaller and smaller and the brought forward balance also gets gradually smaller – but the item never fully depreciates.

Stephanie buys a business van for £16,000, which she decides to depreciate at 25 per cent using the reducing balance method (see Table 9-6).

Table 9-6		Reducing Balance Depreciation Costs Per Annum	
	Asset Cost	Annual Depreciation @ 25 per cent	Net Book Value or Balance
	A	B	
Year 1	£16,000	£4,000	£12,000 (A minus B)
Year 2		£3,000	£9,000
Year 3		£2,250	£6,750
Year 4		£1,687.50	£5,062.50
Year 5		£1,265.63	£3,796.88

This method of depreciation carries on ad infinitum. You can see that the actual amount of depreciation expense reduces as time goes by.

The net book value of an asset is the cost of the asset minus the accumulated depreciation, as shown in Table 9-6.

Table 9-1 shows the accounts of a business at the end of its first year of operations. No depreciation expense for the year has been recorded yet, but obviously some amount of depreciation must be recorded. The business purchases all its fixed assets during the first week of the year and the assets are placed in service immediately; therefore, the business is entitled to record a full year's depreciation on its fixed assets. (Special partial-year rules apply when assets are placed in service at other times during the year.)

The business has the following list of fixed assets:

Buildings	£250,000
Land	£150,000
Plant and Machinery	£500,000
Motor Vehicles	£150,000
Total	£1,050,000

The cost of land and buildings is not depreciated. Land stays on the books at original cost as long as the business owns the land. Ownership of land is a right in perpetuity, which doesn't come to an end; land doesn't wear out in the physical sense and generally holds its economic value over time. Buildings, machines and other fixed assets, on the other hand, wear out with use over time and generally reach a point where they have no economic value.

10. Using the fixed asset list, determine the annual depreciation expense for Plant and Machinery if the business adopts the straight line method of depreciation. Assume that the estimated useful life of the asset is five years.

Solve It

11. Using the fixed asset list, calculate the depreciation expense for years 1–4 for Motor Vehicles. Please use the reducing balance method and a depreciation rate of 25 per cent.

Solve It

Timing Bad Debts Expense

Retailers have to live with some amount of shoplifting losses, despite their best efforts to prevent it. Similarly, businesses that extend credit to their customers and make loans have to live with some amount of bad debts expense, despite their best efforts to screen customers and collect overdue debts. Bad debts is the general term for these uncollectible receivables.

A business has two options for how it records its bad debts expense:

- **Specific write-off method:** No entry is made for bad debts expense until specific debtors are actually written-off as uncollectible. A debt isn't written-off until every conceivable collection effort has been made and the debt has been discharged through bankruptcy proceedings or until the customer (or other debtor) vanishes and can't be traced. One disadvantage of this method is that the debtors asset may be overstated because specific accounts haven't as yet been identified as uncollectible that will prove to be uncollectible in the future.

- **Allowance method:** Based on its collection experience with its credit customers (and other debtors), a business records bad debts expense before individual, specific debts are identified as being uncollectible. The business estimates its bad debts expense, before all the facts are in regarding which particular debtors have to be written-off as uncollectible. This method is more conservative than the specific write-off method because the bad debts expense is recorded sooner. One disadvantage is that the future amount of bad debts (debtors that will eventually be written-off) has to be estimated.

From the data in Table 9-1, you can see that the business's debtors balance is £645,000 at year-end. The business hasn't loaned money to employees, officers or suppliers. (Non-customer loans are recorded in other accounts, such as loans to officers.) The business didn't write-off any debtors during the year; however, at year-end, the amounts owed to the business by a few customers are several months overdue. The business shuts off credit to these customers and sends them overdue debt letters. The customers assure the business that they are going to pay but just need more time.

The business has done everything to get the customers to pay up, short of bringing legal action. As far as the business knows, none of these customers have declared bankruptcy, but the business has heard a rumour that one customer contacted a lawyer about bankruptcy. The total amount overdue from these deadbeat customers is £18,500, and the business is of the opinion that this amount won't be collected.

In addition, some other customers are two or three months overdue in paying their accounts. The business understands that some of these debts may end up being uncollectible but is still hopeful that these overdue accounts can be collected in full.

Q. Given the preceding background information, work out how much bad debts expense the business should record at the end of its first year according to:

a. The *specific write-off method* for bad debts expense.

b. The *allowance method* for bad debts expense (see information below for this part of the question).

A. Frankly, coming up with a bad debts expense amount for the year under either of these methods is somewhat arbitrary. Only time will tell exactly how much of the total £645,000 debtors won't be collected.

a. The £18,500 seriously overdue amount of debtors is written-off by the specific write-off method for recording bad debts expense. The entry is as follows:

	Debit	Credit
Bad Debts Expense	£18,500	
Debtors		£18,500

The specific debtors making up this £18,500 have been identified. Considering that the business has identified specific customers and made reasonable efforts to collect the amounts owed, the debts should be written-off and charged to bad debts expense. This amount of expense is allowed for tax purposes.

After making this write-off entry, the debtors balance is £626,500 (£645,000 balance before write-off – £18,500 write-off = £626,500 adjusted debtors balance). Some of this total amount of debtors is likely to turn out to be uncollectible. But the specific write-off method doesn't record these future write-offs at this time. The bad debts expense for the first year is £18,500 and the debtors balance reported in its year-end balance sheet is £626,500.

b. Using the allowance method for recording the bad debts expense, an additional amount of bad debts expense is recorded for the yet-to-be identified uncollectible receivables. Of course, the accountant has to estimate the amount of future write-offs. (The argument is that some estimate is better than none.) Suppose that a conservative estimate of these additional bad debts is £20,000. However, specific customers' accounts haven't been identified for this estimated bad debts amount.

During the year, £18,500 has already been recorded in the bad debts Expense account. As the specific debtors were identified as uncollectible during the year the business had no option but to write-off the debts and record the bad debts expense. Using the allowance method, the accountant makes the following additional entry at the end of the year, which increases the bad debts Expense account:

	Debit	Credit
Bad Debts Expense	£20,000	
Allowance for Doubtful Accounts		£20,000

The Allowance for Doubtful Accounts account is the contra account to the debtors Asset account. Its balance is deducted from the Asset account's balance in the balance sheet. After giving effect to this year-end entry, the business's bad debts expense for the year is £38,500 (£18,500 actually written-off during the year + £20,000 estimated uncollectible debtors to be written-off in the future). In its year-end balance sheet, the business reports debtors at £626,500 and the £20,000 balance in the allowance for doubtful account is deducted from debtors. So, the net amount of debtors in its ending balance sheet is £606,500.

12. The chief accountant of the business outlined in the example question argues that a customer's debtors should be written-off as uncollectible when it becomes more than 30 days old. The normal credit term that the business offers to customers is 30 days. At the end of its first year, £278,400 of the business's £645,000 debtors is more than 30 days old. What bad debts expense entry would the chief accountant make at the end of the year if he has his way? Do you agree with his approach?

Solve It

13. The Managing Director of the business outlined in the example question (Table 9-1) attends an industry update seminar at which the speaker says that the average bad debts experience of businesses in this field is about 1 per cent of sales. Assume that the business adopts this method. Determine its bad debts expense for the first year and for the balances in its debtors and allowance for doubtful accounts at the end of the year.

Solve It

Answers to Problems on Choosing Accounting Methods

Here are the answers to the questions presented earlier in this chapter.

1 In Table 9-1, the Owners' Capital – Retained Earnings account has a zero balance. Why?

The final entry of the year is the closing entry in which the net profit or loss for the year is entered into the retained earnings account. The closing entry isn't made until all expenses for the year are recorded. Because the business has just concluded its first year, its retained earnings account had a zero balance at the start of the year. The closing entry to transfer net profit or loss for the year into the account hasn't been made, and so retained earnings still has a zero balance. After the accountant records net profit or loss into retained earnings, the account does have a balance, of course.

2 In Table 9-1, note the Prepaid Expenses Asset account at the end of the year. What are three examples of such prepaid costs? Are the methods for allocating these costs to expenses fairly objective and noncontroversial?

Three examples of prepaid expenses are:

 ✔ **Insurance premiums:** Paid in advance of the insurance coverage. When the premium is paid, the amount is recorded in the prepaid expenses Asset account and then the cost is allocated to each month of insurance coverage.

 ✔ **Advertising campaigns:** Often an invoice is sent through for the following years advertising costs (for example, radio advertising). The cost of the advertising is recorded in the prepaid expenses Asset account and then allocated to advertising as an expense on a monthly basis.

 ✔ **Subscriptions: Often** paid at the beginning of the year but relate to the whole year. When the subscription is paid, the amount is recorded in the prepaid expenses Asset account and then the cost is allocated across each month that the subscription covers.

Generally speaking, the allocation of these and other prepaid expenses is objective and noncontroversial. Different accountants use the same allocation methods. However, most businesses don't bother to record relatively minor prepaid costs in the Asset account and instead record the costs immediately as expenses.

3 In Table 9-1, note the Accrued Expenses Payable Liability account at the end of the year. What are three examples of such accrued costs? Are the methods for allocating these costs to expense fairly objective and noncontroversial?

Three examples of accrued costs are:

 ✔ **Holiday and sick pay:** Businesses should accrue the costs of holiday and sick pay that are 'earned' by their employees each pay period. (We stress the word 'earned' because the actual accumulation of these employee benefits may not be clear-cut and definite. If a business has a collective bargaining contract with its employees these benefits usually are well-defined.)

 ✔ **Operating expenses: Businesses may have incurred certain costs for which an invoice hasn't been received yet. They should record that liability by debiting the Expense account and crediting the Accrual account. When the invoice has been received, the accrual can be reversed.**

 ✔ **PAYE/NI tax:** Businesses normally pay across the tax and national insurance deducted from the payroll the month following the date of the payroll. Therefore, seeing one month of PAYE/NI sitting in the balance sheet as unpaid is quite normal.

The accrual of these and other costs isn't cut and dried and tends to be somewhat controversial. The allocation of accrued costs has many shades of grey – no 'bright' lines delineate which particular costs should be accrued and which ones don't have to be.

4 During its first year, a business makes seven acquisitions of a product that it sells. Table 9-3 presents the history of these purchases. Compare the purchases history in Table 9-3 with the one in Table 9-2. Does the average cost method make more sense or seem more persuasive in one case over the other?

This question is a hard one to answer, to be frank, because the appropriateness of the average cost method depends on how you look at it. You can argue that you have a little more reason to use the average cost method in the Table 9-3 scenario, because the purchase price bounces up and down; whereas in the Table 9-2 scenario, the purchase prices are on an upward trend. But, by and large, accountants don't consider whether prices fluctuate up and down or are on a steady up escalator when making the decision to use the average cost method. Accountants like the 'leveling out' effect of the average cost method, and therefore often prefer it.

5 Refer to the purchase history in Table 9-3. The bookkeeper says that he used the average cost method. He calculated the average of the seven purchase costs per unit and multiplied this average unit cost by the 158,100 units sold during the year. His average cost per unit is £24.76 (rounded). Is this the correct way to apply the average cost method? If not, what is the correct answer for Cost of Goods Sold expense for the year?

The bookkeeper made a mistake, because the average cost method doesn't use the simple average of purchases prices. The average cost method uses the *weighted* average of acquisition prices, which means that each purchase price is weighted by the quantity bought at that price. In the Table 9-3 scenario, the £26.15 purchase price carries much less weight because only 6,100 units are bought at this price. The £23.05 purchase price carries more weight because 36,500 units are bought at this price.

The correct average cost per unit is calculated as follows:

(£4,493,140 total cost of purchases ÷ 186,000 units purchased) = £24.1567, or £24.16 rounded

Therefore, the correct Cost of Goods Sold expense for the period is £3,819,169. You can calculate this amount by multiplying the exact average cost per unit by the 158,100 units sold, or you can calculate it as follows:

(158,100 units sold ÷ 186,000 units available for sale) × £4,493,140 total cost of goods available for sale = £3,819,169 Cost of Goods Sold expense

6 Table 9-3 presents the stock acquisition history of a business for its first year. The business sells 158,100 units during the year. By the FIFO method, determine its Cost of Goods Sold expense for the year and its cost of ending stock.

The Cost of Goods Sold expense by the FIFO method is determined as follows:

Cost of Goods Sold Expense Calculation by the FIFO Method

	Quantity (Units)	Cost Per Unit	Total Cost
First purchase	14,200	£25.75	£365,650
Second purchase	42,500	£23.85	£1,013,625
Third purchase	16,500	£24.85	£410,025
Fourth purchase	36,500	£23.05	£841,325
Fifth purchase	6,100	£26.15	£159,515
Sixth purchase	42,300	£23.65	£1,000,395
Totals	158,100		£3,790,535

The cost of ending stock includes some units from the sixth purchase and all units from the seventh purchase, which is summarised in the following schedule:

	Quantity (Units)	Cost Per Unit	Total Cost
Sixth purchase	9,700	£23.65	£229,405
Seventh purchase	18,200	£26.00	£473,200
Totals	27,900		£702,605

7 In the example shown in Table 9-3, the purchase cost per unit bounces up and down over successive acquisitions, and the quantities purchased each time vary quite a bit. Do these two factors play a role in the choice of a Cost of Goods Sold method?

Generally speaking, the volatility of acquisition costs per unit isn't a critical factor when choosing a Cost of Goods Sold expense method, nor is the variation in acquisition quantities. The reasons for selecting one method over another don't depend on these two factors.

8 Table 9-3 presents the stock acquisition history of a business for its first year. The business sells 158,100 units during the year. By the LIFO method, determine its Cost of Goods Sold expense for the year and its cost of ending stock.

The Cost of Goods Sold expense as determined by the LIFO is as follows:

Cost of Goods Sold Expense Calculation by the LIFO Method

	Quantity (Units)	Cost Per Unit	Total Cost
Seventh purchase	18,200	£26.00	£473,200
Sixth purchase	52,000	£23.65	£1,229,800
Fifth purchase	6,100	£26.15	£159,515
Fourth purchase	36,500	£23.05	£841,325
Third purchase	16,500	£24.85	£410,025
Second purchase	28,800	£23.85	£686,880
Totals	158,100		£3,800,745

The cost of ending stock includes all the units from the first purchase and some from the second purchase, which is summarised as follows:

	Quantity (Units)	Cost Per Unit	Total Cost
Sixth purchase	13,700	£23.85	£326,745
Seventh purchase	14,200	£25.75	£365,650
Totals	27,900		£692,395

9 Suppose that the business whose stock acquisition history appears in Table 9-3 sells all 186,000 units that it has available for sale during the year. In this situation, does the business's choice of Cost of Goods Sold expense method make any difference?

No, all three methods (average cost, FIFO and LIFO) give the same result. The £4,493,140 total purchase cost of the 186,000 units would be charged to the Cost of Goods Sold expense.

10 Using the fixed asset list, determine the annual depreciation expense for Plant and Machinery if the business adopts the straight line method of depreciation. Assume that the estimated useful life of the asset is five years.

Plant and Machinery cost = £500,000

Depreciation rate per annum = £500,000 ÷ 5 = £100,000

Thus the annual depreciation rate is £100,000.

11 Using the fixed asset list, calculate the depreciation expense for years 1–4 for Motor Vehicles. Please use the reducing balance method and a depreciation rate of 25 per cent.

Reducing Balance depreciation costs per annum		
Asset Cost *A*	*Annual Depreciation @ 25 per cent* *B*	*Net Book Value* *Or* *Balance*
Year 1 £150,000	£37,500	£112,500 (A minus B)
Year 2	£28,125	£84,375
Year 3	£21,093.75	£63,281.25
Year 4	£15,820.31	£47,460.94

This method of depreciation carries on ad infinitum. You can see that the actual amount of depreciation expense is reducing year on year.

12 The chief accountant of the business outlined in the example question argues that a customer's debtors should be written-off as uncollectible when it becomes more than 30 days old. The normal credit term that the business offers to customers is 30 days. At the end of its first year, £278,400 of the business's £645,000 debtors is more than 30 days old. What bad debts expense entry would the chief accountant make at the end of the year if he has his way? Do you agree with his approach?

If the chief accountant has his way, he would make the following entry:

	Debit	Credit
Bad Debts Expense	£278,400	
Debtors		£278,400

We certainly don't agree with writing-off such a large amount of debtors. In the real world of business, many customers don't pay on time; indeed, late payment by some customers is expected any time credit's extended. The business would like to receive all payments for its credit sales on time, of course, but it knows that many of its customers probably don't make their payments within 30 days. The chief accountant needs to get real and understand that many customers slip beyond the 30-day credit period, but eventually pay for their purchases.

13 The Managing Director of the business outlined in the example question (Table 9-1) attends an industry update seminar at which the speaker says that the average bad debts experience of businesses in this field is about 1 per cent of sales. Assume that the business adopts this method. Determine its bad debts expense for the first year and for the balances in its debtors and allowance for doubtful accounts at the end of the year.

To record bad debts expense equal to 1 per cent of total sales for year, the year-end adjusting entry is as follows:

	Debit	Credit
Bad Debts Expense	£45,850	
Allowance for Doubtful Accounts		£45,850

The business also records the write-off of specific customers' accounts that have been identified as uncollectible. The write-off entry is as follows:

	Debit	Credit
Allowance for Doubtful Accounts	£18,500	
Debtors		£18,500

Based on the information provided in the example, using 1 per cent of sales to estimate bad debts expense seems too high for this particular business.

Part III
Managerial, Manufacturing and Capital Accounting

'Look, Mr Brinkley, you don't fool me —
you don't have a proper accountant in
this company do you?'

In this part . . .

The first chapter in this part explains the accountant's essential role in helping business managers do their jobs well. In broad terms, managers need financial information for planning, control and decision-making. Accountants need to develop profit analysis models that managers can use efficiently – so they make optimal decisions based on the key factors that drive profit.

For manufacturing businesses, accountants have the additional function of determining the product cost of the goods produced by the business. In Chapter 11, we explain manufacturing cost accounting fundamentals. The chapter explains the importance of calculating the burden rate for indirect fixed manufacturing overhead costs that's included in product cost, and how production output (not just sales) affects profit for the period.

Chapter 12 explains nominal and effective interest rates, how compounding works both for and against you, and return on investment (ROI) measures. At their core, interest and investment ratios are based on accounting methods.

Chapter 10

Analysing Profit Behaviour

*B*usiness managers need to possess a sure analytical grip on the fundamental factors that drive profit. And because profit is an *accounting* measure, chief accountants should help the business's managers understand and analyse profit performance. The trick is not to overload managers with so much detail that they can't see the forest for the trees.

Now, don't get us wrong. Detail is necessary for management control; managers need to keep their eyes on a thousand and one details, any one of which can spin out of control and cause serious damage to profit performance. But too much detail is the enemy of profit analysis for planning and decision-making. Management decision-making, in contrast, needs condensed and global information presented in a compact package that managers can get their heads around without getting sidetracked by too many details.

You can do the profit analysis methods that we discuss in this chapter on the back of an envelope. All you need for the number-crunching is a basic handheld calculator. More elaborate and detail-rich profit analysis methods need to be done on computers. These sophisticated profit analysis methods have their place, but before they delve into technical profit analysis, managers should be absolutely clear on the fundamental factors that determine profit. The idea is to make sure that they know how to read the dashboard before going under the bonnet and taking apart the engine.

This chapter tackles three main questions:

✔ How does the business make its profit?

✔ How can the business improve its profit performance?

✔ How do unfavourable changes affect the business's profit performance?

Mapping Profit for Managers

Table 10-1 lays out an internal profit (P&L) report for the business's managers. The revenue and expense information is for the most recent year of a business that we call Firm A. (We introduce two other business examples later in this chapter and call them Firm B and Firm C.) An internal profit report should serve as a profit map that shows managers how to get to their profit destination. The profit report in Table 10-1 is very condensed; it's stripped down to bare essentials. The report includes the five fundamental factors that drive profit performance:

- ✔ **Sales volume**, or the total number of units sold during the period.
- ✔ **Sales revenue per unit** (sales price).
- ✔ **Cost of Goods Sold expense per unit** (product cost).
- ✔ **Variable operating expenses per unit.**
- ✔ **Fixed operating expenses** for the period.

The other sterling amounts in the profit report shown in Table 10-1 depend on these five profit drivers. For instance, the £24,000,000 sales revenue amount equals the w120,000 units sales volume times the £200 sales revenue per unit (or sales price). And, the £25 fixed operating expenses per unit amount equals the £3,000,000 total fixed operating expenses for the period divided by the 120,000 units sales volume.

Table 10-1   Internal Profit and Loss Report Highlighting Profit Drivers

	Firm A	
	Totals	*Per Unit*
Sales volume (units)	120,000	
Sales revenue	£24,000,000	£200.00
Cost of Goods Sold expense	£15,600,000	£130.00
Gross Margin	£8,400,000	£70.00
Variable operating expenses	£3,600,000	£30.00
Contribution Margin	£4,800,000	£40.00
Fixed operating expenses	£3,000,000	£25.00
Operating Profit	£1,800,000	£15.00

Don't confuse the internal profit report presented in Table 10-1 with the Profit and Loss statement in the external financial reports that a business distributes to its owners and creditors. (We discuss externally reported financial statements in Chapters 5, 6 and 8.) The internal profit report includes sales volume and per unit values, which aren't disclosed in externally reported Profit and Loss statements. Also, the internal profit report separates operating expenses into variable and fixed categories, which isn't done in externally reported Profit and Loss statements.

The last line in Table 10-1 is operating profit, which is profit before interest and income tax. Interest and income tax are deducted to reach a business's final, bottom-line net income. (Income tax is a very technical topic, about which generalising is difficult.)

Standard terminology doesn't exist in the area of management profit reporting and analysis. Instead of gross margin, you may see Gross Profit. Instead of operating profit, you may see operating earnings or earnings before interest and income tax (EBIT). You may even see other terms, too. Despite the diversity of terminology, in the context of a profit report, the meanings of the terms used are usually clear enough.

Before using the five profit factors for analysing profit performance, a good thing to do is to 'walk down the profit ladder' in the internal profit report (see Table 10-1). The top rung of the ladder is sales revenue, which equals sales price times sales volume. You can think of sales revenue as profit before any expenses are deducted.

If the business sells products, the first expense deducted against sales revenue is Cost of Goods Sold, which equals product cost (Cost of Goods Sold expense per unit) times sales volume. (Chapter 9 explains the different accounting methods for recording this expense.) Deducting Cost of Goods Sold from sales revenue gives you gross margin. Managers keep a close watch on the gross margin ratio, which for Firm A equals 35 per cent (£70 gross margin per unit ÷ £200 sales price = 35 per cent gross margin ratio). Even a relatively small shift in this ratio can have huge impacts on profit.

Virtually all businesses have variable operating expenses, which are costs that move in tandem with changes in sales revenue. One example of a variable expense is the commissions paid to salespeople, which typically are a certain percentage of sales revenue. Other examples of variable expenses that fluctuate with sales are delivery expenses and bad debts from credit sales. Total variable operating expenses equal variable operating expenses per unit times sales volume. Deducting variable operating expenses from gross margin produces contribution margin, or profit before fixed operating expenses are considered.

Businesses commit to a certain level of fixed operating expenses for the year. Examples of fixed expenses are employees on fixed salaries, insurance, depreciation, legal and accounting, and so on. In the short run, fixed costs behave like the term implies – they're relatively fixed and constant in amount regardless of whether sales are high or low. Fixed costs aren't sensitive to fluctuations in sales over the short term. Firm A's £3,000,000 fixed operating expenses for the period are divided by its 120,000 units sales volume to determine the £25 fixed operating expenses per unit in Table 10-1.

The final step in the walk down the profit ladder is deducting fixed operating expenses from contribution margin. The remainder is the business's operating profit for the year. The business earns £1,800,000 operating profit for the year, which is 7.5 per cent of its sales revenue for the year. Internal operating profit (P&L) reports often include ratios (percentages) for each line item based on sales revenue, so that managers can track changes in these important ratios period to period.

Q. Refer to the Firm A example presented in Table 10-1. Purely hypothetically, suppose that the business has a choice of selling 5 per cent more sales volume or selling the same sales volume at a 5 per cent higher sales price. Assume that other profit factors remain the same. Which change – the 5 per cent higher sales volume or the 5 per cent higher sales price – would be better for operating profit?

A. Well, 5 per cent additional sales volume means that the business would sell 6,000 more units than in the Table 10-1 scenario: 120,000 units sales volume in Table 10-1 × 5 per cent = 6,000 additional units. Each additional unit sold earns £40 contribution margin per unit (see Table 10-1). So, total contribution margin would be £240,000 higher. The business's fixed operating expenses wouldn't increase with such a relatively small increase in sales volume. Therefore, its operating profit would be £240,000 higher. Would the sales price increase be any better? You bet it would!

A 5 per cent jump means sales price would be £10 per unit higher: £200 sales price in Table 10-1 × 5 per cent = £10 increase in sales price. This jump would increase the contribution margin per unit from £40 (see Table 10-1) to £50. Therefore, the business's total contribution margin would be £6,000,000: £50 contribution per unit × 120,000 units sales volume = £6,000,000 contribution margin. This amount is an increase of £1,200,000 over the contribution margin in the Table 10-1 scenario. We have no reason to think that fixed operating expenses would be any different at the higher sales price, and so operating profit would increase £1,200,000.

In short, the 5 per cent gain in sales price would be much better for operating profit, compared with the 5 per cent step up in sales volume.

2. Using the data presented in Table 10-1, suppose that the business has a choice of selling 10 per cent more sales volume or keeping the sales volume at the same level and increasing the selling price by 10 per cent. Assuming all other profit factors remain the same, which change (the higher sales volume or the increased sales price) would be better for operating profit?

Solve It

Analysing Operating Profit

An internal profit report like the one in Table 10-1 is prepared according to the standard accounting approach, which reports totals for sales revenue and expenses for the period and which starts with sales revenue and works its way down to bottom line profit (operating profit in the Table 10-1 example). Nothing's wrong with this sort of report, but an accounting profit report isn't the best format for the efficient analysis of profit behaviour.

Busy business managers can analyse the profit performance of their business more efficiently using compact profit models based on the five fundamental profit drivers. Different analysis methods are available, each having certain advantages. Managers are best advised to be familiar with the following two profit analysis methods:

- Contribution margin minus fixed costs method
- Excess over breakeven method

Analysis method #1: Contribution margin minus fixed costs

The basis of this method is that fixed costs have a first claim on contribution margin, and what's left over is operating profit. This method starts with contribution margin per unit, which is the catalyst of profit. To make profit, the business has to have an adequate margin per unit. The second step of this method is to multiply contribution margin per unit by sales volume. Earning a margin on each unit sold doesn't help much if a business doesn't sell many units. (Which reminds us of the old joke: 'A business loses a little on each sale, but makes it up on volume.')

Using this method, Firm A's profit for the year is analysed as follows:

Analysis method #1: Contribution margin minus fixed costs (see Table 10-1 for data)

Contribution margin per unit	$40
Times annual sales volume, in units	120,000
Equals total contribution margin	4,800,000
Less fixed operating expenses	3,000,000
Equals operating profit	$1,800,000

Analysis method #2: Excess over breakeven

The thinking behind this method is that a business has to recover its fixed costs first by selling enough units before it starts making profit.

This profit analysis technique pivots on the breakeven volume of the business, which you calculate as follows for Firm A (see Table 10-1 for data):

£3,000,000 annual fixed operating expenses ÷ £40 contribution margin per unit = 75,000 units breakeven point (volume)

Every additional unit sold over the breakeven volume brings in marginal profit (also referred to as incremental profit.) The underlying theme of this method is that after you sell enough units to recoup your fixed operating expenses for the year, you're 'home free' as it were. (Of course, you can't forget about interest expense and income tax.)

Using this method, Firm A's profit for the year is analysed as follows:

Analysis method #2: Excess over breakeven (see Table 10-1 for data)

Annual sales volume for year, in units	120,000
Less annual breakeven volume, in units	75,000
Equals excess over breakeven, in units	45,000
Times contribution margin per unit	£40
Equals operating profit	£1,800,000

Q. Suppose that Firm A sells 125,000 units during the year, instead of the 120,000 units in the Table 10-1 scenario. Using both of the analysis methods just explained, determine Firm A's operating profit at the 125,000 units sales volume level. Assume that other profit factors remain the same.

A. The operating profit of Firm A is analysed for this scenario according to the two methods of profit analysis.

Analysis method #1: Contribution margin minus fixed costs (see Table 10-1 for data)

Contribution margin per unit	£40
Times annual sales volume, in units	125,000
Equals total contribution margin	£5,000,000
Less fixed operating expenses	£3,000,000
Equals operating profit	£2,000,000

Analysis method #2: Excess over breakeven (see Table 10-1 for data)

Annual sales volume for year, in units	125,000
Less annual breakeven volume, in units	75,000
Equals excess over breakeven, in units	50,000
Times contribution margin per unit	£40
Equals operating profit	£2,000,000

2. One of Firm A's marketing managers is overheard to comment, 'If we had sold 10 per cent more units than we did in the year, our profit would have been 10 per cent higher'. Do you agree with this comment? (Table 10-1 presents Firm A's operating profit report for the year.)

Solve It

3. Instead of the scenario shown in Table 10-1, assume that Firm A has a bad year. Its internal operating profit report for this alternative scenario is presented below. Using the two methods explained in this section, analyse why the business suffers a loss for the year.

	Totals	*Per Unit*
Sales Volume (units)	120,000	
Sales Revenue	£21,000,000	£175.00
Cost of Goods Sold expense	£15,600,000	£130.00
Gross Margin	£5,400,000	£45.00
Variable operating expenses	£3,150,000	£26.25
Contribution Margin	£2,250,000	£18.75
Fixed Operating expenses	£3,000,000	£25.00
Operating loss	(£750,000)	(£6.25)

Solve It

4. Table 10-2 presents profit performance information for two businesses for their most recent years. Using the two profit analysis methods explained in this section, analyse the profit performance of Firm B. (You may note that both businesses in Table 10-2 earn exactly the same amount of operating profit as in the earlier Firm A business example, for which we explain two profit analysis methods. This similarity allows you to compare the key differences between businesses that earn the same profit.)

Table 10-2	Internal Profit and Loss Report Highlighting Profit Drivers				
	Firm B			Firm C	
	Totals	Per Unit		Totals	Per Unit
Sales volume (units)	50,000			1,500,000	
Sales revenue	£15,000,000	£300.00		£36,000,000	£24.00
Cost of Goods Sold expense	£7,500,000	£150.00		£27,000,000	£18.00
Gross Margin	£7,500,000	£150.00		£9,000,000	£6.00
Variable operating expenses	£3,750,000	£75.00		£4,200,000	£2.80
Contribution Margin	£3,750,000	£75.00		£4,800,000	£3.20
Fixed Operating expenses	£1,950,000	£39.00		£3,000,000	£2.00
Operating Profit	£1,800,000	£36.00		£1,800,000	£1.20

Solve It

5. Please refer to Table 10-2. Using the two profit analysis methods explained in this section, analyse the profit performance of Firm C. (You may note that both businesses in Table 10-2 earn exactly the same amount of operating profit as in the earlier Firm A business example, for which we explain two profit analysis methods. This similarity allows you to compare the key differences between businesses that earn the same profit.)

Solve It

Analysing Return on Capital

Evaluating the financial performance of a business includes looking at how its profit stacks up against the capital used by the business. Table 10-1 presents Firm A's profit performance for the year down to the operating profit before interest and income tax. Does the business earn enough operating profit relative to the capital it uses to make this profit?

Suppose, purely hypothetically, that Firm A uses £100,000,000 capital to earn its £1,800,000 operating profit. In this situation, the business has earned a measly 1.8 per cent rate of return on the capital used to generate the profit:

£1,800,000 operating profit ÷ £100,000,000 capital = 1.8 per cent rate of return

By almost any standard, 1.8 per cent is a dismal return on capital performance.

In general terms, the amount of capital that a business uses equals its total assets minus its operating liabilities that don't charge interest. The main examples of non-interest bearing operating liabilities are creditors from purchases on credit and accrued expenses payable. (We discuss these two liabilities in Chapters 6 and 7.) Operating liabilities typically account for 20 per cent or more or a business's total assets. The remainder of its assets (total assets less total operating liabilities) is the amount of capital the business has to raise from two basic sources: borrowing money on the basis of interest-bearing debt instruments and raising capital (ownership) capital from private or public sources.

Assume the following:

Firm A's Sources of Capital

Debt	£4,000,000
Owners' capital	<u>£8,000,000</u>
Total capital	£12,000,000

Firm A's return on capital for the year is:

£1,800,000 operating margin ÷ £12,000,000 capital = 15 per cent return on capital

Firm A's interest expense for the year on its debt is £240,000. Deducting interest from the £1,800,000 operating profit earned by the business gives £1,560,000 profit before income tax. The rate of return on capital (before income tax) for the business is calculated as follows:

£1,560,000 profit before income tax ÷ £8,000,000 owners' capital = 19.5 per cent return on capital

Q. Firm A earns 15 per cent return on capital (see the preceding calculation), but its return on capital is 19.5 per cent, which is quite a bit higher. How do you explain the difference?

A. The higher rate of return on capital is due to a *financial leverage gain* for the year.

Debt supplies ⅓ of the firm's capital ($4,000,000 ÷ $12,000,000 total capital = ⅓). The business earns 15 per cent return on its debt capital ($4,000,000 debt × 15 per cent rate of return = $600,000 return on debt capital). Because interest is a contractually fixed amount per period, the business has to pay only $240,000 interest for the use of its debt capital.

The excess of operating profit earned on debt capital over the amount of interest is called *financial leverage gain*. Firm A makes $360,000 financial leverage gain for the year ($600,000 operating profit earned on debt capital – $240,000 interest paid on debt = $360,000 financial leverage gain).

The owners supply ⅔ of the total capital of the business, and so their share of the $1,800,000 operating profit that the business earns

equals $1,200,000 ($1,800,000 operating profit × ⅔ = $1,200,000 share of operating profit). In addition, the owners pick up the $360,000 financial leverage gain. Therefore, the profit before income tax for owners equals $1,560,000 ($1,200,000 owners' share of operating profit + $360,000 financial leverage gain = $1,560,000 profit before income tax). The $1,560,000 profit before income tax yields the 19.5 per cent on capital that triggered this question.

Financial leverage is a double-edged sword. Suppose, for example, that in the example scenario, Firm A earns only $240,000 operating profit for the year. Interest is a contractual obligation that can't be avoided. In this situation, all Firm A's operating profit would go to its debt holders, and profit after interest (before income tax) for its owners would be zero. The business would have a financial leverage loss that wipes out profit for its owners. When a business suffers an operating loss, the burden of interest expense compounds the problem and makes matters just that much worse for shareowners.

---

6. Assume the following:

Firm B's Sources of Capital

Debt	$8,000,000
Owners' capital	$4,000,000
Total capital	$12,000,000

See Table 10-2 for Firm B's operating profit performance for the year. The business pays $480,000 interest for the year. Calculate its financial leverage gain (or loss) for the year.

Solve It

7. Assume the following:

Firm C's Sources of Capital

Debt	$6,000,000
Owners' capital	$6,000,000
Total capital	$12,000,000

See Table 10-2 for Firm C's profit data for the year. The business pays $360,000 interest for the year. Calculate its financial leverage gain (or loss) for the year.

Solve It

8. Suppose that Firm B's fixed operating expenses are ₤3,030,000 for the year. Otherwise, other profit factors are the same as in Table 10-2. Using the sources of capital and interest expense presented in Question 5, calculate Firm B's financial leverage gain (or loss) for the year.

Solve It

9. Suppose that Firm C's fixed operating expenses are ₤4,440,000 for the year. Otherwise, other profit factors are the same as in Table 10-2. Using the sources of capital and interest expense presented in Question 6, calculate Firm C's financial leverage gain (or loss) for the year.

Solve It

Improving Profit Performance

Business managers are always looking for ways to improve profit performance (or at least they should be). One obvious way to improve profit is to sell more units – to move more units out the door without reducing sales prices. A business may have to increase its market share to sell more volume, which is no easy task as we're sure you know. Or perhaps the business is in a growing market and doesn't have to increase its market share. In any case, the logical place to begin profit improvement analysis is an increase in sales volume.

Selling more units

Every business wants to sell more units in the current period than during the preceding period. Take the publisher of this book, for example. Wiley Publishing certainly wants to sell more copies of *For Dummies* books this year than were sold during the past year. All businesses are on the lookout for how to increase sales volume, because doing so is a fundamental growth strategy.

Q. According to Table 10-1, Firm A sells 120,000 units during the year. If the business had sold 5 per cent more units, would its profit be 5 per cent higher? You may want quickly to check out the answer to the example question in the earlier section 'Mapping Profit For Managers', because we extend it in the following answer.

A. Before we can answer this question, we need to address an important point: when you start simulating increases in sales volume, you have to make assumptions every step of the way. In this case, the question asks you to simulate a 5 per cent (6,000 additional units) increase in sales volume to see what

happens in the profit example (shown in Table 10-1). In order to answer the question, you have to assume the following:

✔ The sale price (average sales revenue per unit) stays the same at £200 per unit.

✔ The product cost per unit remains the same at £130 per unit.

✔ The variable operating expenses hold the same at 15 per cent of sales revenue.

✔ The fixed operating expenses of Firm A stay the same at £3,000,000 for the year.

The last assumption is an important one to understand because it means that the business has enough unused, or untapped, capacity to sell an additional 6,000 units of product. In other words, you're assuming that some slack exists in the organisation such that it could have sold 6,000 more units without stepping up its fixed costs to support the higher sales volume.

For relatively small changes in sales volume, that circumstance is probably true in most situations. But on the other hand, what if the question asks you to simulate an increase in sales volume of 30, 40 or 50 per cent? With a change of this extent, a business is likely to have to hire more people, buy more delivery vans, buy or rent more warehouse space and so on – with the result that its fixed operating expenses are higher at the higher sales volume level.

Capacity is a broad concept that refers to the capability of a business to handle sales activity. It encompasses all the resources needed to make sales, including employees, machines, manufacturing and warehouse space, retail space and so on. Many of the costs of capacity are fixed in nature.

Keeping in mind the assumptions listed, operating profit would increase much more than 5 per cent if Firm A sold 5 per cent more units during the year. The key point is that the contribution margin would stay the same at £40 per unit because sales price, product cost and variable operating expenses per unit all remain the same (see Table 10-1). So the additional 6,000 units would generate £240,000 additional contribution margin:

£40 contribution margin per unit × 6,000 units sales volume increase = £240,000 contribution margin increase

Assuming that fixed operating expenses remain the same at the higher sales volume, operating profit increases £240,000 from a 5 per cent increase in sales volume. This amount is an increase of over 13 per cent:

£240,000 operating profit increase × £1,800,000 operating profit = 13.3 per cent increase in contribution margin

In the end, a sales volume increase of only 5 per cent would increase operating profit over 13 per cent! How do you like that?

In the example scenario, the bigger 13.3 per cent swing in profit compared with the 5 per cent change in sales volume is referred to as *operating leverage*. At the higher sales volume, the business gets more leverage, or better utilisation, from its fixed operating expenses. At a lower sales volume, the percentage drop in profit would be more severe than the percentage drop in sales volume. In other words, the magnifying effect of operating leverage works both ways.

---

10. Suppose that Firm B sells 10 per cent more units during the year than according to Table 10-2. Determine Firm B's operating profit for this scenario. (Assume that fixed operating expenses remain the same at the higher sales volume.)

Solve It

11. Suppose that Firm B sells 5 per cent fewer units during the year than according to Table 10-2). Determine Firm B's operating profit for this scenario. (Assume that fixed operating expenses remain the same at the lower sales volume.)

Solve It

---

12. Suppose that Firm C sells 5 per cent more units during the year than according to Table 10-2. Determine Firm C's operating profit for this scenario. (Assume that fixed operating expenses remain the same at the higher sales volume.)

Solve It

13. Suppose that Firm C sells 10 per cent fewer units during the year than according to Table 10-2. Determine Firm C's operating profit for this scenario. (Assume that fixed operating expenses remain the same at the lower sales volume.)

Solve It

Improving margin per unit

Another way to improve operating profit is to increase the contribution margin per unit, without increasing sales volume. Improving this factor, however, is very difficult in the real world of business. To increase the contribution margin per unit you have to increase sales price, decrease product cost, decrease variable operating expenses per unit or effect some combination of these factors. None of these items are easy to improve in the real world of business, that's for sure.

Q. Suppose that Firm A (see Table 10-1) wants to improve its contribution margin per unit to increase its operating profit £240,000. Assume that its 120,000 units sales volume remains the same. Assume, further, that the business targets its product cost as the most feasible way to improve the contribution margin per unit. So, assume that sales price, variable operating expenses per unit and fixed operating expenses remain the same. How much would product cost have to improve to achieve the desired £240,000 increase in operating profit?

A. You calculate the needed improvement in the contribution margin per unit as follows:

£240,000 desired increase in operating profit ÷ 120,000 units sales volume = £2 improvement needed in contribution margin per unit

Therefore, the business needs to reduce its product cost (Cost of Goods Sold per unit) by £2, from £130 to £128 per unit. Now, this may not sound like such a difficult task. However, the business may have already cut its product cost to the bone. Trying to squeeze another £2 reduction out of product cost may not be realistic. If the business can't reduce the product cost £2 per unit, it has to look at sales price or variable operating expenses per unit in order to improve the contribution margin. Raising sales price £2 per unit, or lowering variable operating expenses £2 per unit, may be no easier than reducing product cost £2 per unit.

14. Suppose that Firm B is able to improve (lower) its product cost per unit £10 (all other profit factors for Firm B remain the same as shown in Table 10-2). Determine its operating profit for this scenario. Also, how does this change affect the business's breakeven sales volume?

Solve It

15. Suppose that Firm C's product cost increases £0.50 per unit (all other profit factors for Firm C remain the same as shown in Table 10-2). Determine its operating profit for this scenario. Also, how does this change affect the business's breakeven sales volume?

Solve It

In the preceding example, we focus on lowering the product cost as one basic way to improve the contribution margin per unit. Another basic strategy for achieving the same end is to increase the sales price. Sales prices are the province of marketing managers, and we're the first to admit that we aren't marketing experts. Setting sales prices is a complex decision involving consumer psychology and many other factors. Nevertheless, in discussing the general topic of how to improve the contribution margin per unit, we need to say a few words about raising sales price – mainly to show the powerful impact of a higher sales price.

You don't get too far when discussing raising sales price without bumping into a problem concerning variable operating expenses per unit. Most businesses have two types of variable operating expenses: some vary with sales volume (the number of units sold) and some vary with sales revenue (the number of pounds from sales). For example, sales commissions depend on the pounds amount of sales, and in contrast, packing and shipping costs depend on the number of units sold and delivered.

Q. Suppose that Firm B (see Table 10-2 for its profit data) is able to increase its sales price £15 per unit and sell the same number of units. Assume the Firm B's volume-driven variable operating expenses are £15 per unit sold and its revenue-driven variable operating expenses are 20 per cent of sales revenue. How does this £15 sales price increase affect its contribution margin per unit, total contribution margin and operating profit?

A. If the business raises the sales price £15, its volume-driven expenses per unit remain the same, but its revenue-driven expenses increase £3 per unit, which is 20 per cent of

the £15 sales price increase. So, the net gain in contribution margin per unit is only £12. Therefore:

> £12 net increase in the contribution margin per unit × 50,000 units sales volume = £600,000 contribution margin increase

Firm B's fixed operating expenses remains the same (a sales price increase is unlikely to have a bearing on a business's fixed operating expenses). Therefore, the increase in the contribution margin increases the business's operating profit £600,000.

---

16. Suppose that Firm B has to drop its sales price £10 due to competitive pressures. All other profit factors remain the same as shown in Table 10-2. The business's volume-driven variable expenses are £15 per unit sold and its revenue-driven variable operating expenses are 20 per cent of sales revenue. Determine Firm B's operating profit for this scenario. Also, how does this change affect the business's breakeven sales volume?

Solve It

17. Suppose that Firm C increases its sales price £1.50. Sales volume remains the same as shown in Table 10-2. The business's revenue-driven variable operating expenses are 10 per cent of sales revenue and its volume-driven variable operating expenses are £0.40 per unit sold. Determine Firm C's operating profit for this scenario. Also, how does this change affect the business's breakeven sales volume?

Solve It

Making Trade-Offs Among Profit Factors

We used to ask students whether, as future business managers, they would drop sales prices 10 per cent in order to increase sales volume 10 per cent. Invariably, they would answer, 'It depends'. Invariably, we would respond, 'No, it doesn't'. The answer is clear.

Unless you're willing to do anything to increase your market share, trading a 10 per cent decrease in sales prices for a 10 per cent increase in sales volume is stupid . . . and we mean really stupid.

Q. Firm B (see Table 10-2) decides to analyse the impact that dropping its sales price 10 per cent to gain a 10 per cent increase in sales volume would have on its operating profit. What would Firm B's operating profit be in this scenario?

A. The comparative schedule shown in Table 10-3 demonstrates just how devastating this trade-off would be for the business's operating profit.

Table 10-3	Operating Profit Result from 10 per cent Sales Price Decrease in Exchange for 10 per cent Sales Volume Increase		
	Firm B		
	Before	*After*	*Change*
Sales price	£300.00	£270.00	(£30.00)
Product cost	£150.00	£150.00	
Variable operating expenses:			
Volume driven expenses	£15.00	£15.00	
Revenue driven expenses at 20 per cent	£60.00	£54.00	(£6.00)
Contribution margin per unit	£75.00	£51.00	(£24.00)
Times sales volume in units	50,000	55,000	5,000
Equals total contribution margin	£3,750,000	£2,805,000	(£945,000)
Less fixed operating expenses	£1,950,000	£1,950,000	
Operating Profit	£1,800,000	£855,000	(£945,000)

Table 10-3 shows that operating profit would decrease £945,000, which is a decrease of more than 50 per cent of the amount before the trade-off. See why this trade-off is a bad idea? The only argument that we received from our students, especially the marketing ones, was that a business may take such an action to gain market share. But that's another argument. The accountant's job is to calculate the precipitous drop-off in operating profit in this situation.

The reason for the huge drop-off in operating profit is simple enough (although perhaps not immediately obvious). The 10 per cent decrease in sales price causes the contribution margin per unit to drop from £75 to £51 (see Table 10-3), which is a plunge of 32 per cent in Firm B's contribution margin per unit (£24 decrease ÷ £75 contribution margin per unit before sales price decrease = 32 per cent decrease). A paltry 10 per cent increase in sales volume can't make up for such a large drop in contribution margin per unit.

18. Suppose that Firm A (see Table 10-1) offers all customers special rebates as a sales incentive. As a result, assume that the sales price decreases £10 per unit, but that annual sales volume increases to 150,000 units. Assume that the business's fixed operating expenses don't increase at the higher sales volume level (which may be stretching things a bit). Also assume that its variable operating expenses are all revenue-driven and equal to 15 per cent of sales revenue. In terms of the impact on operating profit, would the rebate strategy to increase sales volume be a good trade-off for the business?

Solve It

19. The example question in this section shows a scenario for Firm B that involves a 10 per cent reduction in sales price with a 10 per cent increase in sales volume. The comparative schedule makes clear that a 10 per cent sales volume increase isn't nearly enough. Determine the sales volume level needed at the lower sales price to keep operating profit the same at £1,800,000.

Solve It

Answers to Problems on Analysing Profit Behaviour

Here are the answers to the questions presented earlier in this chapter.

1 Using the data presented in Table 10-1, suppose that the business has a choice of selling 10 per cent more sales volume or keeping the sales volume at the same level and increasing the selling price by 10 per cent. Assuming all other profit factors remain the same, which change (the higher sales volume or the increased sales price) would be better for operating profit?

A 10 per cent increase in sales volume would mean that the business would have sold 12,000 more units than the figure 10-1 scenario. (120,000 units × 10% = 12,000 additional units). Each additional unit sold will earn £40 contribution margin per unit (see Figure 10-1). So total contribution margin would have been £480,000 higher. The business's fixed operating expenses would not have increased with such a relatively small increase in sales volume. Therefore it's operating profit would be £480,000 higher. Would the sales price increase have been any better? You bet it would!

A 10 per cent jump means sales price would be £20 per unit higher: £200 sales price in Table 10-1 × 10 per cent = £20 increase in sales price. This jump would increase the contribution margin per unit from £40 (see Table 10-1) to £60. Therefore, the business's total contribution margin would be £7,200,000: £60 contribution per unit × 120,000 units sales volume = £7,200,000 contribution margin. This amount is an increase of £2,400,000 over the contribution margin in the Table 10-1 scenario. We have no reason to think that fixed operating expenses would be any different at the higher sales price, and so operating profit would increase £2,400,000.

In short, the 10 per cent gain in sales price would be much better for operating profit, compared with the 10 per cent step up in sales volume.

2 One of Firm A's marketing managers is overheard to comment, 'If we had sold 10 per cent more units than we did in the year, our profit would have been 10 per cent higher'. Do you agree with this comment? (Table 10-1 presents Firm A's operating profit report for the year.)

Increasing sales volume 10 per cent would increase the total contribution margin 10 per cent, assuming that sales price, product cost and variable operating expenses remain the same. So far then this answer is relatively straightforward. The next step concerns what would happen to the business's total fixed operating expenses at the higher sales volume level.

Fixed operating costs don't increase with an increase in sales volume *unless* the increase in sales volume is relatively large enough so that the business has to expand its capacity to accommodate the higher sales volume. Generally speaking, a business probably can take on a 10 per cent sales volume increase without having to increase its capacity, at least in the short run. (Remember, an increase in capacity requires an increase in fixed operating expenses.)

Assuming that the business's total fixed operating expenses would be the same, all the increase in total contribution margin would 'fall down' to operating profit. Operating profit, therefore, would increase more than 10 per cent. The increase in total contribution margin is more than 10 per cent of operating profit because operating profit is a smaller amount than the total contribution margin amount.

3 Instead of the scenario shown in Table 10-1, assume that Firm A has a bad year. The internal operating profit report for this alternative scenario is presented below. Using the two methods explained in this section, analyse why the business suffers a loss for the year.

	Totals	Per Unit
Sales volume in units	120,000	
Sales revenue	£21,000,000	£175.00
Cost of Goods Sold expense	£15,600,000	£130.00
Gross Margin	£5,400,000	£45.00
Variable operating expenses	£3,150,000	£26.25
Contribution margin	£2,250,000	£18.75
Fixed operating expenses	£3,000,000	£25.00
Operating profit (loss)	(£750,000)	(£6.25)

Refer to the profit data for Firm A at the end of the question in order to produce this answer.

Analysis method #1: Contribution margin minus fixed costs

Contribution margin per unit	£18.75
Times annual sales volume, in units	120,000
Equals total contribution margin	£2,250,000
Less fixed operating expenses	£3,000,000
Equals operating profit (loss)	(£750,000)

Analysis method #2: Shortfall below breakeven

Annual sales volume for year, in units	120,000
Less annual breakeven volume, in units	160,000
Equals shortfall below breakeven, in units	(40,000)
Times contribution margin per unit	£18.75
Equals operating profit (loss)	(£750,000)

4 Table 10-2 presents profit performance information for two businesses for their most recent years. Using the two profit analysis methods explained in this section, analyse the profit performance of Firm B. (You may note that both businesses in Table 10-2 earn exactly the same amount of operating profit as in the earlier Firm A business example, for which we explain two profit analysis methods. This similarity allows you to compare the key differences between businesses that earn the same profit.)

Refer to the profit data in Table 10-2 in order to produce this answer.

Analysis method #1: Contribution margin minus fixed costs

Contribution margin per unit	£75
Times annual sales volume, in units	50,000
Equals total contribution margin	£3,750,000
Less fixed operating expenses	£1,950,000
Equals operating profit	£1,800,000

Analysis method #2: Excess over breakeven

Annual sales volume for year, in units	50,000
Less annual breakeven volume, in units	<u>26,000</u>
Equals excess over breakeven, in units	24,000
Times contribution margin per unit	<u>$75</u>
Equals operating profit	$1,800,000

5 Please refer to Table 10-2. Using the two profit analysis methods explained in this section, analyse the profit performance of Firm C. (You may note that both businesses in Table 10-2 earn exactly the same amount of operating profit as in the earlier Firm A business example, for which we explain two profit analysis methods. This similarity allows you to compare the key differences between businesses that earn the same profit.)

Refer to the profit data in Table 10-2 in order to produce this answer.

Analysis method #1: Contribution margin minus fixed costs

Contribution margin per unit	$3.20
Times annual sales volume, in units	<u>1,500,000</u>
Equals total contribution margin	$4,800,000
Less fixed operating expenses	<u>$3,000,000</u>
Equals operating profit	$1,800,000

Analysis method #2: Excess over breakeven

Annual sales volume for year, in units	1,500,000
Less annual breakeven volume, in units	<u>937,500</u>
Equals excess over breakeven, in units	562,500
Times contribution margin per unit	<u>$3.20</u>
Equals operating profit	$1,800,000

6 Assume the following:

Firm B's Sources of Capital

Debt	$8,000,000
Owners' capital	<u>$4,000,000</u>
Total capital	$12,000,000

See Table 10-2 for Firm B's operating profit data for the year. The business pays $480,000 interest for the year. Calculate its financial leverage gain (or loss) for the year.

In this case, debt holders provide two-thirds of the business's total capital ($8,000,000 of the total $12,000,000 capital). Thus, two-thirds of its $1,800,000 operating profit can be attributed to the debt capital used by the business, which equals $1,200,000 ($\frac{2}{3} \times $1,800,000 = $1,200,000$).

The business pays only $480,000 interest on its debt capital. So:

$1,200,000 operating profit attributable to debt capital – $480,000 interest on debt capital = $720,000 financial leverage gain

Here's another way to calculate financial leverage gain: the business earns 15 per cent return on capital (£1,800,000 operating profit ÷ £12,000,000 total capital = 15 per cent return on capital). The business pays a 6 per cent interest rate on its debt capital (£480,000 interest ÷ £8,000,000 debt = 6 per cent interest rate). A favourable 9 per cent spread exists between the two rates. Therefore:

9 per cent favourable spread between return on capital and interest rate × £8,000,000 debt = £720,000 financial leverage gain.

7 Assume the following:

Firm C's Sources of Capital

Debt	£6,000,000
Owners' capital	£6,000,000
Total capital	£12,000,000

See Table 10-2 for Firm C's profit data for the year. The business pays £360,000 interest for the year. Calculate its financial leverage gain (or loss) for the year.

In this case, debt holders provide one-half of the business's total capital (£6 million of the total £12 million capital). Thus, one-half of its £1,800,000 operating profit can be attributed to the debt capital used by the business, which equals £900,000 (½ × £1,800,000 = £900,000).

The business pays only £360,000 interest on its debt capital. So:

£900,000 operating profit attributable to debt capital – £360,000 interest on debt capital = £540,000 financial leverage gain

8 Suppose that Firm B's fixed operating expenses are £3,030,000 for the year. Otherwise, other profit factors are the same as in Table 10-2. Using the sources of capital and interest expense presented in Question 5, calculate Firm B's financial leverage gain (or loss) for the year.

For the year, Firm B earns £3,750,000 total contribution margin (see Table 10-2). If its fixed operating expenses are £3,030,000, its operating profit for the year is only £720,000. Based on this operating profit, Firm B's return on capital is only 6 per cent (£720,000 ÷ £12,000,000 total capital = 6 per cent return on capital).

In this case, debt supplies two-thirds of total capital. Therefore, two-thirds of its £720,000 operating profit can be attributed to its debt capital, which is £480,000 (£720,000 operating profit × ⅔ = £480,000). The business pays £480,000 interest in the year. Thus, its financial leverage gain is zero.

Here's another way to calculate the business's financial leverage gain/loss for the year: the business earns only 6 per cent return on capital, and its interest rate on debt is 6 per cent (£480,000 interest ÷ £8,000,000 debt = 6 per cent). So, no spread, or difference, exists between its 6 per cent return on capital and its interest rate. Therefore, the financial leverage gain is zero.

9 Suppose that Firm C's fixed operating expenses are £4,440,000 for the year. Otherwise, other profit factors are the same as in Table 10-2. Using the sources of capital and interest expense presented in Question 6, calculate Firm C's financial leverage gain (or loss) for the year.

For the year, Firm C earns £4,800,000 total contribution margin (see Table 10-2). If its fixed operating expenses are £4,440,000, its operating profit for the year is only £360,000. Based on this operating profit, the business's return on capital is a very low 3 per cent (£360,000 ÷ £12,000,000 total capital = 3 per cent return on capital).

In this case, debt supplies one half of total capital. Therefore, one half of its £360,000 operating profit can be attributed to its debt capital, which is £180,000 (£360,000 operating profit × ½ = £180,000). The business paid £360,000 interest in the year. Thus, it has a financial leverage *loss* equal to £180,000.

Here's another way to calculate the business's financial leverage loss for the year: the business earns only 3 per cent return on capital, and its interest rate on debt is 6 per cent (£360,000 interest ÷ £6,000,000 debt = 6.0 per cent). So, an unfavourable 3 per cent spread exists between return on capital and interest rate. The firm's financial leverage loss for the year is £180,000 (3 per cent unfavourable spread × £6,000,000 debt = £180,000 financial leverage loss for the year).

10   Suppose that Firm B sells 10 per cent more units during the year than according to Table 10-2. Determine Firm B's operating profit for this scenario. (Assume that fixed operating expenses remain the same at the higher sales volume.)

For Firm B, selling 10 per cent additional units equals 5,000 additional units sold. Given that its contribution margin per unit is £75, the increase in its total contribution margin is:

> 5,000 additional units × £75 contribution margin per unit = £375,000 increase in total contribution margin

Fixed operating expenses don't increase at the higher sales volume level, and so the gain in total contribution margin increases operating profit by £375,000. The 10 per cent increase in sales volume increases operating profit by 20.8 per cent (£375,000 gain in operating profit ÷ £1,800,000 operating profit at the original sales volume level = 20.8 per cent increase).

The percentage gain in operating profit is much larger than the percentage increase in sales volume. This magnification effect is called operating leverage.

11   Suppose that Firm B sells 5 per cent fewer units during the year than according to Table 10-2. Determine Firm B's operating profit for this scenario. (Assume that fixed operating expenses remain the same at the lower sales volume.)

For Firm B, selling 5 per cent less units equals 2,500 fewer units sold. Given that its contribution margin per unit is £75, the decrease in its total contribution margin is:

> 2,500 fewer units × £75 contribution margin per unit = £187,500 decrease in total contribution margin

Fixed operating expenses don't decrease at the lower sales volume level, and so the drop in total contribution margin decreases operating profit by £187,500. The 5 per cent decrease in sales volume decreases operating profit by 10.4 per cent (£187,500 fall in operating profit ÷ £1,800,000 operating profit at the original sales volume level = 10.4 per cent decrease).

The percentage drop in operating profit is much larger than the percentage decrease in sales volume, and this magnification effect is called *operating leverage*.

12   Suppose that Firm C sells 5 per cent more units during the year than according to Table 10-2. Determine Firm C's operating profit for this scenario. (Assume that fixed operating expenses remain the same at the higher sales volume.)

For Firm C, selling 5 per cent additional units equals 75,000 additional units sold. Given that its contribution margin per unit is £3.20, the increase in its total contribution margin is:

> 75,000 additional units × £3.20 contribution margin per unit = £240,000 increase in total contribution margin

Fixed operating expenses don't increase at the higher sales volume level, and so the gain in total contribution margin increases operating profit by £240,000. The 5 per cent increase in sales volume increases operating profit by 13.3 per cent (£240,000 gain in operating profit ÷ £1,800,000 operating profit at the original sales volume level = 13.3 per cent increase).

13 Suppose that Firm C sells 10 per cent fewer units during the year than according to Table 10-2. Determine Firm C's operating profit for this scenario. (Assume that fixed operating expenses remain the same at the lower sales volume.)

For Firm C, selling 10 per cent less units equals 150,000 fewer units sold. Given that its contribution margin per unit is £3.20, the decrease in its total contribution margin is:

> 150,000 fewer units × £3.20 contribution margin per unit = £480,000 decrease in total contribution margin

Fixed operating expenses don't decrease at the lower sales volume level, and so the drop in total contribution margin decreases operating profit by £480,000. The 10 per cent decrease in sales volume decreases operating profit by 26.7 per cent (£480,000 fall in operating profit ÷ £1,800,000 operating profit at the original sales volume level = 26.7 per cent decrease).

14 Suppose that Firm B is able to improve (lower) its product cost per unit £10 (all other profit factors for Firm B remain the same as shown in Table 10-2). Determine its operating profit for this scenario. Also, how does this change affect the business's breakeven sales volume?

The complete schedule of changes in this scenario is as follows:

	Firm B		
	Before	**After**	**Change**
Sales price	£300.00	£300.00	
Product cost	£150.00	£140.00	(£10.00)
Variable operating expenses:			
Volume driven expenses	£15.00	£15.00	
Revenue driven expenses at 20 per cent	£60.00	£60.00	
Contribution margin per unit	£75.00	£85.00	+£10.00
Times sales volume in units	50,000	50,000	
Equals total contribution margin	£3,750,000	£4,250,000	+£500,000
Less fixed operating expenses	£1,950,000	£1,950,000	
Operating Profit	£1,800,000	£2,300,000	+£500,000

As the schedule shows, operating profit increases £500,000, which is a 27.8 per cent increase from a 6.7 per cent change in product cost (£10 decrease ÷ £150 = 6.7 per cent decrease).

The business's breakeven decreases because the contribution margin per unit is higher than it was before the product cost change:

> £1,950,000 fixed operating expenses ÷ £85 contribution margin per unit = 22,941 units breakeven volume

At the £75 contribution margin per unit, Firm B's breakeven volume is 26,000 units sales volume.

15 Suppose that Firm C's product cost increases £0.50 per unit (all other profit factors for Firm C remain the same as shown in Table 10-2). Determine its operating profit for this scenario. Also, how does this change affect the business's breakeven sales volume?

The impact on contribution margin and operating profit from the seemingly small increase in product cost is shown in the following comparative schedule:

	Firm C		
	Before	*After*	*Change*
Sales price	£24.00	£24.00	
Product cost	£18.00	£18.50	+£0.50
Variable operating expenses	£2.80	£2.80	
Contribution margin per unit	£3.20	£2.70	(£0.50)
Times sales volume in units	1,500,000	1,500,000	
Equals total contribution margin	£4,800,000	£4,050,000	(£750,000)
Less fixed operating expenses	£3,000,000	£3,000,000	
Operating Profit	£1,800,000	£1,050,000	−750,000

So, operating profit drops £750,000, from £1,800,000 to only £1,050,000, which is a 41.7 per cent decrease! The reason is the relatively large drop in the contribution margin per unit, from £3.20 to only £2.70, which is a 15.6 per cent decline. The importance of maintaining the contribution margin per unit can't be overstated.

If Firm C's product cost increases £0.50 per unit, the business's breakeven also increases because the contribution margin per unit is lower than it was before the product cost change:

£3,000,000 fixed operating expenses ÷ £2.70 contribution margin per unit = 1,111,111 units breakeven volume

At the £3.20 contribution margin per unit, the breakeven volume is 937,500 units sales volume.

16 Suppose that Firm B has to drop its sales price £10 due to competitive pressures. All other profit factors remain the same as shown in Table 10-2. The business's volume-driven variable expenses are £15 per unit sold and its revenue-driven variable operating expenses are 20 per cent of sales revenue. Determine Firm B's operating profit for this scenario. Also, how does this change affect the business's breakeven sales volume?

The circumstances cause the firm's operating profit to decrease £400,000, as shown in the following schedule:

	Firm B		
	Before	*After*	*Change*
Sales price	£300.00	£290.00	(£10.00)
Product cost	£150.00	£150.00	
Variable operating expenses:			
Volume driven expenses	£15.00	£15.00	
Revenue driven expenses at 20 per cent	£60.00	£58.00	(£2.00)
Contribution margin per unit	£75.00	£67.00	(£8.00)
Times sales volume in units	50,000	50,000	
Equals total contribution margin	£3,750,000	£3,350,000	(£400,000)
Less fixed operating expenses	£1,950,000	£1,950,000	
Operating Profit	£1,800,000	£1,400,000	(£400,000)

If Firm B's sales price drops £10, the business's breakeven increases because contribution margin per unit is lower than before the sales price change:

> £1,950,000 fixed operating expenses ÷ £67 contribution margin per unit = 29,104 units breakeven volume

At the £75 contribution margin per unit, the breakeven volume is 26,000 units sales volume.

17 Suppose that Firm C increases its sales price £1.50. Sales volume remains the same as shown in Table 10-2. The business's revenue-driven variable operating expenses are 10 per cent of sales revenue and its volume-driven variable operating expenses are £0.40 per unit sold. Determine Firm C's operating profit for this scenario. Also, how does this change affect the business's breakeven sales volume?

The circumstances cause the firm's operating profit to increase £2,025,000, as shown in the following schedule:

	Firm C		
	Before	**After**	**Change**
Sales price	£24.00	£25.50	+£1.50
Product cost	£18.00	£18.00	
Variable operating expenses	£2.80	£2.95	
Contribution margin per unit	£3.20	£4.55	+£1.35
Times sales volume in units	1,500,000	1,500,000	
Equals total contribution margin	£4,800,000	£6,825,000	(£2,025,000)
Less fixed operating expenses	£3,000,000	£3,000,000	
Operating Profit	£1,800,000	£3,825,000	£2,025,000

If Firm C's sales price increases £1.50, the business's breakeven decreases because the contribution margin per unit is higher than before the sales price change:

> £3,000,000 fixed operating expenses ÷ £4.55 contribution margin per unit = 659,341 units breakeven volume

At the £3.20 contribution margin per unit, the breakeven volume is 937,500 units sales volume.

18 Suppose that Firm A (see Table 10-1) offers all customers special rebates as a sales incentive. As a result, assume that the sales price decreases £10 per unit, but that annual sales volume increases to 150,000 units. Assume that the business's fixed operating expenses don't increase at the higher sales volume level (which may be stretching things a bit). Also assume that its variable operating expenses are all revenue-driven and equal to 15 per cent of sales revenue. In terms of the impact on operating profit, would the rebate strategy to increase sales volume be a good trade-off for the business?

On the surface, this trade-off appears to be a good one that improves operating profit. After all, the business decreases the sales price only 5 per cent for a 25 per cent jump in sales volume. Surely this deal must be a good one. But look closely at the following comparative schedule:

	Firm B		
	Before	*After*	*Change*
Sales price	£200.00	£190.00	(£10.00)
Product cost	£130.00	£130.00	
Variable operating expenses:			
Volume driven expenses	£0.00	£0.00	
Revenue driven expenses at 20 per cent	£30.00	£28.50	(£1.50)
Contribution margin per unit	£40.00	£31.50	(£8.50)
Times sales volume in units	120,000	150,000	+30,000
Equals total contribution margin	£4,800,000	£4,725,000	(£75,000)
Less fixed operating expenses	£3,000,000	£3,000,000	
Operating Profit	£1,800,000	£1,725,000	(£75,000)

As the schedule shows, operating profit actually *decreases* £75,000 in this scenario. One key to understanding this change is that the contribution margin per unit decreases 21.25 per cent (£8.50 decrease ÷ £40.00 contribution margin per unit before sales price decrease = 21.25 per cent). The 25 per cent increase in sales volume (from 120,000 units to 150,000 units) isn't enough to make up for the drop in the all important contribution margin per unit.

19 The example question in this section shows a scenario for Firm B that involves a 10 per cent reduction in sales price with a 10 per cent increase in sales volume. The comparative schedule makes clear that a 10 per cent sales volume increase isn't nearly enough. Determine the sales volume level needed at the lower sales price to keep operating profit the same at £1,800,000.

Obviously, sales volume has to increase more than 10 per cent to keep operating profit at £1,800,000. The following calculation determines the exact sales volume needed to keep operating profit the same:

> £3,750,000 contribution margin target ÷ £51 contribution margin after sales price decrease = 73,529 units sales volume needed to keep operating profit the same

This answer is proven in the following comparative schedule using the 73,529 units sales volume:

	Firm B		
	Before	*After*	*Change*
Sales price	£300.00	£270.00	(£30.00)
Product cost	£150.00	£150.00	
Variable operating expenses:			
Volume driven expenses	£15.00	£15.00	
Revenue driven expenses at 20 per cent	£60.00	£54.00	(£6.00)
Contribution margin per unit	£75.00	£51.00	(£24.00)
Times sales volume in units	50,000	73,529	+23,529
Equals total contribution margin	£3,750,000	£3,750,000	
Less fixed operating expenses	£1,950,000	£1,950,000	
Operating Profit	£1,800,000	£1,800,000	

Chapter 11

Manufacturing Cost Accounting

• •

In This Chapter

▶ Recognising the different types of manufacturing costs

▶ Getting to know manufacturing accounting entries

▶ Calculating product cost

• •

*I*n addition to normal accounting matters, businesses that manufacture products face certain accounting problems that retailers and distributors do not encounter. Throughout this chapter, we use the term *manufacture* in the broadest sense: car makers assemble cars, brewers brew beer, petrol firms refine oil, DuPont makes products through chemical synthesis and so on.

Retailers and distributors, on the other hand, buy products in a condition ready for resale to the end consumer. For example, Asda Wal-Mart and Tescos don't manufacture the products they sell. Other businesses manufacture the products that retailers sell – although the manufacturers may put private labels on the goods (common practice for supermarkets and other retailers).

The chapter focuses mainly on the accounting procedures used to accumulate the basic types of manufacturing costs and how these pools of costs are used to determine product cost. A manufacturer must know product cost in order to determine its Cost of Goods Sold expense for the period and the cost of its stock. This chapter explores certain unavoidable problems that accountants face in determining product cost. To complete the picture, the chapter also explains how unscrupulous managers can set production output in order to manipulate profit for the period.

Minding Manufacturing Costs

A manufacturing business, first of all, must separate between its manufacturing costs and nonmanufacturing costs. Manufacturing costs are the costs of production that are included in the determination of product cost. Non-manufacturing costs include marketing expenses and the general and administration expenses of the business, which are referred to as period costs (we discuss the importance of the distinction between product and period costs in the later section 'Separating period and product costs'). First, we explain the basic types of manufacturing costs that go into the calculation of product cost.

Manufacturing costs consist of four basic types:

✔ **Raw materials:** What a manufacturer buys from other businesses to use in the production of its own products. For example, Ford Motors buys tyres from Goodyear (or other tyre manufacturers) that become part of Ford's cars.

✔ **Direct labour:** Employee costs for those who work on the production line.

✔ **Variable overheads:** Indirect production costs that increase or decrease as the quantity produced increases or decreases. An example is the cost of electricity that runs a business's production machines: if the business increases or decreases the use of those machines, the electricity cost increases or decreases accordingly.

✔ **Fixed overheads:** Indirect production costs that do not increase or decrease as the quantity produced increases or decreases. These fixed costs remain the same over a fairly broad range of production output levels. Fixed manufacturing costs include:

- Salaries for certain production employees who don't work directly on the production line, such as the Managing Director, safety inspectors, security guards, accountants and other admin workers.

- Depreciation of production buildings, equipment and other manufacturing fixed assets.

- Premises costs, such as building insurance, and heating and lighting charges.

Table 11-1 presents an internal operating profit report of a manufacturing business called Firm X; the report includes information about the business's manufacturing activity and costs for the year. A business may manufacture hundreds or thousands of products, but in the example, Firm X manufactures and sells only one product. The example is therefore realistic while avoiding the clutter of too much detail. Table 11-1 is a good platform to illustrate the fundamental accounting problems and methods of all manufacturers.

The information in the operating profit report and manufacturing activity summary in Table 11-1 is confidential and for management eyes only. The business's competitors would love to know this information. For instance, if Firm X enjoys a significant product cost advantage over its competitors, it definitely wouldn't want its cost data to get into their hands.

Table 11-1	Internal Profit and Loss Report for Firm X	
	Firm X	
Operating Profit for Year	*Per Unit*	*Totals*
Sales volume (units)		110,000
Sales revenue	£1,400	£154,000,000
Cost of Goods Sold expense	(£760.00)	(£83,600,000)
Gross Margin	£640.00	£70,400,000
Variable operating expenses	(£300.00)	(£33,000,000)
Contribution Margin	£340.00	£37,400,000
Fixed operating expenses		(£21,450,000)
Operating Profit		£15,950,000
Manufacturing Activity Summary for the Year		
Annual production capacity (units)		150,000
Actual output (units)		120,000
Raw materials	£215.00	£25,800,000
Direct labour	£125.00	£15,000,000
Variable manufacturing overhead costs	£70.00	£8,400,000
Total Variable Manufacturing Costs	£410.00	£49,200,000
Fixed manufacturing overhead costs	£350.00	£42,000,000
Product Cost and Total Manufacturing Costs	£760.00	£91,200,000

Understanding product costs versus period costs

Unlike a retailer that purchases products in a condition ready for resale, a manufacturer begins by purchasing the raw materials needed in the production process. Then the manufacturer pays workers to operate the production machines and equipment and to move the products into warehouses after they're produced. All this work is done in a sprawling plant that has many indirect overhead costs. All these different production costs are funnelled into product cost.

When manufacturing costs are incurred, they're recorded in a stock account – in particular, the work-in-progress stock account. We explain the use of this account in the section 'Taking a Short Tour of Manufacturing Entries' later in this chapter. Product costs are later recorded in the Cost of Goods Sold expense when the products are sold.

Pay special attention to the £760.00 product cost and its components in Table 11-1. In particular, note that the £760.00 is the sum of four separate cost components – raw materials, direct labour, variable manufacturing overheads and fixed manufacturing overheads. All four of the component costs must be correct to end up with the correct product cost.

Product costs are said to be capitalised because they're viewed as a capital investment, which is an investment in an asset. Product costs aren't recorded to expenses until the products are eventually sold, at which time the appropriate amount of cost is removed from the Asset account and recorded in the Cost of Goods Sold expense account.

Costs that are charged to expenses when they're recorded are known as *period costs*. Marketing costs (such as advertising, sales personnel or delivery of products to customers) are period costs. These selling costs are recorded as expenses in the period the costs are incurred. General and administrative costs (such as legal and accounting, compensation of officers or information and data processing) are also period costs. Period costs don't pass through a stock account.

Separating period and product costs

The distinction between period and product costs is very important. What if a business deliberately records some of its manufacturing costs as period costs instead of as product costs? Suppose that for the year just ended, a business records £2,400,000 of its manufacturing costs as marketing expenses. The £2,400,000 should have gone into stock and stayed there until the products are sold. To the extent that the products haven't yet been sold at the end of the year, the business has understated the cost of its ending stock and overstated its marketing expense for the year. Why would a business do this? To minimise its current year's taxable income, that's why.

Wages paid to production line workers are a clear example of a manufacturing cost. Salaries paid to salespeople are a marketing cost and not part of product cost. Depreciation on production equipment is a manufacturing cost, but depreciation on the warehouse in which products are stored after being manufactured is a period cost. Similarly, moving raw materials and partially completed goods through the production process is a manufacturing cost, but transporting the finished products from the warehouse to customers is a period cost. Essentially, product cost stops at the end of the production line – but every cost up to that point is a manufacturing cost.

A manufacturer needs to design and implement a cost accounting system to determine the cost of every product it manufactures and sells. The business must track the costs of all raw materials that go into the production process and the costs of all production line labour (which may involve hundreds or thousands of operations). In addition, the business has to determine and allocate many indirect manufacturing costs to the various products it manufactures (although in the example shown in Table 11-1, the business produces only one product). Tracking and allocating these costs is a very challenging task, to say the least.

Q. How is the £83,600,000 Cost of Goods Sold expense of Firm X determined (see Table 11-1)?

A. In the example in Table 11-1, the business records £91,200,000 total manufacturing costs to produce 120,000 units during the year. Therefore, the product cost per unit is £760.00: £91,200,000 total manufacturing costs ÷ 120,000 units production output = £760.00 product cost per unit. Based on this product cost per unit its Cost of Goods Sold expense for the year is determined as follows:

> £760.00 product cost × 110,000 units sales volume = £83,600,000 Cost of Goods Sold expense

The business uses the LIFO (last-in, first-out) method: all 110,000 units sold are charged out at the £760.00 product cost per unit, which is for the latest batch of units produced. (The example treats the entire year as one production period for determining product cost, whereas in actual practice, product cost is determined monthly or quarterly.) In other words, none of the cost from its Opening Stock is charged to Cost of Goods Sold expense. The cost of Opening Stock most likely is carried on the books at a lower product cost. If the business were to use the FIFO (first-in, first-out) method, some of the units sold during the year would be charged out based on the product cost in Opening Stock. (Turn to Chapter 9 to read more about the LIFO and FIFO methods.)

1. The business's total manufacturing costs for the year are £91,200,000 as shown in Table 11-1), but only £83,600,000 is charged to Cost of Goods Sold expense. What happened to the other £7,600,000 (£91,200,000 manufacturing costs for year − £83,600,000 Cost of Goods Sold expense for year = £7,600,000)?

Solve It

2. As you can see in Table 11-1, Firm X records £42,000,000 fixed manufacturing overhead costs in the year. Suppose, instead, that its fixed manufacturing overhead costs are £45,600,000 for the year, which is an increase of £3,600,000. Would the business's operating profit be £3,600,000 lower? (Assume that variable manufacturing costs per unit and operating expenses remain the same.)

Solve It

3. Suppose that Firm X uses the FIFO method instead of the LIFO method shown in Table 11-1. The business starts the year with 25,000 units of Opening Stock at a cost of £735 per unit according to the FIFO method. During the year, it manufactures 120,000 units and sells 110,000 units (see Table 11-1). Determine Firm X's Cost of Goods Sold expense for the year and its Closing Stock using the FIFO method.

Solve It

4. Firm X produces 120,000 units and sells 110,000 units during the year (see Table 11-1). Therefore, the business increases its stock 10,000 units. Does this increase seem reasonable? Or is the business's production output compared with its sales volume out of kilter?

Solve It

Taking a Short Tour of Manufacturing Entries

When a retailer or wholesaler purchases products, it debits the stock account. The cost of the products is held in a stock account until the products are sold. At that time, the appropriate amount of cost is removed from the stock account and charged to the Cost of Goods Sold expense. The amount of the cost removed from stock is determined by which Cost of Goods Sold expense method is used, such as FIFO or LIFO. (These methods are discussed in Chapter 9.)

In contrast to retailers and wholesalers, a manufacturer has to make more entries to get to its Cost of Goods Sold expense. The following illustrative entries are based on the Firm X manufacturing example, whose operating profit report and manufacturing activity summary appear in the earlier Table 11-1.

Firm X purchases £27,325,000 of raw materials during the year, which is slightly more than the cost of materials released into the manufacturing process. Therefore, its stock of raw materials increases during the year. The business has a good credit rating and purchases all its raw materials on credit. The following entry shows Firm X's raw materials purchases during the year:

	Debit	Credit
Raw materials stock	£27,325,000	
Trade Creditors		£27,325,000

When raw materials are released from stock storage into the manufacturing process, the cost is charged to a particular job order or to a particular department. The transfers of raw materials to production during the year are shown in the following entry:

	Debit	Credit
Work-in-progress stock	£25,800,000	
Raw materials stock		£25,800,000

The work-in-progress stock account is a special account used by manufacturers to accumulate the costs of products working their way through the production process. These products aren't ready for sale until the production process is completed. At that time, an entry is made to move the product cost out of this temporary holding account into the finished goods stock account.

The business's direct labour costs consist of all elements of compensation earned by its production line workers. The largest part of the compensation of production line workers is paid in cash, but payroll taxes are withheld and fringe benefit costs are also recorded in various Liability accounts. In the following entries we use accrued payables as the generic title for various Liability accounts used to record costs incurred by the business that are paid at a later time. The direct labour costs of the business during the period are shown in the following entry:

	Debit	Credit
Work-in-progress stock	£15,000,000	
Cash		£9,000,000
Payroll taxes payable		£4,000,000
Accrued payables		£2,000,000

The bulk of the business's variable manufacturing overhead costs are paid in cash over the course of the year, but two Liability accounts – trade creditors and accrued payables – are involved in recording many of these costs. The business's variable manufacturing overhead costs for the year are shown in the following entry:

	Debit	Credit
Work-in-progress Stock	£8,400,000	
Cash		£5,400,000
Trade Creditors		£2,000,000
Accrued payables		£1,000,000

Most of the business's indirect fixed manufacturing overhead costs for the period are paid in cash during the year, but many involve Liability accounts for unpaid manufacturing costs – such as the two shown in the following entry. Also, depreciation is a major fixed overhead cost, and so the accumulated depreciation account is credited in recording the depreciation cost component of the fixed manufacturing overhead costs. The business's fixed manufacturing overhead costs for the year are shown in the following entry:

	Debit	Credit
Work-in-progress stock	£42,000,000	
Cash		£32,000,000
Accumulated depreciation		£5,000,000
Trade Creditors		£3,000,000
Accrued payables		£2,000,000

When the manufacturing process is complete, products are moved off the production line to the warehouse. The appropriate amount of product cost is removed from the work-in-progress stock account and entered in the finished goods stock account. The transfers of products from the production line to the finished goods warehouse during the year are shown in the following entry:

	Debit	Credit
Finished goods stock	£91,200,000	
Work-in-progress stock		£91,200,000

Note that in these entries, we assume that no work-in-progress applies at the opening or end of the year. This assumption would be accurate, for instance, if the business shuts down its manufacturing activity for a week or two at the end of the year to permit a fumigation of the plant or to give workers a holiday. The entries would be more involved if work-in-progress stock exists at the start and end of the year.

Recording the Cost of Goods Sold during the year is shown in the following entry:

	Debit	Credit
Cost of Goods Sold expense	£83,600,000	
Finished goods stock		£83,600,000

Table 11-2 presents the internal operating profit reports of two sample manufacturing businesses, Firm Y and Firm Z. Their operating profit reports include information about their manufacturing activity for the year.

Table 11-2 — Internal Profit and Loss Report for Firms Y and Z

Operating Profit for Year	Firm Y Per Unit	Firm Y Totals	Firm Z Per Unit	Firm Z Totals
Sales volume (units)		500,000		2,000,000
Sales revenue	£85.00	£42,500,000	£25.00	£50,000,000
Cost of Goods Sold expense	(£56.00)	(£28,000,000)	(£18.45)	(£36,900,000)
Gross Margin	£29.00	£14,500,000	£6.55	£13,100,000
Variable operating expenses	(£12.50)	(£6,250,000)	(£2.50)	(£5,000,000)
Contribution Margin	£16.50	£8,250,000	£4.05	£8,100,000
Fixed operating expenses		(£5,000,000)		(£7,500,000)
Operating Profit		£3,250,000		£600,000
Manufacturing Activity Summary for the Year				
Annual production capacity (units)		800,000		2,500,000
Actual output (units)		500,000		2,500,000
Raw materials	£15.00	£7,500,000	£7.50	£18,750,000
Direct labour	£20.00	£10,000,000	£2.75	£6,875,000
Variable manufacturing overhead costs	£5.00	£2,500,000	£5.00	£12,500,000
Total Variable Manufacturing Costs	£40.00	£20,000,000	£15.25	£38,125,000
Fixed manufacturing overhead costs	£16.00	£8,000,000	£3.20	£8,000,000
Product Cost and Total Manufacturing Costs	£56.00	£28,000,000	£18.45	£46,125,000

5. Refer to Table 11-2 for the operating profit report and manufacturing activity summary of Firm Y for the year. Assume that the business has no work-in-progress stock at the start or end of the year. The business purchases £7,800,000 raw materials on credit during the year. Make the basic manufacturing entries for the business by following the series of entries explained in this section.

Solve It

6. Refer to Table 11-2 for the operating profit report and manufacturing activity summary of Firm Z for the year. Assume that the business has no work-in-progress stock at the start or end of the year. The business purchases £19,500,000 raw materials on credit during the year. Make the basic manufacturing entries for the business by following the series of entries explained in this section.

Solve It

7. Assume that Firm Y uses the LIFO method to charge out raw materials to production. In this question, assume that supply shortages of raw materials mean that Firm Y can't purchase all the raw materials it needs for production during the year, and it has to draw down its raw materials stock. Fortunately, it has an adequate Opening Stock of raw materials to cover the gap in purchases during the year. In this situation, is the cost of raw materials issued to production different to the £7,500,000 shown in Table 11-2?

Solve It

8. Determine Firm Z's operating profit if it sells 2,100,000 units during the year, which is 100,000 more units than in the example shown in Table 11-2. Assume that production output remains the same at 2,500,000 units (the business's production output capacity).

Solve It

Calculating Product Cost: Basic Methods and Problems

Product cost (which is £760.00 in the example shown in the earlier Table 11-1) consists of two quite different types of manufacturing costs: variable costs (including raw materials, direct labour and variable overheads) and fixed overhead costs. Variable manufacturing costs remain the same per unit (except at very low or very high levels of production). Thus, the total of variable manufacturing costs moves up and down with increases and decreases in production output (the number of units produced). In contrast, fixed costs are rigid; these costs remain the same and unchanged over a broad range of production output levels. Many of these fixed costs have to be paid even if the business shuts down its manufacturing for several months.

Refer to the earlier Table 11-1 for Firm X's manufacturing cost information. Its £760.00 product cost consists of £410.00 total variable costs per unit manufactured and £350.00 fixed manufacturing overhead cost per unit.

If Firm X manufactures ten more units than it did during the year, its total variable manufacturing costs would be £4,100 higher (10 additional units × £410 per unit = £4,100). The actual number of units produced drives total variable manufacturing costs, and so even one more unit causes the variable costs to increase £410. But the business's total fixed manufacturing overhead costs would be the same whether it produces ten more units, or 10,000 more units for that matter. Variable manufacturing costs are bought on a per unit basis, as it were, whereas fixed manufacturing costs are bought in bulk at fixed prices for the whole period.

Total manufacturing costs for the year are calculated as follows:

> (variable manufacturing costs per unit × number of units produced) + fixed manufacturing overhead costs = total manufacturing costs

Connecting fixed manufacturing overhead costs and production capacity

Fixed manufacturing overhead costs present certain problems in determining product cost and operating profit (that is, profit before interest and income tax expenses).

Why in the world would a manufacturer in its right mind commit to fixed manufacturing overhead costs? For example, according to Table 11-1, Firm X has £42,000,000 of these cost commitments hanging over its head for the year whether it produces 15,000 or 150,000 units or any number in between. The answer is that fixed manufacturing costs are needed to provide *production capacity* – the people and physical resources necessary to manufacture products – for the year. When the business has the production plant and people in place for the year, its fixed manufacturing costs aren't easily scaled down. The business is stuck with these costs over the short run.

The fixed manufacturing overhead cost component of product cost is called the *burden rate*. The burden rate of Firm X for the year is computed as follows (see Table 11-1 for data):

> £42,000,000 total fixed manufacturing overhead costs for year ÷ 120,000 units production output for period = £350 burden rate

Now, here's a very important twist on the example: suppose that Firm X manufactures only 110,000 units during the period – equal to the quantity sold during the year. Its variable manufacturing costs equal £410.00 per unit. This per unit cost remains the same at the lower production output level. In contrast, the burden rate becomes £381.82 per unit at the lower production output level (£42,000,000 total fixed manufacturing overhead costs ÷ 110,000 units production output = £381.82 burden rate). The higher burden rate causes product cost to be £31.82 higher.

Q. What is the operating profit of Firm X if its production output for the year was 110,000 units (equal to the number of units sold) instead of the 120,000 units production output level assumed in Table 11-1?

A. The operating profit at the 110,000 units production output level is £12,450,000, as shown in Table 11-3.

Table 11-3	Internal Operating Profit Report for Firm X	
		Firm X
Operating Profit for Year	**Per Unit**	**Totals**
Sales volume (units)		110,000
Sales revenue	£1,400	£154,000,000
Cost of Goods Sold expense (see below)	(£791.82)	(£87,100,000)
Gross Margin	£608.18	£66,900,000
Variable operating expenses	(£300.00)	(£33,000,000)
Contribution Margin	£308.18	£33,900,000
Fixed operating expenses		(£21,450,000)
Operating Profit		£12,450,000
Manufacturing Activity Summary for the Year		
Annual production capacity (units)		150,000
Actual output (units)		110,000
Raw materials	£215.00	£23,650,000
Direct labour	£125.00	£13,750,000
Variable manufacturing overhead costs	£70.00	£7,700,000
Total Variable Manufacturing Costs	£410.00	£45,100,000
Fixed manufacturing overhead costs	£381.82	£42,000,000
Product Cost and Total Manufacturing Costs	£791.82	£87,100,000

A key point of this example is that Firm X's product cost is £31.82 higher simply because it produces fewer units. The same total amount of fixed manufacturing overhead costs is spread over fewer units of production output. The higher product cost means that Cost of Goods Sold expense is higher, and therefore, operating profit is lower. At the 120,000 units production output level, operating profit is £15,950,000 (see earlier Table 11-1). But at the 110,000 units production output level, operating profit dips to £12,450,000, which is a decrease of £3,500,000. This decrease gets the attention of business managers, that's for sure!

9. Firm Y is on track to sell 550,000 units in the year, but late in the year, a major customer cancels a large order for 50,000 units. The business reduces its production output to 500,000 units, as you can see in the earlier Table 11-2. Determine the operating profit that Firm Y would earn if it manufactured and sold 550,000 units in the year.

Solve It

10. Assume that Firm Z's production output for the year is 2,000,000 units (instead of 2,500,000 units as in Table 11-2). In other words, the business manufactures the same number of units that it sells in the year. Assume that all other manufacturing and operating factors are the same. Determine the business's operating profit for the year.

Solve It

Boosting profit by boosting production

In the Firm X example shown earlier in Table 11-1, the Cost of Goods Sold expense for the year benefits from the fact that the business produces 10,000 more units than it sells during the year. These 10,000 units absorb £3,500,000 of its total fixed manufacturing overhead costs for the year. The Cost of Goods Sold expense escapes £3,500,000 in fixed manufacturing overhead costs because the business produces 10,000 more units than it sells during the year, thus pushing down the burden rate (see the preceding section for an explanation of burden rate). Until the units are sold, the £3,500,000 stays in the stock Asset account (along with variable manufacturing costs, of course).

The distribution of the business's fixed manufacturing overhead costs for the year is summarised as shown in Figure 11-1.

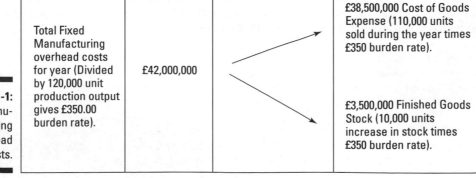

Figure 11-1: Fixed manufacturing overhead costs.

			£38,500,000 Cost of Goods Expense (110,000 units sold during the year times £350 burden rate).
Total Fixed Manufacturing overhead costs for year (Divided by 120,000 unit production output gives £350.00 burden rate).	£42,000,000		
			£3,500,000 Finished Goods Stock (10,000 units increase in stock times £350 burden rate).

Of its £42,000,000 total fixed manufacturing overhead costs for the year, only £38,500,000 ends up in Cost of Goods Sold expense for the year (£350 burden rate × 110,000 units sold = £38,500,000). The other £3,500,000 ends up in the stock Asset account (£350 burden rate × 10,000 units stock increase = £3,500,000). We're not suggesting any funny business, but Firm X helps its operating profit to the tune of £3,500,000 by producing 10,000 more units than it sells. Suppose that the business produced only 110,000 units, equal to its sales volume for the year. All its fixed manufacturing overhead costs would go into the Cost of Goods Sold expense, and operating profit would be that much lower.

Firm X's 120,000 units production output level may well be entirely justified as a way to have more units on hand for sales growth next year. But the production output decision can get out of hand. A manufacturer may deliberately pump up production output, not to prepare for sales growth next year but to pump up profit this year; and that's massaging the numbers, pure and simple, although it falls short of cooking the books (we draw the distinction between the two practices in Chapter 1). Nevertheless, pushing up production output for the sole purpose of boosting profit definitely smacks of accounting manipulation.

You need to judge whether a stock increase is justified. Be aware that an unjustified increase may be evidence of profit manipulation or just good old-fashioned management bungling. The day of reckoning will come when the products are sold and the cost of stock becomes Cost of Goods Sold expense.

In the earlier Table 11-1, Firm X's production capacity for the year is 150,000 units. The business produces only 120,000 units during the year, which is 30,000 units fewer than possible. In other words, it operates at 80 per cent of production capacity (120,000 units output ÷ 150,000 units capacity = 80 per cent utilisation), which is 20 per cent idle capacity. Production capacity, to remind you, is the maximum output that a business can achieve during a period of time given its machinery, equipment, buildings and land, labour force and other necessary manufacturing factors. *Idle capacity* is the difference between actual output during the period and production capacity. As a matter of fact, most manufacturers don't run at full production capacity, and so some idle (unused) production capacity is normal.

Running at 80 per cent of production capacity, this business's burden rate for the year is £350 per unit (£42,000,000 total fixed manufacturing overhead costs ÷ 120,000 units output = £350 burden rate). As we explain earlier in this section, the burden rate would be higher if the business produced only 110,000 units during the year. The burden rate, in other words, is sensitive to the number of units produced. This connection can lead to all kinds of mischief.

Suppose that Firm X manufactures 150,000 units during the year and increases its stock 40,000 units, which may be a legitimate move if the business is anticipating a big jump in sales next year. On the other hand, a stock increase of 40,000 units in a year in which only 110,000 units are sold may be the result of a serious overproduction mistake, and the larger stock may not be needed next year.

Q. In the Table 11-1 scenario, Firm X manufactures 120,000 units during the year, which causes its stock to increase 10,000 units. Suppose, instead, that the business manufactures 150,000 units during the year, which is its production capacity. Assume that sales and other factors are the same in this alternative scenario as shown in Table 11-1 – only production output is different. What is its operating profit for the year if it produces 150,000 units?

A. The operating profit report and summary of manufacturing activity for Firm X (as shown in Table 11-4) indicates what happens at the 150,000 units production output level. Remember that sales volume doesn't change in this scenario; only production output changes. Comparative data is presented for the 120,000 units production output level in the original scenario (see Table 11-1).

Table 11-4	Operating Profit and Summary for Firm X with 150,000 Units Produced	
	Firm X	
Operating Profit for Year	*Per Unit*	*Totals*
Sales volume (units)		110,000
Sales revenue	£1,400	£154,000,000
Cost of Goods Sold expense (see below)	(£690.00)	(£75,900,000)
Gross Margin	£710.00	£78,100,000
Variable operating expenses	(£300.00)	(£33,000,000)
Contribution Margin	£410.00	£45,100,000
Fixed operating expenses		(£21,450,000)
Operating Profit		£23,650,000
Manufacturing Activity Summary for the Year		
Annual production capacity (units)		150,000
Actual output (units)		150,000
Raw materials	£215.00	£32,250,000
Direct labour	£125.00	£18,750,000
Variable manufacturing overhead costs	£70.00	£10,500,000
Total Variable Manufacturing Costs	£410.00	£61,500,000
Fixed manufacturing overhead costs	£280.00	£42,000,000
Product Cost and Total Manufacturing Costs	£690.00	£103,500,000

Check out the £23,650,000 operating profit when production output is 150,000 units, compared with the £15,950,000 operating profit when production output is 120,000 units – a £7,700,000 difference even though sales volume, sales prices and operating expenses all remain the same. Whoa! What's going on here? The simple answer is that the Cost of Goods Sold expense is £7,700,000 less than before. How can the Cost of Goods Sold expense be less if the business sells 110,000 units in both scenarios, and variable manufacturing costs are £410.00 per unit in both cases?

The culprit is the *burden rate* component of product cost. In Table 11-1, total fixed manufacturing costs are spread over 120,000 units of output, giving a £350 burden rate per unit. In the Table 11-4 example, total fixed manufacturing costs are spread over 150,000 units output, giving the much lower £280 burden rate, or £70 per unit less. The £70 lower burden rate multiplied by the 110,000 units sold reduces the Cost of Goods Sold expense by £7,700,000 and increases operating profit the same amount.

If the business produces 150,000 units (production capacity), its stock increases 40,000 units. This increase is quite large compared to the annual sales of 110,000 for the year just ended. Who was responsible for the decision to go full blast and produce up to the production capacity? Do the managers really expect sales to jump up enough next year to justify the much larger stock level? If their guess is right, they look brilliant. But if the output level is a mistake and sales don't go up next year . . . they have you-know-what to pay, even though profit looks good this year. An experienced business manager knows to be on guard when stock takes such a big jump.

11. Towards the end of the year, the Managing Director (MD) of Firm Y looks at the preliminary numbers for operating profit and doesn't like what he sees. He's 'promised' the board of directors that operating profit for the year would come in at £4,850,000. In fact, his bonus depends on hitting that operating profit target. Time is still left before the end of the year to crank up production output for the year. Therefore, he orders that production output be stepped up. The MD asks you, as the chief accountant, to determine what the production output level for the year would have to be in order to report £4,850,000 operating profit for the year. Of course, you have ethical qualms about doing so, but you need the job. Therefore, you reluctantly decide to do the calculation. Determine the production output level that would yield £4,850,000 operating profit for the year.

Solve It

12. Refer to your answer to Question 10, in which Firm Z produces only 2,000,000 units during the year. In the scenario shown in Table 11-2, the business manufactures 2,500,000 units, which is its maximum production output for the year. Do you think that Firm Z cranked up production output to 2,500,000 units mainly to boost its operating profit for the year?

Solve It

Calculating Product Cost in Unusual Situations

The basic calculation model for product cost is:

> total manufacturing costs for period ÷ total units produced during period = product cost per unit

Total manufacturing costs for the period include direct manufacturing costs that can be clearly identified with a particular product and indirect manufacturing costs that are allocated to the product.

This product cost calculation method is appropriate in most situations. However, it has to be modified in two extreme situations:

- ✔ When manufacturing costs are grossly excessive or wasteful due to inefficient production operations.

- ✔ When production output is significantly less than normal capacity utilisation.

Suppose that Firm X has to throw away £1,200,000 of raw materials during the year because they aren't stored properly and end up being unusable in the production process. The manager in charge of the warehouse receives a stiff reprimand.

Q. In Table 11-1, which shows Firm X's operating profit performance and summary of manufacturing activity for the year, we assumed that no wasteful manufacturing costs apply. In this question, assume, instead, that the business has to throw away £1,200,000 of unusable raw materials. How should the £1,200,000 cost of raw materials that are thrown out be presented in the operating profit report and summary of manufacturing activity?

A. The £1,200,000 cost of raw materials that are wasted and not used in production should not be included in the calculation of product cost. The £1,200,000 cost of wasted raw materials should be treated as a *period cost*, which means that it's recorded as an expense in the period. The operating profit report and summary of manufacturing activity for the year in this scenario is shown in Table 11-5.

Table 11-5	Operating Profit and Summary for Firm X – Wasted Raw Materials Scenario	
		Firm X
Operating Profit for Year	*Per Unit*	*Totals*
Sales volume (units)		110,000
Sales revenue	£1,400	£154,000,000
Cost of Goods Sold expense (see below)	(£750.00)	(£82,500,000)
Gross Margin	£650.00	£71,500,000
Variable operating expenses	(£300.00)	(£33,000,000)
Contribution Margin	£350.00	£38,500,000
Fixed operating expenses		(£21,450,000)
Cost of wasted raw materials		(£1,200,000)
Operating Profit		£15,850,000

(continued)

Table 11-5 (continued)

Manufacturing Activity Summary for the Year	Per Unit	Totals
Annual production capacity (units)		150,000
Actual output (units)		120,000
Raw materials	£205.00	£24,600,000
Direct labour	£125.00	£15,000,000
Variable manufacturing overhead costs	£70.00	£8,400,000
Total Variable Manufacturing Costs	£400.00	£48,000,000
Fixed manufacturing overhead costs	£350.00	£42,000,000
Product Cost and Total Manufacturing Costs	£750.00	£90,000,000

As Table 11-5 shows, the £1,200,000 wasted raw materials cost is recorded as an expense in the year. Therefore, the cost of raw materials reduces by the same amount in the manufacturing activity summary for the year, with the result that product cost drops to £750 per unit.

13. The MD of Firm X is puzzled by the operating profit report and summary of manufacturing activity for the year in which £1,200,000 raw materials cost is wasted and charged to expenses. He expected that operating profit would be £1,200,000 lower (as compared to the scenario in Table 11-1, in which no wasted raw materials cost exists). Operating profit in the wasted raw materials scenario is only £100,000 lower than in Table 11-1. Explain to the MD why operating profit is only £100,000 lower.

Solve It

14. After Firm Y's operating profit report and summary of manufacturing activity for the year is prepared (see Table 11-2), you, the chief accountant, discover that £1,000,000 of raw materials were thrown away during the year because the items spoiled and were unusable in the manufacturing process. The MD knows about this loss and insists that no change be made in the operating profit report and summary of manufacturing activity. Do you go along with the MD, or do you argue for changing the operating profit report and summary of manufacturing activity?

Solve It

One argument is that the cost of idle capacity should be charged off as a period cost (that is, charged directly to expenses in the year and not included in product cost). Generally, the cost of idle capacity is calculated as follows:

> percentage of idle capacity × fixed manufacturing overhead costs = cost of idle capacity

Refer to Firm Y's operating profit report and summary of manufacturing activity for the year (see Table 11-2). Its annual production capacity is 800,000 units, but it produces only 500,000 units during the year. The business's idle capacity is 37.5 per cent. In this case, the idle capacity cost is calculated as follows:

> 37.5 per cent idle capacity × £8,000,000 fixed manufacturing overhead costs = £3,000,000 cost of idle capacity

Q. How would Firm Y's operating profit report and summary of manufacturing activity be revised if the cost of idle capacity is treated as a period cost in the year?

A. The £3,000,000 cost of idle capacity is taken out of fixed manufacturing overhead costs and moved up to the operating profit report as an expense in the period. The revised operating profit report and summary of manufacturing activity, which you may find somewhat surprising, is shown in Table 11-6.

Table 11-6	Internal Operating Profit Report for Firm Y	
		Firm Y
Operating Profit Report for Year	*Per Unit*	*Totals*
Sales volume (units)		500,000
Sales revenue	£85.00	£42,500,000
Cost of Goods Sold expense (see below)	(£50.00)	(£25,000,000)
Gross Margin	£35.00	£17,500,000
Variable operating expenses	(£12.50)	(£6,250,000)
Contribution Margin	£22.50	£11,250,000
Fixed operating expenses		(£5,000,000)
Cost of idle capacity		(£3,000,000)
Operating Profit		£3,250,000
Manufacturing Activity Summary for the Year		
Annual production capacity (units)		800,000
Actual output (units)		500,000
Raw materials	£15.00	£7,500,000
Direct labour	£20.00	£10,000,000
Variable manufacturing overhead costs	£5.00	£2,500,000
Total Variable Manufacturing Costs	£40.00	£20,000,000
Fixed manufacturing overhead costs	£10.00	£5,000,000
Product Cost and Total Manufacturing Costs	£50.00	£25,000,000

Note that changing the handling of the cost of idle capacity produces no difference in the business's operating profit for the year. Is this surprising, or what? In this example, the business produces the same number of units it sells during the year. Thus, no 'stock effect' exists. One-hundred per cent of its manufacturing costs for the year end up in expenses regardless of the way in which the idle capacity is handled. In Table 11-2, the entire £8,000,000 fixed manufacturing overhead costs ends up in the Cost of Goods Sold expense. In this example scenario in Table 11-6, £3,000,000 of the fixed costs end up in a period Expense account (Cost of Idle Capacity) and the other £5,000,000 ends up in the Cost of Goods Sold expense.

---

15. Assume that Firm Z manufactures 2,100,000 units during the year (instead of the 2,500,000 units production output shown in Table 11-2). Determine its operating profit for the year. Assume that the cost of idle capacity is treated as a period cost and isn't embedded in product cost.

Solve It

16. Refer to Firm X's operating profit report and summary of manufacturing activity presented in Table 11-1. Note that its annual production capacity is 150,000 units, but the business manufactures only 120,000 units during the year. Therefore, it has 20 per cent idle capacity (30,000 units not produced ÷ 150,000 units production capacity = 20 per cent idle capacity). However, the cost of idle capacity isn't treated as a separate period cost; all the business's fixed manufacturing overhead costs are included in calculating its product cost.

Suppose that the business treats the cost of idle capacity as a period cost. Prepare a revised operating profit report and summary of manufacturing activity for the business.

Solve It

Answers to Problems on Manufacturing Cost Accounting

Here are the answers to the questions presented earlier in this chapter.

1 The business's total manufacturing costs for the year are £91,200,000 as shown in Table 11-1), but only £83,600,000 is charged to Cost of Goods Sold expense. What happened to the other £7,600,000 (£91,200,000 manufacturing costs for year – £83,600,000 Cost of Goods Sold expense for year = £7,600,000)?

The business produces 120,000 units, which is 10,000 more units than the 110,000 units it sells during the year. Therefore, $\frac{1}{12}$ (10,000 ÷ 120,000) of its total manufacturing costs is allocated to the increase in stock, and $\frac{11}{12}$ is allocated to Cost of Goods Sold during the year:

$\frac{11}{12}$ × £91,200,000 total manufacturing costs = £83,600,000 allocated to Cost of Goods Sold expense

$\frac{1}{12}$ × £91,200,000 total manufacturing costs = £7,600,000 allocated to stock

You can also answer this question by using product cost and number of units sold during the year:

£760 product cost × 110,000 units sold during year = £83,600,000 cost allocated to Cost of Goods Sold expense

£760 product cost × 10,000 units increase in stock = £7,600,000 cost allocated to stock

2 As you can see in Table 11-1, Firm X records £42,000,000 fixed manufacturing overhead costs in the year. Suppose, instead, that its fixed manufacturing overhead costs are £45,600,000 for the year, which is an increase of £3,600,000. Would the business's operating profit be £3,600,000 lower? (Assume that variable manufacturing costs per unit and operating expenses remain the same.)

No, operating profit would not be £3,600,000 lower. Table 11-7 shows that operating profit would be £3,300,000 lower. The higher fixed manufacturing overhead costs drive up the product cost per unit, from £760 to £790, or £30 per unit. However, the business sells only 110,000 units, and so the £30 higher product cost per unit increases Cost of Goods Sold expense only £3,300,000 (£30 increase in product cost × 110,000 units sales volume = £3,300,000). Therefore, operating profit decreases £3,300,000.

Table 11-7	Internal Profit and Loss Report for Firm X	
	Firm X	
Operating Profit for Year	*Per Unit*	*Totals*
Sales volume (units)		110,000
Sales revenue	£1,400	£154,000,000
Cost of Goods Sold expense (see below)	(£790.00)	(£86,900,000)
Gross Margin	£810.00	£67,100,000
Variable operating expenses	(£300.00)	(£33,000,000)
Contribution Margin	£310.00	£34,100,000
Fixed operating expenses		(£21,450,000)
Operating Profit		£12,650,000

(continued)

Table 11-7 *(continued)*

Manufacturing Activity Summary for the Year	Per Unit	Totals
Manufacturing Activity Summary for the Year		
Annual production capacity (units)		150,000
Actual output (units)		120,000
Raw materials	£215.00	£25,800,000
Direct labour	£125.00	£15,000,000
Variable manufacturing overhead costs	£70.00	£8,400,000
Total Variable Manufacturing Costs	£410.00	£49,200,000
Fixed manufacturing overhead costs	£380.00	£45,600,000
Product cost and total manufacturing costs	£790.00	£94,800,000

The operating profit decrease still leaves £300,000 of the total £3,600,000 fixed manufacturing overhead costs increase to explain. The 10,000 units increase in stock absorbs this additional amount of fixed manufacturing overhead costs; including fixed manufacturing overhead costs in product cost is called *absorption costing*. Some accountants argue that product cost should include only variable manufacturing costs and not include any fixed manufacturing overhead costs. This practice is called *direct costing*, or *variable costing*, and it isn't generally accepted. Generally accepted accounting principles (GAAP) require that the fixed manufacturing overhead cost must be included in product cost.

3 Suppose that Firm X uses the FIFO method instead of the LIFO method shown in Table 11-1. The business starts the year with 25,000 units of Opening Stock at a cost of £735 per unit according to the FIFO method. During the year, it manufactures 120,000 units and sells 110,000 units (see Table 11-1). Determine Firm X's Cost of Goods Sold expense for the year and its cost of Closing Stock using the FIFO method.

The business starts the year with 25,000 units at £735 per unit for a total cost of £18,375,000, which constitutes one batch of stock. The business manufactures 120,000 units during the year at £760 per unit for a total cost of £91,200,000, which constitutes the second batch of stock.

Under FIFO, the Cost of Goods Sold expense is determined as follows:

25,000 units	× £735	= £18,375,000
85,000 units	× £760	= £64,600,000
110,000 units sold		= £82,975,000

Under FIFO, the Closing Stock consists of one layer:

35,000 units	× £760	= £26,600,000

4 Firm X produces 120,000 units and sells 110,000 units during the year (see Table 11-1). Therefore, the business increases its stock 10,000 units. Does this increase seem reasonable? Or is the business's production output compared with its sales volume out of kilter?

Saying for certain whether the increased stock is reasonable or not is problematic. The key factor is the forecasted sales volume for next year. If the business predicts moderate sales volume growth next year, increasing stock 10,000 units seems reasonable. On the other hand, if the sales forecast is flat for next year, why did the business produce more than it sold during the year just ended? The stock increase may have been a mistake; or taking a more cynical view, perhaps the business deliberately manufactured more units than it sold in order to boost operating profit for the year.

5 Refer to Table 11-2 for the operating profit report and manufacturing activity summary of Firm Y for the year. Assume that the business has no work-in-progress stock at the start or end of the year. The business purchases $7,800,000 raw materials on credit during the year. Make the basic manufacturing entries for the business by following the series of entries explained in the section 'Taking a Short Tour of Manufacturing Entries.'

Note: the following manufacturing entries include short explanations.

	Debit	*Credit*
Raw materials stock	$7,800,000	
Trade Creditors		$7,800,000

Purchase on credit of raw materials needed in the production process.

	Debit	*Credit*
Work-in-progress stock	$7,500,000	
Raw materials stock		$7,500,000

Transfer of raw materials to the production process.

	Debit	*Credit*
Work-in-progress stock	$10,000,000	
Cash		$7,000,000
Payroll taxes payable		$2,000,000
Accrued payables		$1,000,000

To record direct labour costs for period.

	Debit	*Credit*
Work-in-progress stock	$2,500,000	
Cash		$1,500,000
Trade Creditors		$500,000
Accrued payables		$500,000

To record indirect variable manufacturing overhead costs for period.

	Debit	*Credit*
Work-in-progress stock	$8,000,000	
Cash		$5,000,000
Accumulated depreciation		$2,000,000
Trade Creditors		$300,000
Accrued payables		$700,000

To record indirect fixed manufacturing overhead costs for period.

	Debit	*Credit*
Finished goods stock	$28,000,000	
Work-in-progress stock		$28,000,000

To record completion of manufacturing process and to transfer production costs to the finished goods stock account.

	Debit	Credit
Cost of Goods Sold expense	£28,000,000	
Finished goods stock		£28,000,000

To record cost of products sold during year.

6. Refer to Table 11-2 for the operating profit report and manufacturing activity summary of Firm Z for the year. Assume that the business has no work-in-progress stock at the start or end of the year. The business purchases £19,500,000 raw materials on credit during the year. Make the basic manufacturing entries for the business by following the series of entries explained in the section 'Taking a Short Tour of Manufacturing Entries.'

Note: the following manufacturing entries include short explanations.

	Debit	Credit
Raw materials stock	£19,500,000	
Trade Creditors		£19,500,000

Purchase on credit of raw materials needed in the production process.

	Debit	Credit
Work-in-progress stock	£18,750,000	
Raw materials stock		£18,750,000

Transfer of raw materials to the production process.

	Debit	Credit
Work-in-progress stock	£6,875,000	
Cash		£3,875,000
Payroll taxes payable		£2,000,000
Accrued payables		£1,000,000

To record direct labour costs for period.

	Debit	Credit
Work-in-progress stock	£12,500,000	
Cash		£7,000,000
Creditors		£3,500,000
Accrued payables		£2,000,000

To record indirect variable manufacturing overhead costs for period.

	Debit	Credit
Work-in-progress stock	£8,000,000	
Cash		£4,000,000

Accumulated depreciation	$3,000,000
Creditors	$500,000
Accrued payables	$500,000

To record indirect fixed manufacturing overhead costs for period.

	Debit	*Credit*
Finished goods stock	$46,125,000	
Work-in-progress stock		$46,125,000

To record completion of manufacturing process and to transfer production costs to the finished goods stock account.

	Debit	*Credit*
Cost of Goods Sold expense	$36,900,000	
Finished goods stock		$36,900,000

To record cost of products sold during year.

7 Assume that Firm Y uses the LIFO method to charge out raw materials to production. In this question, assume that supply shortages of raw materials mean that Firm Y can't purchase all the raw materials it needs for production during the year, and it has to draw down its raw materials stock. Fortunately, it has an adequate Opening Stock of raw materials to cover the gap in purchases during the year. In this situation, is the cost of raw materials issued to production different to the $7,500,000 shown in Table 11-2?

Yes, the cost of raw materials charged to production is likely to be lower, because the Opening Stock or raw materials is probably on the books at a lower cost per unit compared with current purchase prices. This 'aging' of stock cost is one disadvantage of the LIFO method, which we discuss in Chapter 9. When a business dips into its Opening Stock because it uses more materials than it was able to buy during the period, it has to charge out the raw materials at the costs recorded in its stock account. These costs may go back several years, and in the meantime, the costs of raw materials have probably escalated to higher prices per unit. If the difference is significant, the chief accountant should warn managers that the raw materials component of product cost is lower than normal because of a *LIFO liquidation effect* – not because of more efficient production methods or lower raw material purchase prices during the year.

8 Determine Firm Z's operating profit if it sells 2,100,000 units during the year, which is 100,000 more units than in the example shown in Table 11-2. Assume that production output remains the same at 2,500,000 units (the business's production output capacity).

The business manufactures 500,000 more units than it sells during the year (see Table 11-2). Therefore, it certainly has 100,000 additional units available for sale; indeed, it has 500,000 additional units available for sale without having to reach into its opening quantity of stock. An additional 100,000 units of sales is only a 5 per cent increase (100,000 additional units ÷ 2,000,000 units sales volume = 5 per cent.) So, the business's fixed operating expenses probably would not increase at the higher sales volume level.

The business's product cost is the same at the higher sales level and so its fixed operating costs holds the same. Therefore, its operating profit increases by $405,000:

$4.05 contribution margin per unit × 100,000 additional units sold = $405,000 operating profit increase

In other words, Firm Z's operating profit increases from $600,000 to $1,005,000, which is an increase of 67.5 per cent. But don't get too excited – this large percentage increase is due mainly to the low base of only $600,000 operating profit. Nevertheless, the business certainly can report a much better operating profit than if it had sold just 5 per cent more units.

Firm Y is on track to sell 550,000 units in the year, but late in the year a major customer cancels a large order for 50,000 units. The business reduces its production output to 500,000 units, as you can see in the earlier Table 11-2. Determine the operating profit that Firm Y would earn if it had manufactured and sold 550,000 units in the year.

Firm Y would earn £4,875,000 operating profit, as the schedule in Table 11-8 shows.

Table 11-8	Internal Profit and Loss Report for Firm Y	
	Firm Y	
	Per Unit	Totals
Operating Profit Report for Year		
Sales volume (units)		550,000
Sales revenue	£85.00	£46,750,000
Cost of Goods Sold expense (see the Product Cost and Total Manufacturing Costs in the Per Unit column below)	(£54.55)	(£30,000,000)
Gross Margin	£30.45	£16,750,000
Variable operating expenses	(£12.50)	(£6,875,000)
Contribution Margin	£17.95	£9,875,000
Fixed operating expenses		(£5,000,000)
Operating Profit		£4,875,000
Manufacturing Activity Summary for Year		
Annual production capacity (units)		800,000
Actual output (units)		550,000
Raw materials	£15.00	£8,250,000
Direct labour	£20.00	£11,000,000
Variable manufacturing overhead cost	£5.00	£2,750,000
Total Variable Manufacturing Costs	£40.00	£22,000,000
Fixed manufacturing overhead costs	£14.55	£8,000,000
Product Cost and Total Manufacturing Costs	£54.55	£30,000,000

The cancelled order for 50,000 units hits operating profit hard: the business's operating profit falls £1,625,000 as a result, from £4,875,000 (see Table 11-8) to £3,250,000 (see Table 11-2, in which only 500,000 units are sold).

 The business has unused production capacity (see Table 11-2), and so producing an additional 50,000 units wouldn't increase its fixed manufacturing overhead costs. And, its fixed operating costs wouldn't have increased at the higher sales level. The business's *variable* operating expenses equal £12.50 per unit, and its variable manufacturing costs equal £40.00 per unit. Thus, its total variable costs equal £52.50 per unit. Manufacturing and selling 50,000 additional units causes costs to increase £2,625,000 (£52.50 variable costs per unit × 50,000 units = £2,625,000). Selling an additional 50,000 units increases sales revenue £4,250,000 (£85.00 sales price × 50,000 units = £4,250,000). Therefore,

Incremental sales revenue from additional 50,000 units = £4,250,000

Incremental costs from additional 50,000 units = (£2,625,000)

Incremental operating profit from additional 50,000 units = £1,625,000

This calculation is an example of *marginal analysis*; on analysing things on the edge. The focus is on the 50,000 units that the business didn't sell (but came close to selling).

10 Assume that Firm Z's production output for the year is 2,000,000 units (instead of 2,500,000 units as in Table 11-2). In other words, the business manufactures the same number of units that it sells in the year. Assume that all other manufacturing and operating factors are the same. Determine the business's operating profit for the year.

In this scenario, the business suffers a £1,000,000 operating *loss*; see the schedule in Table 11-9.

Table 11-9	Internal Profit and Loss Report for Firm Z	
	Firm Z	
	Per Unit	*Totals*
Operating Profit Report for Year		
Sales volume (units)		2,000,000
Sales revenue	£25.00	£50,000,000
Cost of Goods Sold expense (see the Product Cost and Total Manufacturing Costs in the Per Unit column below)	(£19.25)	(£38,500,000)
Gross Margin	£5.75	£11,500,000
Variable operating expenses	(£2.50)	(£5,000,000)
Contribution Margin	£3.25	£6,500,000
Fixed operating expenses		£7,500,000
Operating Profit		(£1,000,000)
Manufacturing Activity Summary for Year		
Annual production capacity (units)		2,500,000
Actual output (units)		2,000,000
Raw materials	£7.50	£15,000,000
Direct labour	£2.75	£5,500,000
Variable manufacturing overhead cost	£5.00	£10,000,000
Total Variable Manufacturing Costs	£15.25	£30,500,000
Fixed manufacturing overhead costs	£4.00	£8,000,000
Product Cost and Total Manufacturing Costs	£19.25	£38,500,000

Producing only 2,000,000 units means that the business's burden rate increases to £4.00 per unit from the £3.20 burden rate when it produces 2,500,000 units (see Table 11-2). This increase is £0.80 per unit, which decreases Firm Z's contribution margin per unit from £4.05 to £3.25 per unit. The business records £0.80 less profit on each unit sold, and so on its 2,000,000 units sales volume its operating profit drops £1,600,000 – from £600,000 profit (see Table 11-2) to £1,000,000 loss. The business appears to boost production output to 2,500,000 units in order to show a profit for the year. As the result, Firm Z's stuck with a surplus stock that it has to do something with in the year(s) ahead.

11 Towards the end of the year, the Managing Director (MD) of Firm Y looks at the preliminary numbers for operating profit and doesn't like what he sees. He's 'promised' the board of directors that operating profit for the year would come in at £4,850,000. In fact, his bonus depends on hitting that operating profit target. Time is still left before the end of the year to crank up production output for the year. Therefore, he orders that production output be stepped up. The MD asks you, as the chief accountant, to determine what the production output level for the year would have to be in order to report £4,850,000 operating profit for the year. Of course, you have ethical qualms about doing so, but you need the job. Therefore, you reluctantly decide to do the calculation. Determine the production output level that would yield £4,850,000 operating profit for the year.

Table 11-10 shows that if the business manufactures 625,000 units, its operating profit becomes £4,850,000.

Table 11-10	Internal Profit and Loss Report for Firm Y	
	Firm Y	
	Per Unit	**Totals**
Operating Profit Report for Year		
Sales volume (units)		500,000
Sales revenue	£85.00	£42,500,000
Cost of Goods Sold expense (see the Product Cost and Total Manufacturing Costs in the Per Unit column below)	(£52.80)	(£26,400,000)
Gross Margin	£32.20	£16,100,000
Variable operating expenses	(£12.50)	(£6,250,000)
Contribution Margin	£19.70	£9,850,000
Fixed operating expenses		(£5,000,000)
Operating Profit		£4,850,000
Manufacturing Activity Summary for Year		
Annual production capacity (units)		800,000
Actual output (units)		625,000
Raw materials	£15.00	£9,375,000
Direct labour	£20.00	£12,500,000
Variable manufacturing overhead cost	£5.00	£3,125,000
Total Variable Manufacturing Costs	£40.00	£25,000,000
Fixed manufacturing overhead costs	£12.80	£8,000,000
Product Cost and Total Manufacturing Costs	£52.80	£33,000,000

The MD wants £1,600,000 more profit than shown in Table 11-2 (£4,850,000 profit target − £3,250,000 profit at 500,000 units production level = £1,600,000 additional profit). The only profit driver that changes with a higher production level is the burden rate, which has to decline £3.20 per unit in order to achieve the additional profit (£1,600,000 additional profit wanted ÷ 500,000 units sales volume = £3.20 decrease needed in burden rate). The burden rate has to decrease £3.20, from £16.00 (see Table 11-2) to £12.80. The production output level has to be 625,000 units to get the burden rate down to £12.80 (£8,000,000 fixed manufacturing overhead costs ÷ £12.80 burden rate = 625,000 units).

Whether jacking up production to 625,000 units is ethical when sales are only 500,000 units for the year is a serious question. The members of Firm Y's board of directors should definitely challenge the MD on why such a large stock increase is needed. We certainly would!

12 Refer to your answer to Question 10, in which Firm Z produces only 2,000,000 units during the year. In the scenario shown in Table 11-2, the business manufactures 2,500,000 units, which is its maximum production output for the year. Do you think that Firm Z cranked up production output to 2,500,000 units mainly to boost its operating profit for the year?

No one wants to jump to conclusions, but boosting operating profit appears to be the reason for Firm Z's high production output level. Put another way, the CEO of the business has to justify the large stock increase based on legitimate reasons, such as a big jump in sales forecast for next year or a looming strike of employees that will shut down the business's production for several months. Otherwise, the ugly truth is that the business is engaging in some *earnings management*, also called massaging the numbers. Sophisticated readers of the business's financial statements will notice the large jump in stock in the balance sheet, and they may press top management for an explanation. Therefore, the attempt at accounting manipulation may not work.

13 The MD of Firm X is puzzled by the operating profit report and summary of manufacturing activity for the year in which £1,200,000 raw materials cost is wasted and charged to expenses. He expected that operating profit would be £1,200,000 lower (as compared to the scenario in Table 11-1, in which no wasted raw materials cost exists). Operating profit in the wasted raw materials scenario is only £100,000 lower than in Table 11-1. Explain to the MD why operating profit is only £100,000 lower.

The MD is asking about the impact on operating profit. If the £1,200,000 cost of wasted raw materials is included in the calculation of product cost, £1,100,000 of it ends up in Cost of Goods Sold expense because 110,000 of the 120,000 units produced are sold during the year. The other £100,000 is absorbed in the stock increase. In contrast, if the £1,200,000 is charged to expenses directly, none of it escapes into the stock increase. So in one scenario, profit is hit with a £1,100,000 expense and in the other scenario profit is hit with a £1,200,000 expense. The operating profit difference is only £100,000.

14 After Firm Y's operating profit report and summary of manufacturing activity for the year is prepared (see Table 11-2), you, the chief accountant, discover that £1,000,000 of raw materials were thrown away during the year because the items spoiled and were unusable in the manufacturing process. The business's MD knows about this loss and insists that no change be made in the operating profit report and summary of manufacturing activity. Do you go along with the MD, or do you argue for changing the operating profit report and summary of manufacturing activity?

If you haven't read the answer to Question 13, please read it. In that scenario the net error in operating profit is only £100,000 because most of the cost of wasted materials flowed through to Cost of Goods Sold expense. In this case, *all* the cost of wasted materials ends up in the Cost of Goods Sold expense, and so operating profit is correct. The reason is that all the manufacturing costs for the year are charged to Cost of Goods Sold because all the business's output for the year is sold. Note that its entire £28,000,000 manufacturing costs is charged to Cost of Goods Sold expense. (Remember that the business uses the LIFO method.)

Therefore, the argument in this situation is really about how to classify costs in the internal operating profit report to managers. Should you report a separate cost of wasted raw materials? Yes, we think so. We hope that this cost is one that the business can avoid in the future. If the error isn't corrected, the managers would be misled into thinking that the true product cost is £16.00, when in fact it's £2.00 lower (£1,000,000 cost of wasted raw materials ÷ 500,000 units production output = £2.00 per unit error).

15 Assume that Firm Z manufactures 2,100,000 units during the year (instead of the 2,500,000 units production output shown in Table 11-2). Determine its operating profit for the year. Assume that the cost of idle capacity is treated as a period cost and isn't embedded in product cost.

The business's operating loss is £680,000, as Table 11-11 shows.

Table 11-11	Internal Profit and Loss Report for Firm Z	
	Firm Z	
	Per Unit	*Totals*
Operating Profit Report for Year		
Sales volume (units)		2,000,000
Sales revenue	£25.00	£50,000,000
Cost of Goods Sold expense	(£18.45)	(£36,900,000)
Gross Margin	£6.55	£13,100,000
Variable operating expenses	(£2.50)	(£5,000,000)
Contribution Margin	£4.05	£8,100,000
Fixed operating expenses		(£7,500,000)
Cost of idle capacity		(£1,280,000)
Operating loss		(£680,000)
Manufacturing Activity Summary for Year		
Annual production capacity (units)		2,500,000
Actual output (units)		2,100,000
Raw materials	£7.50	£15,750,000
Direct labour	£2.75	£5,775,000
Variable manufacturing overhead cost	£5.00	£10,500,000
Total Variable Manufacturing Costs	£15.25	£32,025,000
Fixed manufacturing overhead costs – net of idle capacity cost (see above)	£3.20	£6,720,000
Product Cost and Total Manufacturing Costs	£18.45	£38,745,000

The business has 16 per cent idle capacity in this scenario (400,000 units not produced ÷ 2,500,000 units capacity = 16 per cent idle capacity). So, 16 per cent of its £8,000,000 fixed manufacturing overhead costs, or £1,280,000, is removed from the calculation of product cost and treated as a period cost. Of course, this action reduces operating profit for the year by this amount.

16 Refer to Firm X's operating profit report and summary of manufacturing activity presented in Table 11-1. Note that its annual production capacity is 150,000 units, but the business manufactures only 120,000 units during the year. Therefore, it has 20 per cent idle capacity (30,000 units not produced ÷ 150,000 units production capacity = 20 per cent idle capacity). However, in the Table 11-1 scenario, the cost of idle capacity isn't treated as a separate period cost; all the business's fixed manufacturing overhead costs are included in calculating its product cost.

Suppose that the business treats the cost of idle capacity as a period cost. Prepare a revised operating profit report and summary of manufacturing activity for the business.

Firm X's operating profit would be £15,250,000, as Table 11-12 shows.

Table 11-12	Internal Profit and Loss Report for Firm X	
	Firm X	
Operating Profit for Year	*Per Unit*	*Totals*
Sales volume (units)		110,000
Sales revenue	£1,400	£154,000,000
Cost of Goods Sold expense (see the Product Cost and Total Manufacturing Costs in the Per Unit column below)	(£690.00)	(£75,900,000)
Gross Margin	£710.00	£78,100,000
Variable operating expenses	(£300.00)	(£33,000,000)
Contribution Margin	£410.00	£45,100,000
Fixed operating expenses		(£21,450,000)
Cost of idle capacity		(£8,400,000)
Operating Profit		£15,250,000
Manufacturing Activity Summary for the Year		
Annual production capacity (units)		150,000
Actual output, (units)		120,000
Raw materials	£215.00	£25,800,000
Direct labour	£125.00	£15,000,000
Variable manufacturing overhead costs	£70.00	£8,400,000
Total Variable Manufacturing Costs	£410.00	£49,200,000
Fixed Manufacturing Overhead costs (net of idle capacity cost – see above)	£280.00	£33,600,000
Product Cost and Total Manufacturing Costs	£690.00	£82,800,000

Note that the business's operating profit decreases a relatively small amount, only £700,000, due to treating idle capacity as a period cost rather than a product cost. In Table 11-1, operating profit is £15,950,000, and in this schedule, it's £15,250,000, or £700,000 less. This £700,000 is 'buried' in the Closing Stock cost under the method shown in Table 11-1; in other words, in the scenario shown in Table 11-1, the cost of idle capacity is included in the £760 product cost. The product cost is £70 higher than the £690 product cost in Table 11-12 (in which idle capacity is pulled out of manufacturing and treated as a period cost). The business sells 110,000 units, and the other 10,000 units of its production output increase its stock. These 10,000 units absorb £700,000 of the idle capacity cost (10,000 units stock increase × £70 higher burden rate = £700,000 absorbed by stock increase).

Chapter 12

Figuring Out Interest and Return on Investment

*I*n our experience, most people are a little fuzzy on the details of interest and return on investment (ROI). Most people know that interest is the cost of borrowing money or the income from saving money, and that they should earn a return on their investments, but when put in a specific borrowing, saving or investing situation, people aren't sure how interest is calculated and exactly what different interest rates mean. And they're in a fog regarding how rates of return on investments are determined and the assumptions behind these measures of investment performance. Well, that's where this chapter comes to the rescue.

The better you understand interest and ROI, the better economic citizen and intelligent investor you become. In this chapter, we explain how interest works and how investment performance is measured using rates of return. We think that you're going to find more than a few surprises as you read through it.

Getting Down to the Basics of Interest

Any explanation of interest has to start with what's called simple interest – although, the reality isn't as simple as the term implies.

The Apollo 13 astronauts became famous for their message, 'Houston, we have a problem'. The inherent problem in this chapter is that, by their very nature, interest and ROI require calculations. However, most people have their enthusiasm for number-crunching well under control (except for accountants and actuaries).

We don't throw a load of mathematical formulas at you in this chapter (that would certainly turn you off). Instead, we use transparent examples that demonstrate how interest works and how to determine ROI. In sports, becoming a better player takes practice. In accounting, the best means for improving your understanding of interest and ROI is to practise with realistic examples.

Keeping things simple with simple interest

The idea behind simple interest is that a certain amount of interest is paid or earned on a certain amount of money for a certain period of time, say one year. Suppose that you put £1,000 in a savings account at the start of the year. At the end of the year your savings account is credited (increases) £40 for the interest you earned. The simple interest rate you earned is calculated as follows:

£40 interest earned ÷ £1,000 amount invested for one year = 4.0 per cent simple interest rate

But, what if you earned £10 each quarter instead of £40 at the end of the year? Things get more complicated, as we explain in this chapter.

Q. Suppose that you fill out all the forms and convince a bank to loan your business £100,000. The terms of the loan are that the bank put £100,000 in your bank account today; the maturity of the loan is one year later; and the annual interest rate on the loan is 6 per cent. What amount do you have to pay the bank one year later, on the maturity date, to pay off this loan?

A. You can probably solve this problem in your head without doing any calculations on a handheld business/finance calculator or using Excel. But we modify this simple example later in the chapter in order to explore several other important features of interest, and so we want to be very clear about how interest is calculated for this basic example.

In this example, interest is added to the amount borrowed to determine the *maturity value* of the loan, which is the amount payable to the bank on the maturity date. The amount borrowed, which is called the *face value* or *principal* of the loan, is the basis for calculating interest. The amount of interest is calculated as follows:

£100,000 amount borrowed today × 6 per cent annual interest rate = £6,000 interest on loan

£100,000 amount borrowed today + £6,000 interest on loan = £106,000 maturity value of loan one year later

The legal instrument used for the contract between a borrower and a lender is fairly complicated and contains many clauses and provisions. Generally, the borrower signs a loan agreement to the lender. You need a lawyer to explain all the terms, conditions, obligations and rights of each party under the loan agreement.

Q. Suppose, however, that the lender doesn't refer to an annual interest rate or to the amount you borrow. You sign a legal agreement (probably a promissory loan agreement) that calls for the payment of £106,000 at the maturity date of the loan (one year later). The bank puts £100,000 in your bank account today. Is the annual interest rate on this loan still 6 per cent?

A. Yes, the annual interest rate is still 6 per cent. Why? Well, the interest rate is calculated on the basis of the amount received

at the start of the loan. So, the interest rate is calculated as follows:

£106,000 maturity value of loan one year later – £100,000 received today when signing the loan agreement = £6,000 interest for one year

£6,000 interest for one year ÷ £100,000 received at start of loan = 6 per cent annual interest rate

One year later you pay back to the bank 6 per cent more than the bank loaned to you today, which means that the annual interest rate is 6 per cent. Whether this interest rate is too high or not is up to you. You may want to shop around at different banks and other lenders to see whether you can get a better interest rate.

1. Suppose that your business borrows £500,000 from a bank, and that amount is deposited in your bank account today. The loan agreement that you sign calls for a 6.25 per cent annual interest rate. Determine the *maturity value* (the amount you will pay the bank when the loan agreement comes due) of the loan agreement one year from now.

Solve It

2. Suppose that you sign a loan agreement that calls for £868,000 to be paid to the lender one year from today. (In other words, the maturity value of the loan one year from today is £868,000.) The lender gives you £800,000 today. No mention is made of the rate of interest on this loan. What is the annual interest rate on this loan?

Solve It

3. Refer to Question 1. Suppose that the date on the loan agreement is 1 March, 2009 – this date is when the agreement was signed and the money was put in the business's bank account. Today is 31 August, 2009, which is the close of the business's accounting year. Should an adjusting entry for interest expense be recorded? If so, make the journal entry.

Solve It

4. Refer to Question 2. Because the loan agreement calls for a payment of £868,000 at the maturity date, the bookkeeper thinks that this amount should be recorded as a liability and that the difference between this liability amount and the £800,000 proceeds received by the business should be debited to the prepaid expenses Asset account. Do you agree?

Solve It

Distinguishing nominal and effective interest rates

Assume that a business borrows £100,000 for one year at an annual interest rate of 6 per cent. One alternative is that the bank charges 6 per cent simple interest that's payable at the end of the year. In this case, the business pays the bank £106,000 (which includes £6,000 interest) at the maturity date one year later.

Now here's a twist that happens all the time: instead of 6 per cent simple interest figured once a year, assume that the bank quotes a 6 per cent annual interest rate that's compounded quarterly, which means that it wants to be paid interest every three months. Does this change make a difference? It certainly does, and it makes the calculation of interest more complicated.

When used in reference to an annual rate of interest, *compounding* refers to the frequency of charging (or earning) interest during the year. The annual rate has to be converted into the interest rate per period. Assuming that the lender charges interest quarterly, the 6 per cent annual rate is divided by four to get the 1.5 per cent interest rate per quarter. In the example just introduced, the business can pay £1,500 at the end of each quarter (£100,000 × 1.5 per cent interest rate per quarter = £1,500 interest per quarter). This way, the bank collects interest income earlier and can put the money to work sooner. On the other hand, the main reason for quarterly compounding may be to raise the effective annual interest rate.

Suppose that the business doesn't want to pay interest quarterly; it prefers to make just one payment at the maturity date of the loan one year later. The bank readily agrees as long as the compounding effect is included in the payoff amount (maturity value) of the loan. The bank demands quarterly compounding, which means four interest periods apply during the year.

Q. A business has a bank loan for £100,000. Assuming quarterly compounding of the quoted 6 per cent annual interest rate, determine the amount the business has to pay the bank at the maturity date of the loan agreement one year from now.

A. The 6 per cent annual interest rate quoted by the bank is often referred to as the *nominal* rate. Nominal means in name only. In the example, the lender insists on quarterly compounding, which means that it charges a 1.5 per cent rate each quarter. If the business doesn't pay interest at the end of each quarter, the unpaid interest is added to the loan balance for the next quarter.

Accordingly, the amount owed to the bank one year later is calculated as shown in Table 12-1:

Table 12-1	Calculating the Amount Owed to the Bank at the End of Year 1		
Quarter	Loan Balance at Start of Period	Interest at 1.5 per cent	Loan Balance at End of Period
1	£100,000.00	£1,500.00	£101,500.00
2	£101,500.00	£1,522.50	£103,022.50
3	£103,022.50	£1,545.34	£104,567.84
4	£104,567.84	£1,568.52	£106,136.36

The business owes the bank £106,136.36 at the maturity date of the loan agreement. Therefore, interest on the loan agreement is £6,136.36, which is £136.36 higher than the £6,000.00 simple interest the bank would have charged if the entire year had been treated as just one interest period.

So, two interest rates are at work in this loan: the nominal rate (6 per cent per year in this example) and the effective annual interest rate that gives effect to the compounding of the nominal rate. The effective annual interest rate on the loan in the example is 6.13636 per cent, and is calculated as follows:

> £6,136.36 interest for one year
> ÷ £100,000.00 borrowed at the start of year = 6.13636 per cent effective annual interest rate on loan

The true interest rate is the effective interest rate because this rate determines the actual payment of interest. The nominal interest rate is simply the point of departure for calculating the effective interest rate.

If the business in this example had agreed to a 6.13636 per cent annual interest rate on the loan in the first place, the bank would have been willing to compound annually, which means once a year. At this higher rate, the bank ends up with the same amount of money. Essentially, the bank should be indifferent about whether it charges a 6.13636 per cent annual interest rate that's compounded annually, or a nominal 6 per cent annual rate compounded quarterly; it's six of one, half dozen of the other.

Is it misleading to quote a nominal annual interest rate of 6 per cent that in fact is compounded quarterly? The effective or 'real' annual interest rate isn't 6 per cent, but 6.13636 per cent. You can argue that compounding is a sleight of hand trick for jacking up the true annual interest rate. Financial institutions have to be careful not to mislead borrowers and savers; but you should always read the small print of any agreement you're about to sign, because this text informs you of the terms and conditions associated with your transaction. All we can do is to caution you that featuring nominal annual interest rates is common practice. If you're loan-shopping, be sure to find out whether the nominal annual interest rate is compounded more frequently than once a year.

---

5. Suppose that a business borrows £100,000 for one year. The lender quotes a 6 per cent annual interest rate that's compounded biannually (twice a year). Determine the annual effective interest rate on the loan. You may find Table 12-2 helpful.

Table 12-2	Calculating the Annual Effective Interest Rate on the Loan		
Quarter	Loan Balance at Start of Period	Interest at ? per cent	Loan Balance at End of Period
1	£100,000.00		
2			

Solve It

6. A business borrows £250,000 from its bank for one year. At the maturity date, one year after the money's deposited in the business's bank account, the firm writes a cheque to the bank for £268,324 to pay off the loan. Determine the effective annual interest rate and the nominal annual interest rate assuming biannual compounding. You may find Table 12-3 helpful.

Table 12-3	Calculating the Effective Annual Interest Rate and the Nominal Annual Interest Rate Assuming Biannual Compounding		
Half Year	**Loan Balance at Start of Period**	**Interest at ? per cent**	**Loan Balance at End of Period**
1	£250,000.00		
2			£268,324.00

Solve It

Lifting the Veil on Compound Interest

In the 'Distinguishing nominal and effective interest rates' section earlier in this chapter, we explain how quarterly compounding increases the effective annual interest rate compared with the quoted nominal annual interest rate. In the rest of this chapter, the effective interest rate is taken for granted. Instead of focusing on what happens within one year, the following discussion looks at the effects of compounding over multiple years for investing and borrowing examples.

Be careful: 'compounding' in these longer-term contexts (which run 5, 10, 20 or more years) takes on a different emphasis. Compounding in these long range settings refers to the exponential growth idea – that if something grows at a certain rate from year to year, over enough years, its size end ups being two or more times larger than the starting point. For example, if you start with a population of, say, 10,000 people in a town and its population grows 6 per cent per year, the population doubles to 20,000 in 12 years.

Q. You just invested your £10,000 year-end bonus in a savings account. You plan to leave this money in the account for 20 years, because you view it as a nest egg. The savings account pays 5 per cent annual effective interest. (The interest rate may change in the future, but assume that the interest rate remains the same over all 20 years.) Assuming that your savings account earns 5 per cent annual interest for 20 years, what is the balance in your account at the end of 20 years?

A. In order to answer the question for the 20-year lifespan of the investment, you need to understand how year-to-year compounding works. Compounding means that you don't withdraw your interest earnings each year. Instead, you reinvest the annual earnings. The result of compounding for, say, the first four years is shown in Table 12-4:

Table 12-4	Your Savings Balance at the End of 4 Years with a 5% Interest Rate		
Quarter	Savings Balance at Start of Period	Interest at 5 per cent	Savings Balance at End of Period
1	£10,000.00	£500.00	£10,500.00
2	£10,500.00	£525.00	£11,025.00
3	£11,025.00	£551.25	£11,576.25
4	£11,576.25	£578.81	£12,155.06

The total amount of your earnings over the first four years is £2,155.06. Someone may think that, at 5 per cent, you earn £500.00 each year on your £10,000.00 investment, and over four years you earn £2,000.00. But as you can see in the schedule, you earn £2,155.06. You reinvest your annual earnings, which means that, year-to-year, you have more money invested in your savings account.

Over 20 years, your savings account balance grows to £26,532.98. This amount assumes an annual 5 per cent annual earnings rate and assumes that the financial institution holding your savings account doesn't go belly up. (The government may insure your account, but that still doesn't guarantee that you get all your earnings.)

Your total amount of earnings over 20 years is £16,532.98 (the future value less the £10,000.00 you started with). Try thinking of your total earnings as follows: at £500.00 per year interest, based on your initial investment, you earn £10,000.00 (£500.00 per year × 20 years = £10,000.00). The other £6,532.98 of earnings over the 20 years comes from compounding (reinvesting) your earnings every year.

How did we get the answer? To prepare the four-year schedule, we grab our trusty scientific calculator and enter 20 for N (the number of periods), 5 for I/YR (interest rate), negative 10,000 for PV (the present value of the amount borrowed) and then punch the FV (future value) key to get the answer. (By the way, be sure that the PMT [payment] key has zero entered.)

Before computer spreadsheet programs and handheld business/financial calculators came along, you had to use a table look-up method to solve problems like this one. Some of the biggest disadvantages of this method are that tables of future values and present values don't cover every situation, they're clumsy to use and they require you to do pencil and paper calculations by hand. Surprisingly, many college accounting and finance textbooks still include these tables. For the life of us, we don't know why – the situation is like teaching the Morse code when everyone has a telephone.

7. Refer to the savings account example in which you invest £10,000 today and earn 5 per cent annual interest (compounded annually) for 20 years. That example assumes that the 5 per cent annual interest remains the same over all years. Instead, assume that you earn 4.5 per cent annual interest during the first ten years and 5.5 per cent annual interest during the last ten years. Are you better off in this situation?

Solve It

Borrowing and Investing in Instalments

Borrowing and investing are most commonly done in instalments. With this method, payments are made regularly to pay off a loan or build an investment. In this section, we stick with interest-based investments and examples of fixed income investments and loans. (In the section 'Measuring Return on Investment (ROI)' later in the chapter, we cover investments in which changes in the market value of the investment are an important part of the return (earnings or loss) on the investment.)

Paying off a loan

Q. Your business borrows £100,000 from a bank. You and the bank negotiate an instalment loan in which you will pay off the loan over four years. The effective annual interest rate is 6 per cent. The bank wants your business to amortise one-fourth of the principal amount each year. *Amortise* means to pay down the principal value of the loan. At the end of the first year, for instance, your business has to pay £25,000 on the principal balance of the loan plus interest for that year, and so on for the following three years. You sign the loan agreement to the bank and receive £100,000, which is deposited in your business's bank account. How much is each annual payment to the bank?

A. Probably the best approach to answering this question is to prepare an Excel spreadsheet to do the year-by-year calculations. (Of course, you can do the calculations with pencil and paper by hand, but the Excel program is much faster and less prone to calculation mistakes.) The loan payment schedule is shown in Table 12-5:

Quarter	Loan Balance at Start of Period	Interest at 6 per cent	Principal Payment	Total Payment to the Bank	Loan Balance at End of Period
1	£100,000.00	£6,000.00	£25,000.00	£31,000.00	£75,000.00
2	£75,000.00	£4,500.00	£25,000.00	£29,500.00	£50,000.00
3	£50,000.00	£3,000.00	£25,000.00	£28,000.00	£25,000.00
4	£25,000.00	£1,500.00	£25,000.00	£26,500.00	£0.00

Table 12-5   **Loan Payment Schedule for £100,000 Loan Over 4 Years at a Rate of 6%**

Q. Using the basic premise of the preceding question, suppose the bank wants *equal* payments at the end of each year. (In the preceding answer, the total payment varies year to year.) What is the annual payment on the loan under these terms?

A. A question like this one shows the value of a handheld business/financial calculator, which is designed for the express purpose of solving this type of problem. You enter

4 for N (the number of periods); 6 in INT (the I/YR key on your scientific calculator); 100,000 in PV (the present value of the loan, or the amount borrowed); and 0 in FV (future value). The reason for entering 0 in FV is that you want the loan completely paid off and reduced to a zero balance at the end of the fourth year. Press the PMT (payment) key, and the answer pops up on the screen – £28,859.15. Each payment to the bank should be £28,859.15.

Table 12-6 shows the proof of this answer. The payments to the bank are the same each year. This compares to the previous example where the amounts paid each year were different and on a gradual reducing basis.

Table 12-6   Loan Payment Schedule Showing Equal Amounts Paid Each Year

Quarter	Loan Balance at Start of Period	Interest at 6 per cent	Principal Payment	Total Payment to the Bank	Loan Balance at End of Period
1	£100,000.00	£6,000.00	£22,859.15	£28,859.15	£77,140.85
2	£77,140.85	£4,628.45	£24,230.70	£28,859.15	£52,910.15
3	£52,910.15	£3,174.61	£25,684.54	£28,859.15	£27,225.61
4	£27,225.61	£1,633.54	£27,225.61	£28,859.15	£0.00

You can see that the principal balance reduces to zero at the end of the fourth quarter. In this schedule, as the amount of interest goes down each quarter, the amount of principal amortisation goes up.

8. Suppose a business borrows £1,000,000 from a bank. The annual interest rate is 7.5 per cent and the loan is for four years. The bank wants the business to make payments at the end of each year such that the principal of the loan is amortised in four equal amounts. Determine the annual payments required under the terms of this loan. You may find Table 12-7 helpful:

Table 12-7 Loan Payment Schedule for £1,000,000 Loan Over 4 Years at a Rate of 7.5%

Quarter	Loan Balance at Start of Period	Interest at 7.5 per cent	Principal Payment	Total Payment to the Bank	Loan Balance at End of Period
1	£1000,000.00	£75,000.00	£250,000	£325,000	£750,000
2					
3					
4					£0.00

Solve It

9. Suppose that a business borrows £1,000,000 from a bank. The annual interest rate is 7.5 per cent and the loan is for four years. The bank wants the business to make equal payments at the end of each year such that the principal of the loan is completely amortised (paid off) by the end of the fourth year. Determine the amount of annual payment required under the terms of the loan. You may find Table 12-8 helpful:

Table 12-8	Loan Payment Schedule for £1,000,000 Over 4 Years at a Rate of 7.5% with Equal Payments				
Quarter	Loan Balance at Start of Period	Interest at 7.5 per cent	Principal Payment	Total Payment to the Bank	Loan Balance at End of Period
1	£1000,000.00	£75,000.00			
2					
3					
4					£0.00

Solve It

Measuring Return on Investment (ROI)

You can invest in many different ways – precious metals, property, art, small businesses, government bonds, life insurance policies, retirement annuities, stocks, hedge funds and so on. One thing all these investment alternatives have in common is that the investor wants to take more money out of the investment than the amount of money put into the investment.

Measuring investment performance can be as simple as reading a comic strip or as perplexing as reading a book on nuclear physics. The primary measure of investment performance is the annual rate of return on investment (ROI). 'Return' in ROI refers to the earnings, income, profit or gain, depending on the type of investment.

One fundamental point in measuring investment performance is that you have to recover, or recoup, the amount of capital you put in the investment venture. Only the excess over and above recovery of capital is return on the investment. Another crucial point is that calculating ROI focuses on cash flows into and out of the investment – unless changes in the market value of the investment are an integral and important part of the investment, such as investments in marketable securities (stocks and bonds, for example).

The ROI for a period is calculated as follows, and is usually expressed as a percentage:

Return for period ÷ Amount invested at start of period = Rate of ROI

If you invest £100,000 at the start of the year, and your investment provides £2,500 cash flow income and the market value of your investment increases by £7,500 during the year, your return is as follows:

Return of £10,000 (£7,500 + £2,500) ÷ £100,000 = 10 per cent ROI

Individuals, financial institutions and businesses always account for the cash income element of investment return. However, they may not record the market value gain or loss of an investment. For example, most people who invest in property, stocks/bonds and so on don't record the gain/loss of their investment during the period, which means that they don't have a full and complete accounting of ROI during the period.

The type of investment accounting that most individuals carry out is largely governed by income tax requirements. Unrealised market gains aren't taxed, and so most investors don't record this information. However, property investors may well keep an eye on market values for comparative purposes.

In contrast, financial institutions including banks, insurance businesses and pension funds are governed by generally accepted accounting principles (GAAP). GAAP requires that changes in market values of marketable securities should be recognised. The situation isn't quite as straightforward as this summary suggests, however, and you really need to be clear about what is and what isn't included in ROI calculations.

Q. Here's an example of a property investor evaluating her ROI. Sam buys a property for £100,000. She pays a deposit of 25 per cent. She negotiates rent on this property of £700 per month and has mortgage costs and management charges totalling £480 per month. What is her ROI at the end of year one?

A. The return can be calculated as £700 rent – £480 costs equals £220 per month, which equates to an annual return of £2,640.

If we divide the annual return by the sum of money invested, the rate of return is as follows:

£2,640 ÷ £25,000 = 10.6 per cent

This rate of return is better than leaving the money in the bank, and so Sam considers this investment to be a good one.

10. Paul buys a house for £250,000. He pays a deposit of 25 per cent. He negotiates rent of £1,400 per month and has associated mortgage costs and management fees of £1,125 per month. Calculate the return on his investment.

Solve It

Answers to Problems on Interest and Return on Investment

Here are the answers to the questions presented earlier in this chapter.

1 Suppose that your business borrows $500,000 from a bank, and that amount is deposited in your bank account today. The loan agreement that you sign calls for a 6.25 per cent annual interest rate. Determine the *maturity value* (the amount you will pay the bank when the loan agreement comes due) of the loan agreement one year from now.

$500,000 × 6.25 per cent annual interest rate = $31,250 interest for year

$500,000 borrowed + $31,250 interest = $531,250 maturity value of loan agreement

2 Suppose that you sign a loan agreement that calls for $868,000 to be paid to the lender one year from today. (In other words, the maturity value of the loan one year from today is $868,000.) The lender gives you $800,000 today in exchange for this loan agreement. No mention is made of the rate of interest on this loan. What is the annual interest rate on this loan?

$868,000 maturity value of loan agreement – $800,000 proceeds from loan = $68,000 interest on loan agreement

$68,000 interest ÷ $800,000 amount of loan = 8.5 per cent annual interest rate

3 Refer to Question 1. Suppose that the date on the loan agreement is 1 March, 2009 – this date is when the loan agreement was signed and the money was put in the business's bank account. Today is 31 August, 2009, which is the close of the business's fiscal year. Should an adjusting entry for interest expense be recorded? If so, make the journal entry.

Yes, an adjusting entry should be made to record the accrued interest – six months' worth – on the loan. The following adjusting entry should be made:

	Debit	*Credit*
Interest expense	$15,625	
Accrued interest payable		$15,625

To record six months interest on loan agreement payable:

$31,250 annual interest × 1/2 = $15,625 interest through 31 August, 2009

4 Refer to Question 2. Because the loan agreement payable calls for a payment of $868,000 at the maturity date, the bookkeeper thinks that this amount should be recorded as a liability and that the difference between this liability amount and the $800,000 proceeds received by the business should be debited to the prepaid expenses Asset account. Do you agree?

Accountants don't agree with this recording practice. Of course, all loan agreements payable have a maturity value greater than the amount borrowed, but only the amount borrowed, equal to the face value or principal of the loan, is recorded as a liability at the time of signing the loan. Then, as time passes, an additional liability (accrued interest payable) is recorded for the accrued (accumulated) interest on the loan. In a simple bookkeeping sense, recording the $68,000 interest on the loan agreement as a prepaid expense and then crediting (decreasing) this account as an interest expense is recorded is fine, but interest isn't really prepaid. Financial statement readers expect that the balance in the prepaid expense Asset account is, in fact, for expenses that have been prepaid.

5 Suppose that a business borrows £100,000 for one year. The lender quotes a 6 per cent annual interest rate that's compounded biannually (twice a year). Determine the annual effective interest rate on the loan. You may find the following form helpful.

The annual effective interest rate is 6.09 per cent, which can be seen in Table 12-9:

Table 12-9   Calculating the Annual Effective Interest Rate on the Loan

Half Year	Loan Balance at Start of Period	Interest at 3 per cent	Loan Balance at End of Period
1	£100,000.00	£3,000.00	£103,000.00
2	£103,000.00	£3,090.00	£106,090.00

At the end of the year, the loan balance is £106,09.00, and so interest for the year is £6,090. Therefore,

> £6,090 interest for year ÷ £100,000 amount borrowed = 6.09 per cent effective annual interest rate

6 A business borrows £250,000 from its bank for one year. At the maturity date, one year after the money's deposited in the business's bank account, the firm writes a cheque to the bank for £268,324 to pay off the loan. Determine the effective annual interest rate and the nominal annual interest rate assuming biannual compounding.

> £268,324 maturity value of loan agreement – £250,000 proceeds of loan agreement = £18,324 interest on loan agreement for one year

> £18,324 interest ÷ £250,000 proceeds of loan agreement = 7.33 per cent effective annual interest rate

Because the effective interest rate is 7.33 per cent, the nominal annual interest rate is slightly less – 7.2 per cent, which means 3.6 per cent per half year. Table 12-10 proves that this rate is correct:

Table 12-10   Calculating the Effective Annual Interest Rate and the Nominal Annual Interest Rate Assuming Biannual Compounding

Half Year	Loan Balance at Start of Period	Interest at 3.6 per cent	Loan Balance at End of Period
1	£250,000.00	£9,000.00	£259,000.00
2	£259,000.00	£9,324.00	£268,324.00

7 Refer to the savings account example in which you invest £10,000 today and earn 5 per cent annual interest (compounded annually) for 20 years. That example assumes that the 5 per cent annual interest remains the same over all years. Instead, assume that you earn 4.5 per cent annual interest during the first ten years and 5.5 per cent annual interest during the last ten years. Are you better off in this situation?

The 'trick' to answering this problem is doing it in two steps and carrying over the answer from the first step to the second step.

For the first step, use your business/financial calculator to determine that £10,000.00 invested for ten years at 4.5 per cent annual interest accumulates to £15,529.69 at the end of the tenth year (assuming *compounding*, or reinvesting of annual earnings).

For the second step, enter your answer from the first step as the starting amount (the PV, or present value) for the second leg of the investment, which is ten years at 5.5 per cent annual interest. Your investment accumulates to £26,526.96 at the end of this second ten years (assuming compounding, or reinvesting of annual earnings.

You may be interested that the average annual interest rate that would take a £10,000.00 investment to £26,526.96 at the end of 20 years is 5 per cent. But your actual investment balance wouldn't grow at this constant rate; instead, it would grow at the 4.5 per cent and 5.5 per cent rates during the first and second ten-year segments of the investment.

8 Suppose that a business borrows £1,000,000 from a bank. The annual interest rate is 7.5 per cent and the loan is for four years. The bank wants the business to make payments at the end of each year such that the principal of the loan is amortised in four equal amounts. Determine the annual payments required under the terms of this loan.

Table 12-11 shows the annual payments on the loan. We determine the annual amounts by adding the interest on the loan for the year and £250,000, which is one-fourth of the amount borrowed. A bank may or may not insist on equal principal reductions each year.

Table 12-11 — **Loan Payment Schedule for £1,000,000 Loan Over 4 Years at a Rate of 7.5%**

Quarter	Loan Balance at Start of Period	Interest at 7.5 per cent	Principal Payment	Total Payment to the Bank	Loan Balance at End of Period
1	£1,000,000.00	£75,000.00	£250,000.00	£325,000.00	£750,000.00
2	£750,000.00	£56,250.00	£250,000.00	£306,250.00	£500,000.00
3	£500,000.00	£37,500.00	£250,000.00	£287,500.00	£250,000.00
4	£250,000.00	£18,750.00	£250,000.00	£268,750.00	£0.00

9 Suppose that a business borrows £1,000,000 from a bank. The annual interest rate is 7.5 per cent and the loan is for four years. The bank wants the business to make equal payments at the end of each year such that the principal of the loan is completely amortised (paid off) by the end of the fourth year. Determine the amount of annual payment required under the terms of the loan.

The annual payments on the loan are £298,567.51. As you can see in Table 12-12, the loan is fully amortised (paid off) after the business makes the fourth payment. You can determine the annual payment on the loan by using a business/financial calculator or using the PMT function in the financial functions in Excel. The important thing, however, is to make sure that you understand how each payment is divided between interest and principal reduction.

Table 12-12 — **Loan Payment Schedule for £1,000,000 Over 4 Years at a Rate of 7.5% with Equal Payments**

Quarter	Loan Balance at Start of Period	Interest at 7.5 per cent	Principal Payment	Total Payment to the Bank	Loan Balance at End of Period
1	£1,000,000.00	£75,000.00	£223,567.51	£298,567.51	£776,432.49
2	£776,432.49	£58,232.44	£240,335.07	£298,567.51	£536,097.42
3	£536,097.42	£40,207.31	£258,360.20	£298,567.51	£277,737.22
4	£277,737.22	£20,830.29	£277,737.22	£298,567.51	£0.00

10   Paul buys a house for £250,000. He pays a deposit of 25 per cent. He negotiates rent of £1,400 per month and has associated mortgage costs and management fees of £1,125 per month. Calculate the return on his investment.

Paul's monthly return is calculated as follows:

Rent	£1,400
Less mortgage costs and management fees	£1,125
Monthly income	£275

Annual income = £275 × 12 = £3,300

ROI = £3,300 ÷ £62,500 (25 per cent of £250,000) = 5.3 per cent

Does Paul consider this investment to be a good one? Well, that depends on what other opportunities are available to invest his funds. At the time of writing, the bank base rate is 0.5 per cent (an all-time low) and savings rates are equally low – therefore achieving an investment return of anywhere near 5 per cent would be seen as a huge benefit.

Part IV
The Part of Tens

'I hate the end of the financial year.'

In this part . . .

The Part of Tens contains two shorter chapters: one directed to business investors and the other to accountants in carrying out their responsibilities to business managers. The former presents ten things everyone reading a business financial report should know and keep in mind. The latter chapter provides accountants with a ten-point checklist for helping managers in their planning, control and decision-making.

Chapter 13

Ten Things You Need to Know about Business Financial Statements

*I*nternal financial statements used by managers don't circulate outside the business when they contain confidential and proprietary information. These statements are distributed on a need-to-know basis within the business; they contain more-detailed information than the summary-level information presented in external financial statements distributed to the lenders and shareholders of a business. But both the internal and external financial statements use the same accounting methods. Businesses keep only one set of books, but they 'keep secrets' that aren't disclosed in their external financial reports.

Business managers, business lenders and business investors need to understand certain characteristics and limitations of financial statements. We explain ten of these important points in this chapter.

Rules and Standards Matter

We have seen very, very few maverick financial statements. Almost all financial statements are prepared using *generally accepted accounting principles* (GAAP). These principles are the approved and authoritative methods and standards that businesses must follow when preparing financial statements.

An auditor calls to the attention of the business any deviations from the standards and then advises the appropriate solutions to report the figures correctly. If the business decides that it doesn't want to accept the auditors suggested changes, the auditor reports this fact in the firm's accounts as part of the auditor's report. Auditors don't allow their good name to be associated with accounts that they know may be misleading. In extreme cases, auditors have withdrawn their services where they feel that their reputation is being compromised.

These accounting rules and standards don't put a business in an accounting straitjacket. A business still has some options in the application of GAAP; they can choose which accounting methods to apply. For example, they can choose reducing balance or straight-line depreciation expense methods because they are both equally acceptable (we describe both methods in Chapter 9). The different choices that a business makes regarding accounting policies affect the values reported for assets and liabilities in its balance sheet. As long as the business follows recognised accounting standards, everyone is happy (shareholders and lenders included).

Exactitude Would Be Nice, but Estimates Are Key

Looking at all the numbers in a financial statement, you may assume that they're accurate down to the last penny. Not true. The balance in the cash account is exact, but virtually every other number you see in a financial report is based on an estimate. The amounts of expenses, revenue, assets and liabilities are calculated down to the last penny, but they're based on estimates, and estimates never turn out to be entirely accurate.

For example, consider the depreciation expense. A business estimates the future useful life of a fixed asset (long-term operating asset) and allocates its cost over this useful life. Another example is debtors – the business estimates how much of the total balance of its debtors will turn out to be bad debts. Yet another example is the accrued liability for product warranty and guarantee costs that will be paid in the future. This amount is only an educated guess.

Estimates are unavoidable in accounting. Most businesses have enough experience to make pretty good estimates, and they consult experts when necessary. A business can nudge an estimate toward the conservative side or the liberal side. For instance, it can estimate that its future product warranty and guarantee costs are going to be fairly low or fairly high. Usually, arguments exist on both sides, and the business ends up having to make a somewhat arbitrary estimate.

Some estimates are particularly difficult to make, such as the liability for future post-retirement medical and health benefits that a business promises its employees. Another difficult estimate concerns product recalls. Estimating the cost of a major lawsuit in which the decision may go against the business is also very difficult. Our advice is to be alert when reading financial statements to see whether the business is facing any issue that's particularly difficult to estimate.

Financial Statements Fit Together Hand in Glove

The three primary financial statements – the Profit and Loss statement, the balance sheet and the cash flow statement – appear on separate pages in a financial report and therefore may seem freestanding. In fact, the three financial statements are intertwined and interconnected (check out Chapters 7 and 8 for more details).

Accountants assume that the reader understands these connections, and so they don't connect the dots between corresponding accounts in different financial statements. Understanding these tentacles of connection between the statements is extremely important, especially for interpreting the statement of cash flows (see Chapter 8). For example, an increase in debtors during the year that's reported in the balance sheet causes a decrease in cash flow from operating activities.

Accrual Basis Is Used to Record Profit, Assets and Liabilities

The vast majority of businesses must use accrual-based accounting to determine profit or loss and to keep track of their assets and liabilities. Simply put, the accrual basis must be used to reflect economic reality. Here are three examples of the accrual basis at work:

- A business makes a sale on credit, accepting the customer's promise to pay at a later date and delivering the product. The accountant records the sale by an increase to an asset called debtors.

- A business buys a building or machine that's going to be used for many years in its operations and pays cash for the asset. The cost of the asset isn't charged to expenses right away. Instead, the cost is allocated to expenses over the estimated useful life span of the asset.

- A business records an expense now even though it won't pay for the expense until sometime later. To record the expense, a liability is increased; later, when the expense is paid, the liability is decreased.

Some small businesses don't sell on credit, don't carry stock, don't invest in fixed assets (long-term operating resources) and pay their bills quickly. They may use cash-based accounting instead of accrual-based. Basically, all they do is keep a chequebook.

Cash Flow Differs from Accrual Basis Profit

Even though it reflects economic reality, accrual-based accounting (see the preceding section) causes one point of confusion: many people look at the bottom-line profit or loss number in the Profit and Loss statement and jump to the conclusion that this number is the amount that cash increased or decreased for the period. Indeed, the expression 'a business makes money' suggests that making a profit increases the business's cash account the same amount. But cash flow from profit – the net increase or decrease in cash from the sales and expense activities of a business for a period – almost always differs from the amount of bottom-line profit or loss reported in its Profit and Loss statement.

In one sense, you can blame accounting for speaking with a forked tongue: the Profit and Loss statement reports one number for profit (net income), and the cash flow statement reports another number for profit (cash flow from operating activities). The accrual-based accounting number is in the Profit and Loss statement and the cash-based accounting number is in the cash flow statement. Essentially, a financial report has two versions of profit.

The amount of cash flow from profit (operating activities) in the cash flow statement tells you what profit would have been on cash-based accounting. The statement of cash flows explains why the cash flow from profit is different from the net income for the period.

The main (but not only) difference between cash-based and accrual-based profit accounting is depreciation. On the accrual basis, depreciation expense is deducted from sales revenue to determine profit, which is correct of course. From the cash flow point of view, in contrast, depreciation isn't bad but good. The cash inflow from sales revenue, in part, reimburses the business for using its fixed assets. In other words, depreciation for the year is the recovery of the cash invested in fixed assets in prior years. Money is returning to the business.

Profit and Balance Sheet Values Can Be (and Often Are) Manipulated

Massaging the numbers is expected, and one may even argue that business lenders and investors encourage it – mainly on the grounds that a business is entitled to put its best face forward. Managers may try and pump up sales revenue or deflate expenses for the year in order to meet pre-established profit goals or dampen the volatility of reported earnings year to year. Independent auditors go along with a reasonable amount of accounting manipulation.

Cooking the books, however, is completely different to massaging the numbers. Cooking the books is the playful name for a serious crime, accounting fraud, in which fictitious sales are recorded, expenses aren't recorded, liabilities are hidden or assets are overstated. Accounting fraud is illegal and should be avoided at all costs.

Financial Statements Are Historical

You need to bear in mind that financial statements are prepared using information about events that have already happened. They present a historical interpretation of how the business performed. As everyone knows, past performance isn't an indication of what may happen in the future. If you're reading financial statements that have been downloaded from Companies House, remember the following point:

> A limited company which has a year-end of say 31 January 2009 (accounting reference date) isn't expected to file its accounts with Companies House until nine months after. The deadline for delivery to Companies House is midnight on 1 October 2009.

You can see from these dates that the information held within these accounts is already quite dated. Bear this fact in mind when you're using the latest filed set of accounts to try to establish how well a business has performed. Given the current economic climate, the financial position of a business can change very quickly, and what may have been a profitable firm nine months ago, may now be suffering huge losses.

Some Asset Values Are Current, but Others May Be Old

The balance (amount) of an asset in a balance sheet is the result of the entries (increases less decreases) recorded in the account. A balance sheet doesn't disclose whether the ending balance in an asset is from recent entries or from entries made years ago.

How recent an ending balance is depends on which asset you're talking about and which accounting method is used for the asset. For example, if a business uses the First-In-First-Out (FIFO) method for its Cost of Goods Sold expense, its stock balance is from entries recorded recently. In contrast, if the business uses the Last-In-First-Out (LIFO) method, its stock balance is from older entries. How much older? Well, a business may have been using LIFO for many years and part of its stock balance may go back more than 50 years.

The balance of property and plant and machinery typically consists of fixed assets that have been on the books for five, ten, 20 or more years. You should never confuse the original costs in this Asset account with the current replacement value of the assets. On the other hand, the debtors balance is current, as is cash, of course.

The Accounting Standards Board in the UK is currently debating whether an asset should be shown as fair value in the accounts rather than historical cost accounting (that is, we know what the cost of the asset was, but it would be better to know what the asset is worth now).

Financial Statements Leave Interpretation to Readers

One guiding rule of financial reporting is to let the financial statements speak for themselves. The financial statements and footnotes report the facts but don't interpret what the facts mean or what the facts may foreshadow. The assessment and forecast of a business's financial performance and condition are left for the readers to tackle.

Having said that, the CEO and other top-level officers of public companies include a good deal of commentary and their interpretations of the business's financial performance in annual financial reports. But keep in mind that getting the top officers' take is like asking the captain of a ship how the voyage went when the passengers may have quite a different opinion.

Financial Statements Tell the Story of a Business, Not Its Individual Shareholders

Financial statements tell the story of the business. You can't find out from the financial statements how well or poorly individual investors in the business have done. Some shareholders in a business may have had their money invested in the business from day one, whereas other original investors may have sold their shares. The business doesn't record the prices they received for the shares; in other words, the business doesn't record the dealings and transactions among shareholders. This activity is none of the business's business.

The owners' Capital accounts in a balance sheet report only the original amounts invested by shareholders. What has happened since then in the trading of these ownership shares isn't captured in the financial statements – unless the business itself bought some of the shares from its shareholders.

You may find that comparing the current market price of stock shares you own with the stockholders' capital balances reported in the business's balance sheet is very interesting. In a rough sort of way, this process is like comparing the current market value of your home with the cost you paid many years ago.

Chapter 14

A Ten-Point Checklist for Management Accountants

This chapter offers a ten-point checklist for accountants in fulfilling their functions for managers, somewhat like the checklist for pilots before take off.

Accountants are saddled with several functions, and under the pressures of time they may end up giving short shrift to their duties to managers – which is understandable. However, the very continuance of the business depends on accountants providing managers with the information they need to know for making decisions and maintaining control. If managers don't get what they need from their accountants, the business can fail or spin out of control. In this sense, management accounting functions are the most central duties – if the business fails, the other accounting functions become beside the point.

Designing Internal Accounting Reports

When designing internal management accounting reports, the accountant should ask, 'Who's entitled to know what?'. Generally speaking, the board of directors, the Chief Executive Officer (CEO) and the Managing Director are entitled to know anything and everything. (This sweeping comment is subject to exceptions in business organisations that tightly control the flow of financial information.) By virtue of their positions, the Finance Director and chief accountant (often called the Financial Controller) have access to all financial information about the business.

Other managers in a business have a limited scope of responsibility and authority. The accountant should report to them the information they need to know, but no more. For example, the Production Director receives a wide range of manufacturing information but doesn't receive sales and marketing information.

The accountant should identify a particular manager's specific area of authority and responsibility in deciding the information content of accounting reports to that manager. The reporting of information to individual managers should follow the organisational structure of the business; this practice is called *responsibility accounting*.

From the accounting point of view, the organisational structure of a business consists of profit centres and cost centres:

- A *profit centre* can be a product line, or even a specific product model. For example, a profit centre for Apple Computer is its iPod line of products; another profit centre is its iTunes Music Centre (where customers download audio and video files). Within each broad product line, Apple has sub-profit centres. For example, each type of iPod is a sub-profit centre.

- A *cost centre* is an organisation unit that doesn't directly generate sales revenue. For example, the accounting department of a business is a cost centre.

The accounting reports that go to the manager of a profit centre should be oriented to the profit performance of that organisation unit. The accounting reports that go to a manager of a cost centre should be oriented to the cost performance of that organisation unit.

Helping Managers Understand Their Accounting Reports

Most managers have limited accounting backgrounds; their backgrounds are usually in marketing, engineering, law, human resources and other fields. In addition, most business managers don't want to find out more about accounting – and in all actuality, don't really need to.

Accountants often act as if managers fully understand the accounting reports they receive and have all the time in the world to read and digest the detailed information they contain. Accountants are dead-wrong on this point.

One of the main functions of the management accountant is to serve as the translator of accounting jargon and reports to business managers – to take the technical terminology and methods of accounting and put it all into terms that non-accounting managers can clearly understand. Of course, being authors of accounting books for non-accountants, we may be biased, but we believe that management accountants can perform a very valuable service by improving their communication skills with non-accounting managers.

Involving Managers in Choosing Accounting Methods

Some business managers take charge of every aspect of the business, including choosing accounting methods for their businesses. But many business managers are passive and defer to their chief accountants regarding the accounting methods their businesses should use.

In our opinion, the hands-off approach is a mistake. Chapter 9 explains three critical accounting issues (how to deal with Cost of Goods Sold expense methods, depreciation and bad debts) each have alternative accounting methods which a business must choose. Ultimately, CEOs are responsible for these decisions, because they're responsible for all fundamental decisions of businesses. But such accounting decisions may not be on their radar screen.

In choosing accounting methods, the chief accountant shouldn't allow managers to sit on the sidelines and remain spectators. The chief accountant shouldn't select an accounting method without the explicit approval and understanding of top-level managers. In particular, the head accountant needs to explain the differences in profit and asset and liability values between alternative accounting methods. The business's accounting methods must reflect its philosophy and strategies, and so if the business is conservative in its policies and strategies, it needs to use conservative accounting methods.

Chief accountants can find themselves between a rock and a hard place when top-level managers intervene in the normal accounting process. This interference may be referred to as massaging the numbers, managing earnings, smoothing earnings or old-fashioned accounting manipulation.

Any accountant acceding to management pressure must emphasise to the manager what the consequences are for the following year. Generally speaking, a compensatory effect, or tradeoff, exists between years; pumping up profit this year, for instance, causes profit deflation next year. Massaging the numbers produces a robbing Peter to pay Paul effect, and the accountant needs to make this fact very clear.

Creating Profit Performance Reports for Managers

The accountant needs to read the mind of the manager in designing the layout and content of reports to the manager. Ideally, the profit report should reflect the manager's profit strategy and tactics. For example, a manager of a profit centre focuses on two main things: margin and sales volume. Therefore, the profit report should emphasise those two key factors. This process sounds simple enough, but one impediment exists in designing internal profit reports for managers based on management thinking.

When creating internal profit reports for managers, accountants too often follow the path of least resistance. They use the format and content of the Profit and Loss statement reported outside the business, but this practice is unacceptable. External Profit and Loss statements conceal much information; they don't disclose information about margins and sales volumes for each profit centre of the business.

Accountants have to break out of their external Profit and Loss statement mentality and think in terms of what managers need to know for analysing profit performance and making profit decisions.

Our main advice on this point is straightforward: listen to how managers explain their profit strategy, which is called the 'business model'. Get inside the manager's head. Do your best to understand the mindset of managers as regards how they see the formula for making profit. Listen carefully to which particular factors managers think are the most important drivers (determinants) of profit. Don't try to remodel the manager's thinking into the accountant's way of thinking. Don't forget that managers are in charge – even though you may think they should go back and study accounting. In short, don't try to educate managers on accounting; let them educate you on what they need to know in order to make profit.

Formulating Cash Flow Reports for Managers

The conventional cash flow statement is far too technical and intimidating for most managers to make sense of. What managers don't understand, they don't use. In our view, accountants are too bound by their 'debits and credits' thinking as regards the cash flow statement. This statement is designed to reconcile changes in the balance sheet during the period with the amounts reported in the statement. But should its function also be the purpose of reporting this financial statement to managers? We don't think so.

In mid-size and large businesses, the financial officers of the business manage cash flow. Other managers don't have any direct responsibility over cash flow – although their decisions impact cash flow. Managers of profit and cost centres should have a basic understanding of the cash flow impacts of their decisions. They don't necessarily need cash flow statements, but they need to know how their decisions impact cash flow.

The cash flow reports to managers of profit and cost centres should focus mainly on the key factors that affect cash flow from operating activities (check out Chapter 8 for more details). These internal management reports should concentrate on changes in debtors, stock and operating liabilities (creditors and accrued expenses payable). These factors are the main reason for the difference between cash flow and profit for which managers of profit and cost centres have control and responsibility.

Devising Management Control Reports

Management control is usually thought of as keeping a close watch on a thousand and one details, any one of which can spin out of control and cause problems. First and foremost, however, management control means achieving objectives and keeping on course towards the goals of the business. Management control covers a lot of ground – motivating employees, working with suppliers, keeping customers satisfied and so on. But no doubt exists that managers need control reports that include a lot of detail.

The trick in management control reports is to separate the wheat from the chaff. Being very busy people, managers can't afford to waste time on relatively insignificant problems. They have to prioritise problems and deal with the issues that have the greatest effect on the business.

Therefore, the accountant needs to design management control reports that differentiate significant problems from less serious problems. In control reports, the accountant should use visual pointers to highlight serious problems. In other words, control reports shouldn't be flat, with all lines of information appearing to be equally important.

Developing Models for Management Decision-Making Analysis

For decision-making purposes, business managers need a model of operating profit that, theoretically, fits on the back of an envelope. Here's an example of such a compact profit model, which we adapt from 'Analysis method #1' in Chapter 10:

(Unit Margin × Sales Volume) – Fixed Expenses = Operating Profit

Suppose the sales price is £100 and variable costs equal £65 per unit. Therefore, unit margin is £35. Assume the business sells 100,000 units, so that its total contribution margin for the period is £3,500,000 (£35 unit margin × 100,000 units = £3,500,000 total contribution margin). Now assume that its fixed expenses for the period equal £2,500,000. So its operating profit is £1,000,000 for the period.

The accountant should develop a condensed profit model, which is limited to the critical factors that tip profit one way or the other. This profit model helps the manager focus on the key variables that drive profit behaviour. For example, continuing with the example just mentioned, suppose the manager is contemplating cutting sales price by 10 per cent to boost sales volume by 20 per cent. Using the profit model the manager can quickly do a before and after comparison of the proposed sales price cut:

Before: (£35 Unit Margin × 100,000 units) – £2,500,000 Fixed Expenses = £1,000,000 Operating Profit

After: (£25 Unit Margin × 120,000 units) – £2,500,000 = £500,000 Operating Profit

Giving up 10 per cent of sales price for a 20 per cent gain in sales volume may have intuitive appeal, but this decision cripples profit. Operating profit would drop from £1,000,000 to only £500,000; the manager would give up £10, or 29 per cent of the £35 margin per unit. The sacrifice is too great in exchange for only 20 per cent gain in sales volume.

Working Closely with Managers in Planning

The vital function of collaborating with managers has two parts:

- ✔ Forecasting changes that will affect the business
- ✔ Planning the future of the business

These tasks include plotting the sales trajectory of the business, the need for additional capital, and shifts in size and makeup of its workforce and other factors.

The accountant should be involved in the planning process from the beginning, otherwise the accountant is at a disadvantage in preparing budgets and financial projections. The better the accountant understands the planning process, and the closer the accountant works with managers in developing plans, the more useful the financial forecasts and budgets are going to be.

Establishing and Enforcing Internal Controls

Internal controls are the forms and procedures established in a business to deter and detect errors and dishonesty (we cover internal controls in Chapter 4). (Internal control certainly isn't the most glamorous accounting function in a business organisation.) Even if everyone in the business and everyone the business deals with are as honest as the day is long every day of the year, errors are bound to happen.

For example, in payroll if a tax code is incorrectly entered when processing an individual's payroll, it can lead to the incorrect amount of tax being deducted from that persons payslip. (People soon shout if their payroll is wrong!) Internal controls need to ensure that more than one person is processing the payroll. One person should be responsible for checking that tax code changes have been entered accurately; the same person who enters the tax codes should not then processes the payroll. This control is known as *segregation of duties*.

A business is the natural target of all sorts of dishonest schemes and scams by its employees, managers, customers, suppliers and others. To minimise its exposure to losses from embezzlement, pilfering, shoplifting, fraud and burglary, the accountant should establish and enforce effective internal controls in the business. Internal controls are an example of the principle that an ounce of prevention is worth a pound of cure.

Keeping Up-to-Date on Accounting, Financial Reporting and Tax Changes

Accountants are very busy people because they carry out many functions in a business. Like business managers, they don't have a lot of time to spare. One thing that gets short shrift in a crowded schedule is keeping up with changes in accounting and financial reporting standards. However, doing so is absolutely essential in order for accountants to stay informed of the latest changes.

Accountants simply have to set aside time to read professional journals, peruse websites and keep alert regarding developments in accounting and financial reporting. Accounting practices don't stand still.

Index

• •

Notes

Notes

Notes

Notes

Notes

FOR DUMMIES®

Making Everything Easier!™

UK editions

BUSINESS

Starting a Business For Dummies
978-0-470-51806-9

Business Plans Kit For Dummies
978-0-470-74381-2

Consulting For Dummies
978-0-470-71382-2

FINANCE

Investing For Dummies
978-0-470-99280-7

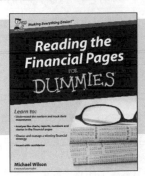

Reading the Financial Pages For Dummies
978-0-470-71432-4

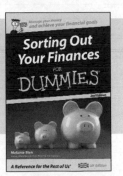

Sorting Out Your Finances For Dummies
978-0-470-69515-9

HOBBIES

Growing Your Own Fruit & Veg For Dummies
978-0-470-69960-7

Researching Your Family History Online For Dummies
978-0-470-74535-9

Origami Kit For Dummies
978-0-470-75857-1

British Sign Language For Dummies
978-0-470-69477-0

Business NLP For Dummies
978-0-470-69757-3

Competitive Strategy For Dummies
978-0-470-77930-9

Cricket For Dummies
978-0-470-03454-5

CVs For Dummies, 2nd Edition
978-0-470-74491-8

Digital Marketing For Dummies
978-0-470-05793-3

Divorce For Dummies, 2nd Edition
978-0-470-74128-3

eBay.co.uk Business All-in-One For Dummies
978-0-470-72125-4

Emotional Freedom Technique For Dummies
978-0-470-75876-2

English Grammar For Dummies
978-0-470-05752-0

Flirting For Dummies
978-0-470-74259-4

Golf For Dummies
978-0-470-01811-8

Green Living For Dummies
978-0-470-06038-4

Hypnotherapy For Dummies
978-0-470-01930-6

IBS For Dummies
978-0-470-51737-6

Lean Six Sigma For Dummies
978-0-470-75626-3

Available wherever books are sold. For more information or to order direct go to www.wiley.com
or call +44 (0) 1243 843291

08049_p1

FOR
DUMMIES®

A world of resources to help you grow

UK editions

SELF-HELP

Cognitive Behavioural Therapy FOR DUMMIES
Rob Willson
Rhena Branch
A Reference for the Rest of Us!
978-0-470-01838-5

Neuro-linguistic Programming FOR DUMMIES
Romilla Ready
Kate Burton
A Reference for the Rest of Us!
978-0-7645-7028-5

Boosting Self-Esteem FOR DUMMIES
Rhena Branch
Rob Willson
978-0-470-74193-1

STUDENTS

Study Skills FOR DUMMIES
Doreen du Boulay
978-0-470-74047-7

Student Cookbook FOR DUMMIES
Oliver Harrison
978-0-470-74711-7

Writing Essays FOR DUMMIES
Mary Page
Dr Carrie Winstanley
978-0-470-74290-7

HISTORY

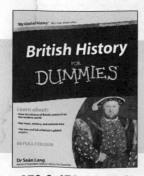

British History FOR DUMMIES
Dr Seán Lang
978-0-470-99468-9

Twentieth Century History FOR DUMMIES
Dr Seán Lang
A Reference for the Rest of Us!
978-0-470-51015-5

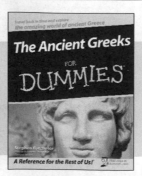

The Ancient Greeks FOR DUMMIES
Stephen Batchelor
A Reference for the Rest of Us!
978-0-470-98787-2

Motivation For Dummies
978-0-470-76035-2

Overcoming Depression For Dummies
978-0-470-69430-5

Personal Development All-In-One For Dummies
978-0-470-51501-3

Positive Psychology For Dummies
978-0-470-72136-0

PRINCE2 For Dummies
978-0-470-51919-6

Psychometric Tests For Dummies
978-0-470-75366-8

Raising Happy Children For Dummies
978-0-470-05978-4

Sage 50 Accounts For Dummies
978-0-470-71558-1

Succeeding at Assessment Centres For Dummies
978-0-470-72101-8

Sudoku For Dummies
978-0-470-01892-7

Teaching English as a Foreign Language For Dummies
978-0-470-74576-2

Teaching Skills For Dummies
978-0-470-74084-2

Time Management For Dummies
978-0-470-77765-7

Understanding and Paying Less Property Tax For Dummies
978-0-470-75872-4

Work-Life Balance For Dummies
978-0-470-71380-8

Available wherever books are sold. For more information or to order direct go to www.wiley.com or call +44 (0) 1243 843291

FOR DUMMIES®

COMPUTER BASICS

978-0-470-27759-1

978-0-470-13728-4

978-0-470-49743-2

DIGITAL PHOTOGRAPHY

978-0-470-25074-7

978-0-470-46606-3

978-0-470-45772-6

MAC BASICS

978-0-470-27817-8

978-0-470-46661-2

978-0-470-43543-4

Access 2007 For Dummies
978-0-470-04612-8

Adobe Creative Suite 4 Design
Premium All-in-One Desk Reference
For Dummies
978-0-470-33186-6

AutoCAD 2010 For Dummies
978-0-470-43345-4

C++ For Dummies, 6th Edition
978-0-470-31726-6

Computers For Seniors For Dummies ,
2nd Edition
978-0-470-53483-0

Dreamweaver CS4 For Dummies
978-0-470-34502-3

Excel 2007 All-In-One Desk Reference
For Dummies
978-0-470-03738-6

Green IT For Dummies
978-0-470-38688-0

Networking All-in-One Desk Reference
For Dummies, 3rd Edition
978-0-470-17915-4

Office 2007 All-in-One Desk Reference
For Dummies
978-0-471-78279-7

Photoshop CS4 For Dummies
978-0-470-32725-8

Photoshop Elements 7 For Dummies
978-0-470-39700-8

Search Engine Optimization
For Dummies, 3rd Edition
978-0-470-26270-2

The Internet For Dummies,
11th Edition
978-0-470-12174-0

Visual Studio 2008 All-In-One Desk
Reference For Dummies
978-0-470-19108-8

Web Analytics For Dummies
978-0-470-09824-0

Windows Vista For Dummies
978-0-471-75421-3